CW01454746

Successful Global Lea

Ramon Henson

Successful Global Leadership

Frameworks for Cross-Cultural Managers and Organizations

palgrave
macmillan

Ramon Henson
Rutgers Business School
USA

ISBN 978-1-349-95482-7   ISBN 978-1-137-58990-3   (eBook)
DOI 10.1057/978-1-137-58990-3

© The Editor(s) (if applicable) and The Author(s) 2016
Softcover reprint of the hardcover 1st edition 2016
This work is subject to copyright. All rights are solely and exclusively licensed by the
Publisher, whether the whole or part of the material is concerned, specifically the rights of
translation, reprinting, reuse of illustrations, recitation, broadcasting, reproduction on
microfilms or in any other physical way, and transmission or information storage and retrieval,
electronic adaptation, computer software, or by similar or dissimilar methodology now
known or hereafter developed.
The use of general descriptive names, registered names, trademarks, service marks, etc. in this
publication does not imply, even in the absence of a specific statement, that such names are
exempt from the relevant protective laws and regulations and therefore free for general use.
The publisher, the authors and the editors are safe to assume that the advice and information
in this book are believed to be true and accurate at the date of publication. Neither the publisher nor the authors or the editors give a warranty, express or implied, with respect to the
material contained herein or for any errors or omissions that may have been made.

Cover illustration: © Tetra Images / Alamy Stock Photo

Printed on acid-free paper

This Palgrave Macmillan imprint is published by Springer Nature
The registered company is Nature America Inc. New York

PREFACE

Two beliefs that managers with limited global experience sometimes express are the following:

Managing people is not that different in different countries, because underneath we are all the same.

Managers everywhere should learn how we do things here because we have the best management techniques. Besides, if you are working for an American company, you have to follow its management practices.

These misguided beliefs and assumptions about what it means to manage and lead in today's global business environment are among several stumbling blocks for those in global leadership roles. I suspect that more will disagree with the second statement than the first, regardless of whatever nation a company's origin happens to be. Just because a company's home base is American (or Swedish, Dutch, or Chinese) does not mean that the management practices in its home country should be followed in the countries where these corporations have subsidiaries.

During a meeting with a group of Japanese managers in Tokyo, when I was working for a subsidiary of a U.S.-based company, I was introducing the concept of goal-setting in the context of performance management. The focus on individual goals seemed alien to these managers. In explaining the Western management practice of performance management to the Japanese managers, I pointed to the importance of accountability when evaluating performance. My translator turned to me, somewhat perplexed, remarking to me that she did not think there was a Japanese translation for the word "accountability." I then had to describe the concept without actually using the word, although eventually, like many other English words for which there is no direct translation (e.g., the Japanese word for baseball is *besuboru*), the Japanese word for accountability became *akauntabiriti.*

IKEA is a Swedish company that had tried for a long time to impose its Swedish management practices throughout all its subsidiaries. It found that it had to adjust and in some cases delay implementing some of its practices because of a lack of cultural fit (Daft 2008). And there are many other examples of adjustments corporations have had to make to adapt its practices when doing business across borders (e.g., Ricks 2006).

Most of us are aware that no nation owns a monopoly on the best management techniques. In the 1970s, when I was working for Citibank, my department was responsible for introducing quality circles, and for a while we were quite successful in rolling out this concept to many retail branches and back-office operations. It was exciting to watch tellers and back-office support people who had never been asked for their opinions participate in teams and make presentations to branch management, who actually listened to what they had to say. For many of them, this was the first time they had even seen a member of management visiting the local branch. The quality circle concept actually came from the Japanese (Munchus 1983). In 1950, the Japanese government invited W. Edwards Deming to lecture on statistical methods and quality control. Along with Joseph Juran, Deming was so influential with the Japanese that they established the Deming Prize to award quality achievements (Hutchins 1985).

This book is for managers around the world who are interested in learning about global leadership based on current research and practice and in developing their ability to work effectively across cultures. Whether you are an American, a Mexican, an Italian, or a Thai, my hope is that there will be some learning, a number of insights, as well as helpful strategies and advice in this book that will help you to become a successful global leader. This book is also intended for human resources leaders and other executives interested in helping to create a global mindset culture in their organizations. Finally, this book is intended for researchers who may get additional ideas for investigating relevant topics based on the concepts, examples and practices discussed here.

Part of this book is based on the author's own personal experiences, coming from the Philippines over 30 years ago as a graduate student and arriving in the USA for the first time. As a graduate student, I was fortunate to meet a tremendously diverse group of students and faculty from many different countries at the University of Michigan. While there, I became involved with General Motors' efforts to put into practice the writings of one of my professors, Rensis Likert, who at that time had just written an influential book called *New Patterns of Management* (Likert 1967). Those were interesting times, especially since GM had such a large market share then and believed it would dominate the industry in a few years' time.

I have also been fortunate in having worked for several companies that assigned me to work on important projects overseas, in a few cases helping to open new markets or expand into existing markets. I have learned a great deal from colleagues and clients in these different countries.

Over the past few years, I have been teaching MBA courses both in the USA and overseas, as well as continuing my consulting work. I owe my students and clients a tremendous debt for all the insights I have gained from their observations and our discussions. Many of the cases and examples in this book come from these sources; the names and affiliations have been changed to respect confidentiality, but they are based on actual incidents and events. In this book, I have also made an attempt to integrate the most relevant and current research on global leadership, and I owe much to the impressive body of work from the leading scholars of the field. In the past several decades, our knowledge of global leadership has accelerated greatly, thanks to these researchers.

This book is organized in three broad sections. In the first (Chaps. 1–3), I review the context of global leadership by discussing the rise of the global manager and highlighting selected global trends impacting the practice of global leadership. In the second (Chaps. 4–6), I cover selected cultural frameworks, a proposed model of global leadership, and the importance of global mindset. In the third (Chaps. 7–9), I discuss the implications for individuals and organizations, and make some recommendations for improving our future understanding of global leadership and its practice.

Ramon Henson
Newark, NJ

ACKNOWLEDGMENTS

This book is the result of years of thinking, doing, and collaborating with many colleagues, executives, and students. From my undergraduate and graduate years, I would like to acknowledge the intellectual debt I owe to several of my professors: Aurelio Cálderon, Charles Cannell, Basil Georgopoulus, Robert Kahn, Edward Lawler, Rensis Likert, Stanley Seashore, J. E. Keith Smith, and Bernardo Villegas. From my corporate and consulting experience, I have learned much from, and have had great conversations, support and partnerships with the following: Roger Allen, Jaime Angueira, Patricia Barlow, Salmah Basri, Michael Beer, Henry Brenner, Jean Casner, Ron Chan, Emmanuel Charron, Gary Cohen, Kitty Cymore, Deb Dagit, Phyllis Davis, Edana Desatnick, Monica Díaz, Penny Dobson, Rojali Edris, Alison Eyring, Forrest Fryer, JP Gagnon, Jay Galbraith, Peter Garrucho, Yosinori Goto, Próspero Hernandez, John Hinrichs, Claire Hofer, Susan Kropf, Hiroko Kuriyama, Farrokh Langdana, Paul Lee, Mei Ling Lo, Paul Madsen, Paul Markovits, Spencer McIlmurray, Antonio Mendez, Enrico Midali, Bill Mobley, Chris Moore, Alfonso Mostacero, David Nadler, Joel Ospa, James Preston, Bill Pyle, Maria Ramos, Steve Rhinesmith, David Rodriguez, Hal Rush, Marshall Sashkin, Russ Shaner, David Sirota, George Szybillo, Motomi Takayama, Dorothy Tao, Anne Tidball, Masato Taniguchi, Roosevelt Thomas, Luís Torres, Jim Walker, Grey Warner, and Helen Zhang.

Thanks to my editor Stacy Noto for her faith in this book, and to my students at Rutgers Business School (New Jersey, Shanghai, and Singapore) for their patience with my passion on this topic. Thanks also to those students who contributed to the interviews, especially Commander James

Crate, Kristin Couch, Giselle Montero, Kavita Ramachandran, and Jon Roberts. And thanks most of all to my family—Phil, Emma, and Greg. A special thanks to my wife Sandra, an Industrial-Organizational psychologist herself, who provided me with great ideas, insights, critiques, and support all throughout this journey.

CONTENTS

LIST OF FIGURES

LIST OF TABLES

CHAPTER 1

The Rise of the Global Manager

At the end of the semester, as students were sharing with each other what they had learned from my course in cross-cultural management, one of my students, Tom, an American in his mid-40s who was going back to school for an MBA after having worked in the corporate world, made a telling comment. He said: "Before this course, I never thought of the U.S. as having a culture. I thought what we did here was what everybody else in the world did, at least in terms of business practices. Now I realize that I am to some extent a product of my culture." Tom has never traveled abroad, and so he has never had to face the day-to-day realities of managing others from different cultures.

Charles Munger, Warren Buffett's friend and close business associate at Berkshire Hathaway, was quoted in a Wall Street Journal interview[1] as saying:

> People chronically misappraise the limits of their own knowledge; that's one of the most basic parts of human nature. Knowing the edge of your circle of competence is one of the most difficult things for a human being to do. Knowing what you don't know is much more useful in life and business than being brilliant.

The real voyage of discovery consists not in seeking new landscapes, but in having new eyes. (Marcel Proust)

© The Editor(s) (if applicable) and The Author(s) 2016
R. Henson, *Successful Global Leadership*,
DOI 10.1057/978-1-137-58990-3_1

For those managers like Tom, who may never have spent any time outside their own country, taking Mr. Munger's advice to know what you don't know may be difficult. It certainly was for me, as I was born and raised in the Philippines, and other than a trip to Hong Kong as a teenager, had never left my home country.

After I graduated from college, I went to work for the Philippine Refining Company, a subsidiary of Unilever. One of my best friends accepted an offer from Procter & Gamble (P&G) Philippines. These two companies were fierce competitors in the Philippines, and we would often compare notes on what it was like working for our respective companies. The Philippine Refining Company shared some of the Dutch cultural characteristics; managers took a long time making decisions because they valued consensus. And the directness of some of the Dutch expatriates working there seemed jarring to the Filipinos. P&G Philippines had a very different culture; decisions were made quickly, risk-taking was encouraged, and there was a more informal working relationship between managers and employees. At the time, I did not realize the extent to which the cultures of these companies reflected the cultures of the countries in which they were based.

Many years later, after having moved to the USA, obtaining my Ph.D., and then working for several Fortune 500 companies where I had international assignments in over 15 different countries (including a three-year stint in Japan), I have a little more perspective on the subject of global leadership and managing across cultures. I have met, worked with, and interviewed several hundred individuals from many different nationalities who have had various leadership roles in their global organizations: as traditional expatriates (going from home country to host country), reverse expatriates (going from host country to home country), third-country expatriates (going from one subsidiary to another), managers with either short-term or rotational assignment roles, as well as leaders of global virtual teams. I have also had various global leadership roles, as well as having led global face-to-face and virtual teams, in different corporations.

In the early part of my career, it seemed like the traditional expatriate model was the prevailing one for global organizations that were expanding. In the Philippines, there were American, Dutch, British, German, and Mexican expatriates sent by their global companies to oversee the local subsidiaries and to educate them on the policies and procedures of the parent company. At about that same time, Japanese car executives were also sending their expatriates to the USA to open sales offices (Cusumano

1988). Today, this is only one of several models for expatriate assignments. In this traditional model, the typical expatriate was one who came from the home country of the multinational, and who was sent overseas, many times for a two- to three-year stint. Depending on the business goals of the company, the expatriate could be expected to accomplish one of several objectives, for example: find a local agent to sell the company's products, meet with local distributors, select local franchisees, negotiate with a joint venture partner, hire a local manager to run an overseas office, or lay the groundwork for setting up a production plant.

In almost all cases, the expatriates would "export" their knowledge and the company's competencies, especially if their firm was setting up an overseas subsidiary and hiring local employees. There was an unwritten assumption that the locals had to be molded and educated on the company's products, policies, and practices. After a period of time, the expatriate would leave, with another one taking his or her place. Eventually, there might be someone in the local office who would be given greater responsibility but invariably, the country manager would be an expatriate (Inkson et al. 1998; Peterson et al. 2000).

At times, the selection of the expatriate to send abroad seemed unusual. For example, in one company, a Latin American executive was selected to head the company's German subsidiary. On the surface, this appeared to be a poor fit, since the two countries are culturally very dissimilar. In this particular case, however, the selection was quite astute. The German subsidiary had lacked a passionate leader who could inject some energy into the business, and he provided that. He was just what the German employees needed; he energized the organization, and excited the employees in that subsidiary. After two years, he had improved the subsidiary's performance and profitability.

At another company, a female from New Zealand working in Australia was selected to lead the marketing organization of a subsidiary of a US company in Japan. Despite the paucity of female executives in Japan, and the concerns some senior managers had about how older Japanese executives would react to interacting with a *gaijin* female executive, she did quite well in Japan.

Peter Drucker (1973) wrote that a manager has five critical responsibilities: set objectives, organize (e.g., analyze activities, structure, and select people for jobs), motivate and communicate, measure, and develop people. It is challenging enough to do these without adding the complexity of managing in a complex, global environment. Yet this is what more and more companies are demanding of their leaders today. In the many interviews my students and I have conducted with executives, the ability to lead globally is increasingly one of the most important requirements for those interested in senior management positions. In a speech many years ago, Jack Welch said (Black and Gregersen 1999):

> The Jack Welch of the future cannot be like me. I've spent my entire career in the United States. The next head of GE will be somebody who has spent time in Bombay, in Hong Kong, in Buenos Aires. (p. 56)

And General Petraeus (2006), in an entirely different context, said:

> Working in another culture is enormously difficult if one doesn't understand the ethnic groups, tribes, religious elements, political parties and other social groupings—and their respective viewpoints; the relationships among the various groups; governmental structures and processes; local and regional history; and, of course, local and national leaders. (p. 8)

In one of his observations about soldiering in Iraq, Petraeus noted that cultural awareness is a force multiplier, and that knowledge of the cultural terrain is sometimes even more important than knowledge of the geographic terrain.

Goldman Sachs, which has a large office in Tokyo, started a program several years ago to help its Japanese staff interact more effectively with colleagues around the world. It's referred to as a "culture dojo."[2] The program provides a forum for people to get together to share their experiences of working for a global business and to learn from each other. There are similar efforts by companies like Accenture and General Electric to help Japanese executives overcome cultural barriers. Mr. Takashi Yoshimura, managing director of Goldman's compliance division in Tokyo, observes that there is a language and a cultural challenge for many Japanese. In my own experience working in Japan, both are present. Many Japanese were not comfortable speaking in English, and I often had a translator in many of the meetings I led in Tokyo. In fact, senior management in one company had set a policy that to be promoted to a *kacho* level (similar to a manager level in other countries), the candidate also needed to score at least 900 in a standardized English Proficiency test.

The cultural issue is around the discomfort many Japanese have about "thinking out loud," "jumping to discussions," and hesitating to say something unless it is important. According to Mr. Yoshimura, "In my college (in Japan), people didn't say anything that might make them look foolish, but at Harvard Law School people said whatever they wanted to say."

A commonly accepted definition of leadership, paraphrasing Yukl (2009), is that it involves a process of influence over others to guide, structure, and facilitate activities and relationships in the pursuit of certain outcomes. How does global leadership differ from leadership in general? Some managers we interviewed claim that leadership is leadership everywhere, and that the major difference is the greater diversity of situations, including cultural issues. However, there are several reasons why global leadership is more than just a difference in degree from leadership in general.

First, the context that global leaders face is very different and more complex than that faced by domestic leaders (Canals 2014; Steers et al. 2012). The cultural, economic, environmental, political, and religious differences are generally greater than those faced by leaders managing within their own country. Youssef and Luthans (2012) have pointed out that global leaders experience three types of distance: physical distance (due to geographical dispersion), structural distance (due to organizational factors like decentralization and span of control), and psychological or social distance (due to status or power differentials), and these have a cumulative effect on the complexity of the global leadership role.

Second, the cognitive, attitudinal, and behavioral requirements of global leaders differ significantly from those of domestic leaders (Alon and Higgins 2005; Jokinen 2005). Third, the challenges and experiences that global leaders face are decidedly different from those needed to become an effective domestic leader (Adler and Bartholomew 1992; Hollenbeck 2001). These include going overseas to establish a joint venture, acquiring a local business, start a subsidiary, and working for or leading a global team. Based on their review of the research, Mendenhall et al. (2012) propose the following definition of global leadership:

> The process of influencing others to adopt a shared vision through structures and methods that facilitate positive change while fostering individual and collective growth in a context characterized by significant levels of complexity, flow and presence. (p. 500)

They then propose the following definition of a global leader, which flows from the definition above:

> An individual who inspires a group of people to willingly pursue a positive vision in an effectively organized fashion while fostering individual and collective growth in a context characterized by significant levels of complexity, flow and presence. (p. 500)

While adding clarity to the construct of global leadership, the definition seems to be missing or downplaying two important elements. One, there is no explicit mention of the leader's desire to achieve important organizational goals or objectives; this "results orientation" is a quality of leaders that many organizations seek when management is deciding who their future leaders will be. The definition instead seems to lean more toward Kotter's (2001) description of a leader versus a manager, whereas a global leader needs to do both.

Two, this definition does not explicitly address the multi-country or multi-cultural nature of the work of global leaders. In other words, this definition could very well apply to leaders in domestic organizations that are characterized by conditions of complexity, flow, and presence. To make these more explicit, I propose modifying this definition by *defining a global leader as one who influences and inspires a group of people to pursue organizational objectives while fostering individual and collective growth in a multi-cultural context characterized by significant levels of ambiguity, uncertainty, complexity, and distance.*

In an early formulation, Bartlett and Ghoshal (1991) stated that "there is no such thing as a universal global manager," and proposed instead that there are actually four different global manager roles: the business (or product-division) manager, the country manager, the functional manager, and the global manager. Each of these roles, according to them, requires different approaches: the business manager is a strategist, architect, and coordinator; the country manager is a sensor, builder, and contributor; the functional manager is a scanner, cross-pollinator, and champion; and the corporate manager is a leader, talent scout, and developer. However, in addition to differences in these roles based on purpose, global leadership roles can also differ along the following dimensions:

1. Face-to-face versus virtual. Many global leaders today have members reporting to them who are dispersed geographically. The dynamics

of leading virtual teams differ significantly from the leadership of face-to-face teams (Kayworth and Leidner 2002). Cultural preferences also make virtual global leadership more complex than face-to-face leadership (Hardin et al. 2007; Mukherjee et al. 2012).

2. Direct versus indirect or matrix. In a number of organizations, global leaders are leading teams whose members do not report directly to them. Many of these are in a matrix relationship, where team members may have two bosses. An example is Fujitsu's recent reorganization (Fig. 1.1), which restructured the company into five geographic regions, three business lines, and two global functions[3]:

3. Headquarters (HQ) versus non-HQ. Bartlett and Ghoshal's model implies that with the exception of the country manager, the other roles originate from the center. Over the past decade, however, more managers from various locations around the world and who are of different nationalities from senior management in headquarters are being asked to take on global assignments.

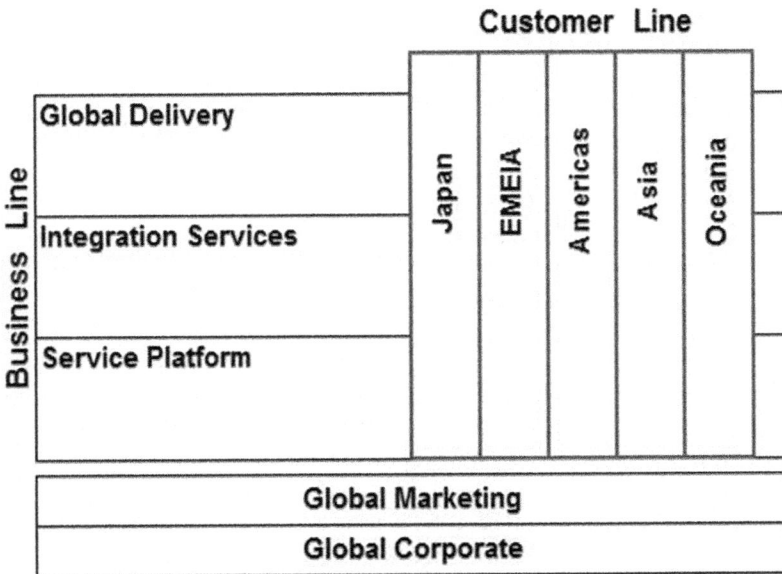

Fig. 1.1   Fujitsu's organization

4. Single versus dual roles. Many organizations have been giving dual roles to some of their global leaders. Here are two examples. In one organization, the country manager of Malaysia also became responsible for another country (Thailand, in this case). In another organization, a regional marketing leader was given the additional responsibility for leading a global project team to recommend innovations for a certain product category within the company's portfolio of products.

5. Senior versus other levels. Bartlett and Ghoshal imply that these global roles are primarily at senior levels. As Mendenhall et al. (2012) have suggested, global leaders are not necessarily limited to individuals in senior positions in their organizations. Many individuals in various levels of their organization have taken on global leadership roles.

If we took all these different combinations, there would theoretically be 32 different types of global managers! Among all these combinations, four composite roles seem to prevail among today's multinationals:

- A senior-level global manager in headquarters heading a function or a product division.
- A senior-level global manager outside headquarters heading a country or a region, or both. In some cases, this global manager might also be responsible for a global initiative and have worldwide responsibility.
- A global team leader, not necessarily at a senior level, who heads a face-to-face global team or a virtual team. In some cases, the team members may be matrixed to the leader and/or may not report directly to the team leader.
- An individual, not necessarily at a senior level, whose role it is to interact or work with one or several of the following groups in other cultures: employees, peers, managers, customers, suppliers and other stakeholders, and who has the potential to make a positive impact through his/her leadership actions.

As Bartlett and Ghoshal have suggested, we need to rethink the roles of global managers as well as the types of assignments global managers have. These roles and assignments have important implications for the requirements of global leadership.

Notes

1. Jason Zweig, "A Fireside Chat with Charlie Munger," The Wall Street Journal, September 12, 2014: http://blogs.wsj.com/moneybeat/2014/09/12/a-fireside-chat-with-charlie-munger/
2. "Cross-Cultural Conversations" by Michiyo Nakamoto, The Financial Times, January 11, 2012.
3. http://www.fujitsu.com/global/about/resources/news/press-releases/2014/0313-05.html

References

Adler, Nancy J., and Susan Bartholomew. 1992. Managing Globally Competent People. *Academy of Management Executive* 6(3): 52–65.

Alon, Ilan, and James M. Higgins. 2005. Global Leadership Success Through Emotional and Cultural Intelligences. *Business Horizons* 48(6): 501–512.

Bartlett, Christopher, and Sumantra Ghoshal. 1991. What Is a Global Manager? *Harvard Business Review* 70(5): 124–132.

Black, J. Stewart, and Hal B. Gregersen. 1999. The Right Way to Manage Expats. *Harvard Business Review* 77(2): 52–63.

Canals, Jordi. 2014. Global Leadership Development, Strategic Alignment and CEOs Commitment. *Journal of Management Development* 33(5): 487–502.

Cusumano, Michael A. 1988. Manufacturing Innovation: Lessons from the Japanese Auto Industry. *Sloan Management Review* 30(1): 29–39.

Drucker, Peter. 1973. *Management: Tasks, Responsibilities, Practices*. New York: Harper & Row.

Hardin, Andrew, Mark Fuller, and Robert Davison. 2007. I Know I Can, but Can We? Culture and Efficacy Beliefs in Global Virtual Teams. *Small Group Research* 38(1): 130–155.

Hollenbeck, George P. 2001. A Serendipitous Sojourn Through the Global Leadership Literature. In William Mobley and Morgan McCall (Eds.), *Advances in Global Leadership*. 2. 15-47. Stamford, CT: JAI Press.

Inkson, Kerr, Michael B. Arthur, Judith Pringle, and Sean Barry. 1998. Expatriate Assignment Versus Overseas Experience: Contrasting Models of International Human Resource Development. *Journal of World Business* 32(4): 351–368.

Jokinen, Tiina. 2005. Global Leadership Competencies: A Review and Discussion. *Journal of European Industrial Training* 29(3): 199–216.

Kayworth, Timothy R., and Dorothy E. Leidner. 2002. Leadership Effectiveness in Global Virtual Teams. *Journal of Management Information Systems* 18(3): 7–40.

Kotter, John P. 2001. What Leaders Really Do. *Harvard Business Review*. 75(11): 75–96.

Mendenhall, Mark E., B. Sebastian Reiche, Allan Bird, and Joyce S. Osland. 2012. Defining the 'Global' in Global Leadership. *Journal of World Business* 47(4): 493–503.

Mukherjee, Debmalya, Susan C. Hanlon, Ben L. Kedia, and Prashant Srivastava. 2012. Organizational Identification Among Global Virtual Team Members. *Cross Cultural Management* 19(4): 526–545.

Peterson, Richard B., Nancy K. Napier, and Won Shul-Shim. 2000. Expatriate Management: Comparison of MNCs Across Four Parent Countries. *Thunderbird International Business Review* 42(2): 145–166.

Petraeus, Lieutenant General David. 2006. Learning Counterinsurgency: Observations from Soldiering in Iraq. *Military Review*, January–February, 2–12.

Steers, Richard M., Carlos Sanchez-Runde, and Luciara Nardon. 2012. Leadership in a Global Context: New Directions in Research and Theory Development. *Journal of World Business* 47(4): 479–482.

Youssef, Carolyn M., and Fred Luthans. 2012. Positive Global Leadership. *Journal of World Business* 47(4): 539–547.

Yukl, Gary. 2009. *Leadership in Organizations*, Seventh edn. Upper Saddle River, NJ: Prentice Hall.

CHAPTER 2

The Context: What's Changing

In 2005, six of the ten largest companies in the world by revenue came from the USA. The four exceptions were Royal Dutch Shell (Netherlands), BP (Great Britain), Daimler Chrysler (Germany), and Toyota Motor (Japan).

By 2010, only two of the top ten had their headquarters in the USA: Wal-Mart (now the largest, from third in 2005) and Exxon Mobil (which dropped from first to fifth). There are now three Chinese companies in the top ten list (all state-owned), along with a Dutch company (Royal Dutch Shell), a Swiss company (Glencore), a German company (Volkswagen), a British company (BP), and a Japanese company (Toyota).[1]

This should come as no surprise to many. The dual drivers of falling trade barriers and technological change have accelerated the globalization of businesses today, as companies look for competitive advantage through expanding their customer base and supply chains. At the same time, the increase in multinational corporations has contributed to the acceleration of globalization; corporations sell their products worldwide, and the capital flows through them perpetuate the global financial system (Moore 2005). Regardless of their industry, managers have to pay attention to the implications of globalization on their business, especially since virtually all countries still embrace the principles of international trade and invest-

---

Globalization is no longer an option but a strategic imperative for all but the smallest corporations. (Gupta et al. 2008) (Reprinted with permission)

© The Editor(s) (if applicable) and The Author(s) 2016
R. Henson, *Successful Global Leadership*,
DOI 10.1057/978-1-137-58990-3_2

ment.[2] The following are selected macro trends that are affecting global businesses and global leaders today.

THE RISE OF EMERGING MARKETS

In his book, *Global Tilt*, management consultant Ram Charan (2013) describes the shift in economic power not from the West to the East, but from the North to the South. He places countries above and below the 31st parallel (a rough division, he admits), with the USA, Western Europe, and Japan above, and countries like Mexico, Brazil, the Middle East, sub-Saharan Africa, India, China, and South Africa (among others) below. As he points out, "Wealth is moving from North to South, and so are jobs. Companies in the South, big and small, have a fierce entrepreneurial drive. Many are reveling in double-digit revenue growth … they are building scale and challenging companies of the North on all fronts." (p. 5).

Latin America's economy grew by 4.6 % a year over the past decade, East Asia by 5.4 %, and Southeast Asia by 5.9 %—in contrast to the USA (1.6 %) and the European Union (1.7 %).[3] In fact, 2013 was the first year in which emerging markets accounted for more than half of world GDP on the basis of purchasing power, according to the International Monetary Fund (Fig. 2.1). For the Economist, "The remarkably rapid

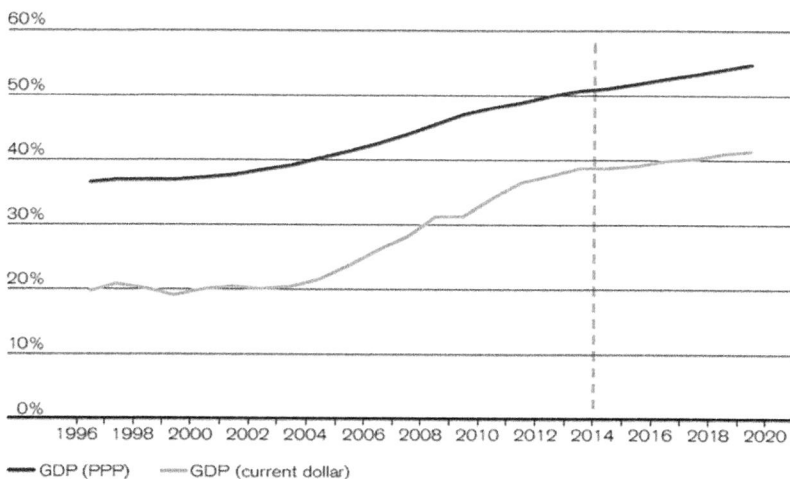

Fig. 2.1 Emerging market share of global GDP (%)
Source : IMF forecasts, Credit Suisse research

growth the world has seen in these two decades (2003–2011) marks the biggest economic transformation in modern history."

The Economist's Economic Intelligence Unit (EIU) forecasts that China will replace the USA as the top economy in the world by 2050, with India just below the USA, and Indonesia and Japan following India. According to the EIU, Asia will account for 52 % of global GDP by 2050.[4] The Corporate Executive Board and Russell Reynolds predict that the compound annual growth rate for emerging economies in Asia between 2011 and 2030 will be 5.34 %, versus 3.45 % for emerging economies outside of Asia, and 2.04 % for advanced economies.[5]

Subramanian (2011) has traced the economic dominance of various countries historically using an index he has created. In 1870, he writes, the UK was the most dominant economic power in the world, much greater than Germany and France. Not only were they a dominant exporter, but also a substantial net creditor. By 1913, the gap between the UK and its closest rivals had narrowed, and by 1929, the USA had become the world's dominant economic power. By 2010, however, China's index had become close to the USA: " demography works overwhelmingly in China's favor. China is as big as the United States in terms of economic size and trade, but the United States is a large net debtor while China is a large net creditor." (p. 49)

He then predicts that, if emerging markets keep on growing three percentage points a year faster than the USA, they will account for two-thirds of the world's output by 2030, with the four most populous emerging markets (China, India, Indonesia, and Brazil) making up two-fifths of global GDP. In their report on megatrends,[6] the consulting firm Ernst &Young predicts that global economic power will continue shifting to rapid-growth economies such as China, India, and Brazil, and that developing countries will continue to grow their share of capital inflows and outflows. By their estimates, these "rapid-growth" markets will account for 47 % of gross global inflows by 2030, up from 23 % in 2010.[7]

Organizations are well aware of these trends, although in at least one study, some multinationals from the developed markets appear to be lagging in their response.[8] In Fig. 2.2, note the differences between developed and emerging market executives on the strategies their companies use when operating in emerging markets:

McKinsey Global Institute (2015) has identified some of the advantages that emerging market competitors have over their developed market counterparts. They are nimble and lean, with workers who are younger,

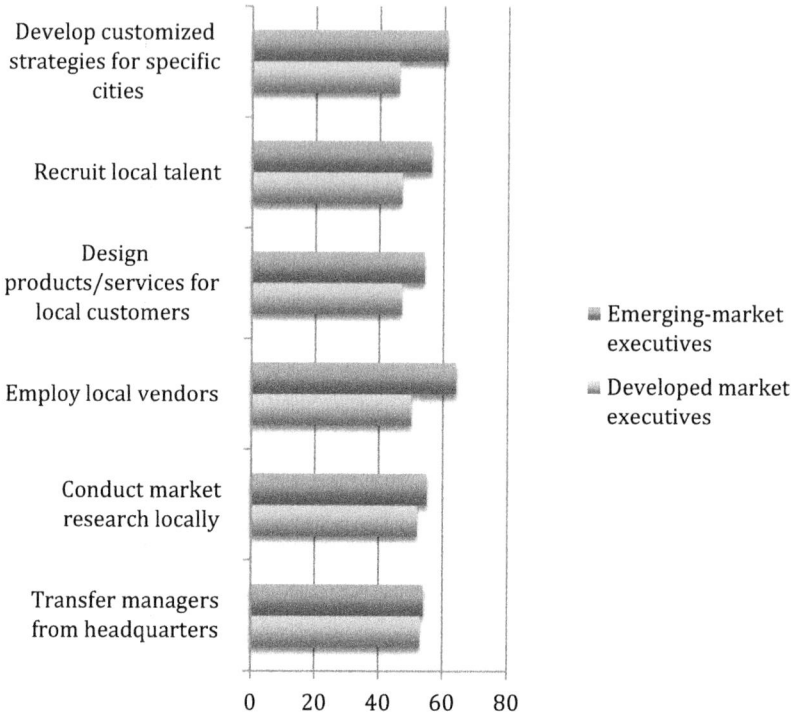

Fig. 2.2 Strategies reported by emerging-market and developed market executives

skilled, and highly motivated. They are aggressive in going to underserved markets, and because of the business history with large conglomerates in emerging markets, many of these emerging-market competitors are able to diversify their risks and protect themselves against market instability.

SHIFTING DEMOGRAPHICS ACROSS AND WITHIN COUNTRIES

Several trends are worth noting here. First, the earth's population is expected to grow to 6.5 billion by 2025 (Beamish et al. 2003). The Population Reference Bureau[9] has charted the world's population from

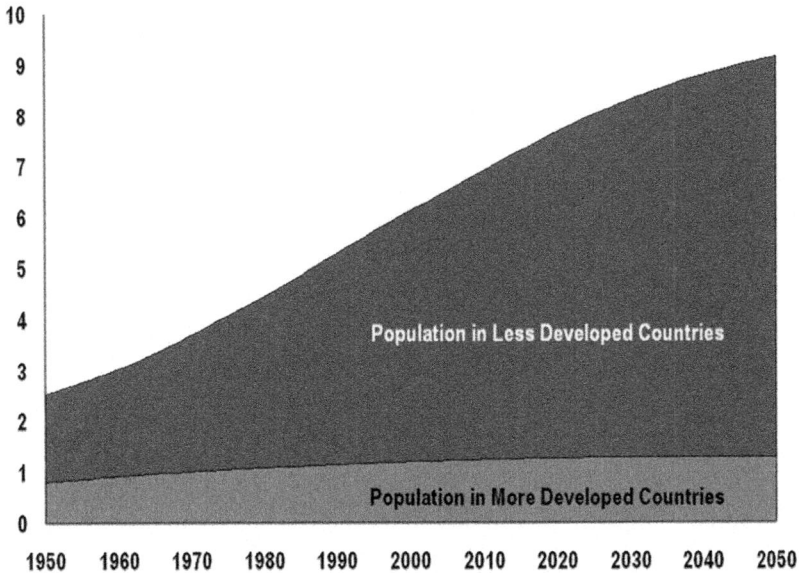

Fig. 2.3 Population growth in less and more developed countries

1950 to 2050 (in billions), and much of the growth will come from the less developed countries (Fig. 2.3):

A second trend is the growth of the middle class. There are various definitions of what constitutes the middle class; an Ernst & Young report[10] suggests a range of $10–$100 per day per day in purchasing power parity terms, as do Kharas and Gertz (2010). By these estimates, at least 50 % of the world's population will become middle class by 2030 (from 29 % in 2008), with two-thirds of that growth coming from the Asia Pacific region. By 2021, for example, there are expected to be over two billion Asians in middle-class households (670 million of them in China alone). While there are still pockets of poverty in many places, more than half of the world is now "middle class"—for the first time in history[11] (Fig. 2.4):

What this means is best summarized by Eduardo Giannetti da Fonseca, the Brazilian economist[12]: "Members of the middle class are people who are not resigned to a life of poverty, who are prepared to make sacrifices to create a better life for themselves but who have not started with life's material problems solved because they have material assets to make their lives easy."

*If trends continue, the middle class in low and middle income countries will grow from 5% in 2005,
to 25% in 2030. China alone will add one billion people to the middle class*

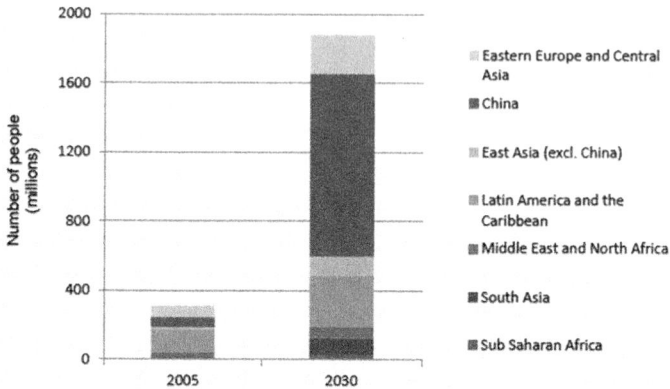

Fig. 2.4   Middle-class growth forecasts, 2003–2030

Also important to consider is the concept of the "growth sweet spot" (see E&Y Report referred to earlier), which is when a huge influx of people start earning over $10 per day or $6000 per capita income:

> At this point, purchasing habits should attract the attention of companies accustomed to supplying to middle-class markets in the developed world. The power of the sweet spot also produces a 'middle-class effect,' where the size of the middle class is directly proportional to the rate of economic growth. Hitting the sweet-spot level accelerates growth, which, in turn adds more people to the middle class, producing a virtuous circle. The economist Surjit Bhalla has claimed that every 10 percentage-point increase in a nation's middle class results in a 0.5 percentage-point rise in its growth rate.

Similarly, Goldman and Kelly (2015) refer to this "consuming class" and projects that this group will grow to 3.2 billion by 2020 (from 1.8 billion in 2009); many of them will come from the emerging economies and will be increasingly urban.

While poverty is still a major issue around the world, the number of poor people has been decreasing at a rapid rate. According to research by the Brookings Institution (Chandy and Gertz 2011), the number of poor people between 2005 and 2010 fell from 1.3 billion to under 900 million.

Most economists agree that poverty levels have indeed dropped world-wide. The Millennium Developing Goal 1 of halving extreme poverty (defined as those living below $1.25 a day) between 1990 and 2015 was actually reached five years ago although, as a World Bank analysis points out, the drop in poverty has been caused mainly by China and India.

The rise of the middle class will mean not only more discretionary income that could fuel growth but perhaps also a desire for stability and a more civilized world. Corporations will need to think even more differently about how to serve these new consumers; the traditional models of scaling or globalizing may no longer be sufficient. Of course, this new middle class will still be poorer than the middle class in advanced economies, which account for 40 % of the growth in consumer spending power.[13]

A third trend is the aging of the population, particularly in developed economies. What demographers refer to as the "demographic transition" (Dyson 2010) is the decline in mortality and fertility rates. Decreasing fertility, combined with lengthening life expectancy, has significant implications for the future. The fertility rate is now below the replacement level of 2.1 children in virtually all of the developed economies. Life expectancy, on the other hand, is expected to increase to 76 years by 2050 from its current average of 66 (as of 2005). In the developed countries, there is an unprecedented increase in the number of people aged 65 and over, as well as declines in birth rates and in the overall population. The age group of 50–55 will become the largest single group of older people in America by 2030. Many organizations and industries—especially health care, hospitality, and financial services—have already started paying attention to the needs of the elderly.

Dobbs et al. (2015) point out that about 60 % of the world's population lives in countries below the fertility rate of 2.1 children per woman. Even in China, the labor work force actually peaked in 2012. Chand and Tung (2014) cite research that the overall median age in developed countries was 29.0 in 1950, but is forecasted to rise to 45.5 by 2050. The overall worldwide population of people over 60 will reach two billion by 2050, and 25 % of them will be people over the age of 65. At the same time, in 55 countries, 40 % or more of the population is now under the age of 15—and most of these are in the emerging markets.

As The Economist[14] has indicated:

In future there will almost certainly be two distinct workforces, broadly made up of the under-50s and the over-50s respectively. These two workforces are likely to differ markedly in their needs and behaviour, and in the jobs they do. The younger group will need a steady income from a permanent job, or at least a succession of full-time jobs. The rapidly growing older group will have much more choice, and will be able to combine traditional jobs, non-conventional jobs and leisure in whatever proportion suits them best.

The figures below show the age distribution in more developed countries[15] (Figs. 2.5 and 2.6):

Figure 2.7 shows the percentage of the population that is aged 65 and over worldwide as well as in different regions.[16]

With the shrinking and graying of the employee labor pool, organizations have begun to rethink their human resources policies, from hiring, retention, and retirement. Some organizations have begun to raise their retirement age, while others are bringing back retired workers (Paul and Townsend 1993).

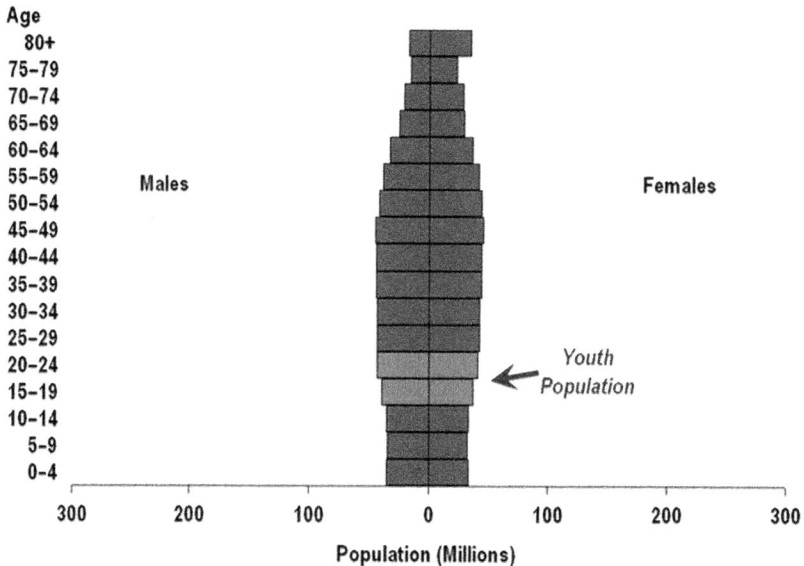

Fig. 2.5   Age distribution in more developed countries

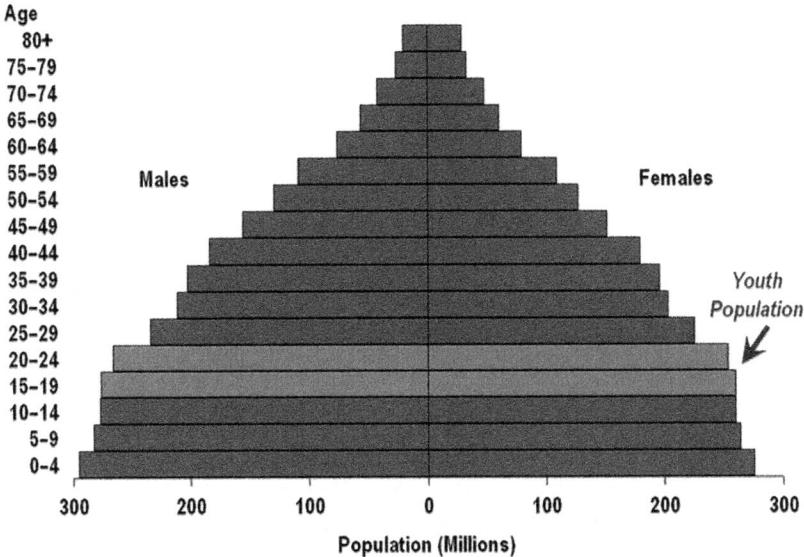

Fig. 2.6   Age distribution in less developed countries

A fourth trend is the urbanization of the world's population. According to a United Nations report, over half of the world's population now lives in urban areas (54 %), and this percentage is expected to increase to 66 % by 2050.[17] Regionally, Asia leads the world with 53 % of the world's population in urban areas. In 2014, there were 28 "mega-cities" (cities with over ten million inhabitants) worldwide; by 2030, there will be 41 of these mega-cities. Tokyo has 38 million inhabitants, followed by Delhi with 25 million and Shanghai with 23 million. Almost all of the urban population growth in the next 30 years will come from cities of developing countries. The United Nations' estimates are that the urban population will increase to 5.2 billion in 2050 from 2.5 billion in 2009; for developed countries, there will be a little over one billion by 2050, and over 67 % of this growth will come from immigration (legal and illegal).

Urbanization is generally beneficial for economic development, and urban populations are on average better off than their rural counterparts in terms of such indicators as access to health services, literacy rates, and life expectancy. There are of course some challenges as well, especially in terms of inequality and environmental issues. However, these concentrations of

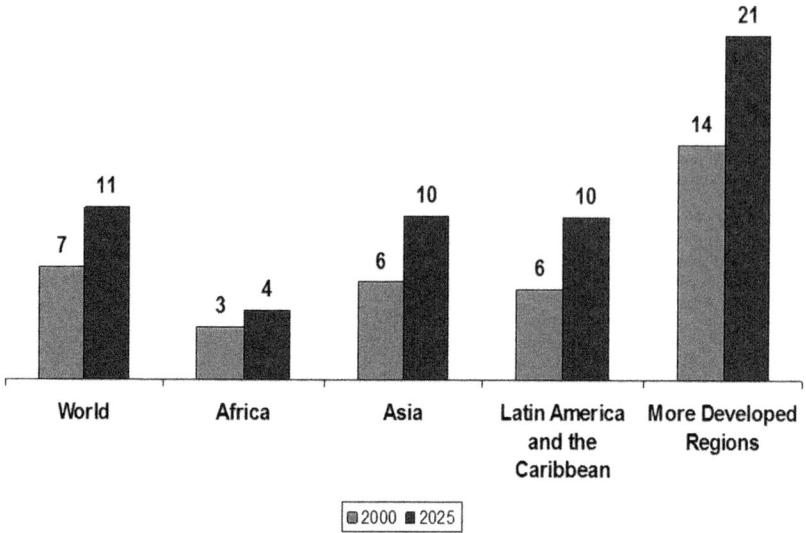

Fig. 2.7 Percentages 65 and over regionally—2000 and 2025 (Projected)

people will mean that organizations can take advantage of clusters of consumers as well as talent pools in urban areas.

ACCELERATING TECHNOLOGICAL CHANGES

Historians over the years have documented the enormous impact resulting from new technologies. The introduction of agriculture led to the proliferation of cities, the printing press created mass readership, and the computer has changed many aspects of our lives. New technologies seem to be spreading much more quickly than they did in the past. For example, according to Dobbs et al. (2015), it took 38 years for the radio to reach 50 million users, but only one year for Facebook to reach that many users (of course, the world's population is much greater today than when radio was first introduced).

The Internet has accelerated change and facilitated connections across individuals, organizations, and nations. It has made information more readily available, with consumers having more knowledge about product features than they otherwise would. Employees working in companies have close to real-time information about company activities that may impact them. Advances in computing technology have enabled organizations to become more sophisticated in data analytics. Many companies now have Chief Digital Officers who are responsible for such activities as e-commerce and digital marketing.[18] Advances in transportation technology—especially with containerization, large container ships, and airplanes—have made worldwide competition even more intense for many firms.

Technology is impacting the lives of many especially in continents such as Africa. Mobile phones are becoming commonplace there, and by 2020, just about every African will have a mobile phone.[19] What this means for technology companies, among other things, is that they are having to create what Govindarajan and Trimble (2012) call "reverse innovation" to build their market share. For example, some firms are using mobile money to sell life-insurance policies; a Singapore-listed company called Olam " has signed up 30,000 farmers in Tanzania as suppliers of coffee, cotton and cocoa through a mobile-phone system" (p. 45).

Technology is also changing the nature of work and the way organizations are designed. Dobbs et al. (2015) have pointed to the increase in jobs today that require more interactions, that is, the searching, coordinating, and monitoring required to exchange ideas, goods, and services. These interaction jobs cover both relatively low-skilled jobs (such as corrections officers) to high-skilled jobs (such as surgeons). According to them, between 2001 and 2009, close to five million of these jobs were created in the USA, while three million production jobs disappeared. Within these interaction jobs, tasks that are routine and low-value-added are either assigned to workers whose wages are less expensive, or outsourced outright. In many Human Resources departments, for example, management has outsourced routine activities such as resume screening and benefits processing. In the past decade, the automobile industry has replaced many of the routine activities associated with assembling cars with robots, while hiring workers with higher-level skills to oversee the automation.

The skills gap for these high-level jobs has been well documented by many (e.g., Bernard and Jensen 1997; Dobbs et al. 2012). Not only is there increasing demand for graduates in science, technology, engineering, and mathematics (otherwise called STEM), but the demand for skilled factory workers is also increasing. Some companies especially in Silicon Valley have been urging changes in the US Government's immigration policies to expand quotas for high-skilled foreign workers. Other companies have created centers of expertise in various places around the world where clusters of desired talent are located.

CONTINUED GLOBALIZATION AND TRADE

The global recession of 2008 no doubt impacted globalization. World exports as a share of GDP have been flat since 2008, and capital flows are about a third of what they were prior to 2008. These are troubling signs, and the Economist has coined a term called "gated globalization" to describe recent trends.[20] First, regional and bilateral trade liberalization pacts are emerging in place of multilateral WTO trade agreements. Second, restrictions on foreign direct investment seem to be increasing as well. Third, while borders have not been closed to immigrants, the flow of people between countries is being managed more carefully. For example, the Singaporean government has made it more difficult for expatriates to secure working permits.

Fourth, recent geopolitical events (e.g., Russia's invasion of Ukraine and the West's subsequent sanctions on Russia) have created tensions and challenges for many multinationals. For example, McDonald's has over 400 restaurants in Russia, from Moscow to Eastern Siberia. Recently, Russia's national consumer-safety regulator ordered the closure of at least nine McDonald's outlets, including its flagship Pushkin Square location, for alleged violations of sanitary rules. The regulators also have conducted inspections of over 200 McDonald's stores for potential sanitation and health violations.[21] Even so, McDonald's has signed a license agreement with a Russian franchisee to open more restaurants, this time in Siberia.[22]

Nonetheless, the latest evidence is that globalization is back, at least as measured by the DHL Global Connectedness Index.[23] This index measures several types of cross-border flow: trade (in both goods and services), information, people (including tourists, students, and migrants) and capital. It also tracks the depth of international connections (how much activity crosses borders), their breadth (how many different borders are being crossed), and their direction (how outward and inward flows compare). As the chart below shows, depth has rebounded from the global recession although breadth has declined, suggesting that there are fewer cross-border transactions (Fig. 2.8).

Many multinationals are generally aware of the risks they undertake when entering foreign markets, and they have risk mitigation strategies in place. Yet some events may not be foreseen, and their occurrence could

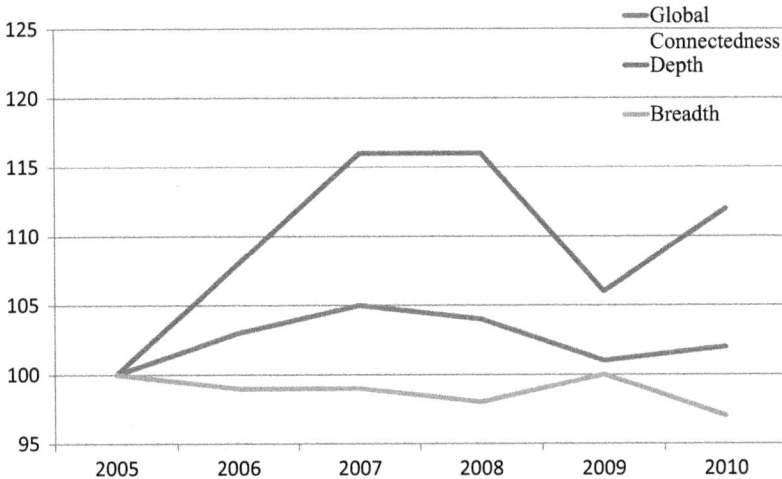

Fig. 2.8   Global connectedness, depth and breadth, 2005–2013

send red flags to other multinationals on increasing their foreign direct investment, at least in some markets. Still, the potential for growth in these markets is too great to ignore, and the prospects of multinationals dramatically reducing their foreign direct investments remain low. As examples: Tata Motors acquired Jaguar and Land Rover from Ford for 2.3 billion dollars.[24] Geeley of China acquired Volvo, also from Ford, for $1.3 billion in cash. They also acquired London Taxi Co. (famous for the black cabs) for 17.5 million dollars.[25] Shuanghai International Holdings acquired the world's largest producer of pork, Smithfield Foods, for 4.7 billion dollars.[26]

Beyond trade, Erez and Drori (2009) point out that globalization impacts organizations and people through three global cultural processes or trends: rationalization, professionalization, and actorhood. Rationalization drives organizations to compare themselves through rankings and profitability measures to value standardization, and to become more customer-focused. Professionalization reinforces interdependence through the sharing of professional knowledge and values. Actorhood emphasizes the need for personal development and recognition of cultural diversity. According to Erez and Drori, these global trends complement many multinationals' cultural values, such as risk-taking, customer orientation, interdependence, trust, and acceptance of cultural diversity.

EVOLVING ORGANIZATIONAL FORMS

To adapt to changes in the global marketplace and align their strategies, global organizations continuously reorganize and reconfigure their structures. Two basic principles of organizational design are that structure should follow strategy, and that structures should not be built around individuals. Unfortunately, we see examples of these principles being violated by organizations on a regular basis. In some cases, senior management decides to reorganize for one of several reasons: they want to shake up the company because it has become too complacent; they see that their competitors are reorganizing so they follow suit, whether this structure makes sense for them or not; or they force-fit a structure as a result of an acquisition or a joint venture. At other times, senior management organizes around individuals, either to give selected executives more of an "empire" (and enhance their power), or to test executives for future promotional roles.

Invariably, these structures don't align with the organizations' strategies or their capabilities. Senior management then decides to reorganize once again, in an endless if futile quest to find the right formula. With the average tenure of today's CEOs being about five years (the exact number seems to vary depending on the samples studied, but the trend is there for both US and non-US CEOs),[27] there are only so many opportunities for senior management to get their organization structure right.

There is no question, however, that organizational structures are continuing to evolve, especially for global companies. However, in a recent survey of senior executives, 78 % replied that their organizations still had to find the right operating model for their global business.[28] In another survey[29] 42 % of executives felt that their organization was not aligned with the strategy. When Jack Welch was CEO of General Electric, he used the term "boundaryless organization" to reinforce what he wanted GE to become—flat, non-hierarchical, empowered (Slater 1998). Finding the right structure and operating model is also challenging due to various corporate governance mechanisms and their lack of alignment with companies' operating models. In a recent Deloitte survey of global companies, for example, close to 50 % of companies reported that they were centralized at the global level but held their country and regional units accountable for P&L.[30]

Hamel (2007) goes so far as to assert that we are going to be transitioning into a "post-organizational" society and he questions the model of organizations that has served business well over the past 100 years or so. He argues that we need a revolution in management because businesses still think in terms of the old, traditional paradigm that Max Weber, Frederick Taylor, and Henry Ford pioneered. For Hamel, business needs to leapfrog and create a new paradigm. He is less clear on what this management innovation will look like, although he does cite companies like Whole Foods, Google, and W.L. Gore as organizations that are truly empowering their people, creating a community of spirit, and building an enlarged sense of purpose.

In advocating for more management innovation, he has formulated some of his rules for innovators (p. 239):

> To solve a systemic problem you need to understand its systemic roots.
> Commit to revolutionary goals, but take evolutionary steps.
> Be clear about the performance metrics your innovation is designed to improve.

There does not seem to be anything particularly revolutionary about these very sensible rules, and good managers can certainly apply them within their organizations today. General Stanley McChrystal (McChrystal et al. 2015) describes how his Joint Special Operations Task Force, organized along traditional military command-and-control structures, had to transform itself in order to meet the challenges of dealing with Al Qaeda in Iraq, which operated as a decentralized network and could strike quickly. He and his team created strong lateral ties between units and partner organizations to encourage cooperation across these silos and establish trust, and developed a structure he called a "team of teams—an organization within which the relationships between constituent teams resembled those between individuals on a single team; teams that had traditionally resided in separate silos would now have to become fused to one another via trust and purpose." (p. 132)

One clear trend is around the flattening of layers and increasing spans of control (Littler et al. 2003). Many years ago, the common management wisdom was that a manager's span of control should be no greater than five. Larger than that and a manager would not be able to devote the time to "manage" his or her direct reports effectively. These days, some CEOs have direct reports of over 20. At Google, Schmidt and Rosenberg (2014) report on their rule of seven—managers should have a minimum of seven direct reports. One reason for pushing the span of control outward is to prevent managers from doing too much micromanaging, thus providing more autonomy for employees.

In an interesting analysis, Wulf (2012) investigated whether this flattening (or delayering) has in fact occurred in corporations. She sampled 300 large US firms over a 15-year period and found that indeed flattening has occurred, at least at the higher levels of organizations. She found, for example, that the number of firms with COO positions decreased by around 20 % over this period, and the number of positions between division head and CEO decreased by about 25 %. She also found that the number of positions reporting directly to the CEO almost doubled (from 4.5 to almost 7), and more recent data suggest that this trend is continuing (with average span of control up to 9.8).

However, she also found that this flattening had some unintended consequences. Specifically, decision-making actually became more centralized, and CEOs of these flattened companies became even more hands-on. Perhaps part of the reason for this is her finding that the composition of the types of positions reporting to the CEO has also changed. That is, the C-suite started to expand to include executives with global functional responsibility in such areas as human resources, information technology, and marketing. If this is in fact a result of flattening, lower-level managers may feel more disempowered, and the tensions between headquarters and subsidiaries perhaps increasing. Her finding is not surprising given the trend in global organizations to "globalize" and integrate certain core functions such as human resources and supply chain. This has led to multiple tensions between the corporate center and the subsidiaries and operating units, and occasional confusion as to whether this is part of a pendulum swinging back to centralization from decentralization.

In one multinational, senior management decided to globalize some of its functions such as Marketing and Procurement while creating line functions responsible for P&L in its various geographies; the latter were called Operating Business Units or OBUs. The restructuring was announced with great fanfare, but roles and responsibilities were not clearly defined between the global functions and these OBUs, thus leading to confusion and many concerns. Several line executives commented that the size of the global organization "smacked of control" and that they perceived that more power was going to the center. They were unclear as to what their levels of authority were, and what they were going to be held accountable for. It took several years, and a number of executive changes, before the new structure began to operate smoothly and the achieved cost and innovation benefits began to pay off.

CHANGING NATURE OF GLOBAL ASSIGNMENTS

Historically, as noted previously, most individuals with overseas responsibilities in organizations were traditional expatriates, assigned abroad for a period of time (typically, two to three years) to open a subsidiary, hire local workers, and train them on the company's products and processes so they could operate successfully within the company's guidelines. There are still many of these individuals around, and some of them have built their international careers by moving from one location to another. In the past, such individuals were typically male, and they came from the head office. This follows the traditional "missionary" model, where religious clergy from the home country traveled, at great sacrifice, to an unknown land to convert the natives. There is a conversion role that expatriates play, as one of their duties is to make sure that they pass on the corporate culture and norms, and not just the technical aspects of running the business, to the local subsidiaries.

Baliga and Jaeger (1984) suggest that multinationals attempt to control subsidiaries through bureaucratic and cultural control. The presence of expatriates in subsidiaries represents a type of cultural control, and firms tend to rely on a greater number of expatriates especially when they are culturally distant from the subsidiary (Colakoglu and Caligiuri 2008). There is some evidence, however, that at least for companies with "low" distance (e.g., cultural, institutional) relative to their home country, subsidiary performance might in fact be better if they are managed by host country nationals versus parent country nationals (Dörrenbächer et al. 2013).

As discussed previously, different models of global managers have evolved over the past 30 years or so, partly due to changing organizational and business conditions. In addition to the traditional expatriate model, there is the reverse expatriate, someone from the subsidiary who is assigned to the home office for a period of time. These reverse expatriates often have an assigned role, although part of the reason for a headquarters assignment is for them to learn and absorb the corporate culture. When they return, they not only have had several years of formal and informal education, but have also developed a network of important people from corporate headquarters.

A third model, now increasingly common among global companies, takes managers from subsidiaries and assigns them to other subsidiaries. As a global company increases its presence in overseas locations, and its talent pool deepens, they realize that there are significant benefits in applying this model, not only for the organization but also for individuals. For example, Jan (a Polish national) was an executive running the Eastern European organization for a global pharmaceutical company when an opportunity arose to become the country manager for the company's China operation. Jan had actually spent four years in China earlier in his career for a different company, and in fact was married to a Chinese woman. With his background and experience, it made a lot of sense for the company to send him to China, and of course Jan was delighted to return.

These three models of global managers can be very expensive for companies. Estimates of the costs of expatriate assignments run anywhere from $100,000 to over $1 million a year (Black and Gregersen 1999). At times, these assignments are necessary investments, of course. There is sometimes no substitute for having a manager on the ground immersed in the local culture, and who will stay for a couple of years to get the subsidiary up and running. Expatriates can hire and train local personnel, negotiate business deals with local suppliers and partners, and work with local government officials. Some of these assignments may be in developed countries, while others may be in quite remote areas of emerging markets. I know a company that sent expatriates to rural parts of China to hire local sales representatives. They had to introduce themselves to the local town officials, and explain the basics of how their company operated and how they selected and hired employees. These officials, and the local population, were familiar only with the state-run model of managing an organization, and it was a challenge even explaining a common management practice such as the interviewing and hiring of applicants for employment. Nonetheless, these expatriates learned valuable lessons that they were able to apply in subsequent assignments.

The demands on these expatriate managers will vary depending on the scope of the assignment. For example, some expatriates are sent overseas because they have a special technical or functional expertise (e.g., manufacturing, marketing), while others are sent overseas to run and lead a specific subsidiary or division within that subsidiary.

With short-term assignments, managers may be sent overseas for a short period of time with a specific, very focused task. They will "parachute" in to provide their expertise to a subsidiary and solve whatever short-term problems the subsidiary may be facing. For example, corporations in the service and hospitality industries, including McDonald's and Marriott, will assign experts to different locations worldwide and set up local franchises. Sometimes there will be different waves of these experts sent, depending on the business challenges required. Some will have expertise in setting up joint ventures, others will have expertise in building supply chains, while still others will have expertise in store or hotel design. When the subsidiaries start operating, other expatriates may be brought in to address specific business problems, such as a marketing campaign. Traditionally, such global managers came from headquarters because that was where all the expertise resided.

From interviews with executives, an increasing number of these short-term assignments seem to be staffed by individuals from other subsidiaries. For example, a global company that has developed a strong center of expertise in Marketing in Mexico will more than likely send someone from the Mexican subsidiary to another subsidiary in its Latin American operation for an assignment. This makes sense because of the geographical proximity as well as linguistic similarity between Mexico and other countries in the region. At other times, individuals with expertise in one emerging market may be sent to another emerging market in some other part of the world. For example, Carlos was a Chilean manager who had developed strong marketing expertise in building his company's Santiago subsidiary. When the company needed help with its marketing operations in Beijing, Carlos flew to China and spent three months helping the subsidiary there.

Fernando Lanzer is a Brazilian national and coach who stated, in a recent *Financial Times* article[31]: "Many emerging markets have cultures which are more similar than different in terms of management practices. In broad terms, Brazil, Russia, India and China are all hierarchical and collectivistic cultures. People are managed rather similarly in such cultures."

In that same article, Nadir Karanjia, an Indian consultant suggested: "Since the emerging countries have similar social drivers, managers from other emerging countries will find it easier to understand the needs and expectations of the emerging-market target."

Perhaps as a recognition of this, McDonald's recently reorganized its global business into four segments: " the U.S., 'international lead markets' such as Australia and the U.K., 'high-growth markets' such as China and Poland, and a grab bag of other countries called 'foundational markets.'"[32]

Because of advanced technology tools (and a desire to reduce costs), companies are also giving managers regional or global responsibilities while they remain in their home offices. Yang is one such manager. His home office is in Singapore where he is the regional head for his company's marketing operation. His direct reports are located in eight different Asian countries. While he travels occasionally to each of these countries, most of the interactions with his team are via video conferencing. Other global managers may have direct reports who are in different continents, such as Juan Carlos, who works in Mexico, but whose team members come from, among other countries, India, Canada, and Italy.

Steers et al. (2014) categorize global assignments into three types: expatriates (such as the traditional model referred to above), frequent flyers (managers with short-term assignments), and virtual managers. The virtual manager model has certainly had benefits for global companies. In many cases, they have been able to reduce costs while at the same time improve the level of global talent and reinforce the importance of recognizing and spreading internal best practices, regardless of where the practice originated. Reducing face-to-face time however has some trade-offs; managers need to become even more skilled at being able to build relationships and trust.

Corporations are not immune to occasional accounts of hype and exaggeration, and we are no doubt familiar with the inflated claims that some firms make about their products and services. The Food and Drug Administration (FDA) and other government agencies sometimes have had to intervene and dismiss firms' claims about the supposed efficacy of their products. Recently, for example, the FDA had warned a genetic testing company, 23andMe (co-founded by the spouse of Google's Sergey Brin), to stop sales of its genetic tests because the tests had not been clinically or analytically validated. The FDA did shift its position after several discussions.[33]

Other corporations make two additional questionable and sometimes exaggerated claims about their firms. The first is that people are their most important assets, and the second is that they always operate ethically. It is not that these claims are always false, but that we should not be naive enough to accept these statements at face value. We need to ask for evidence and what proof these corporations have for making these statements. At times, the rhetoric fails to catch up with reality. Johnson & Johnson (J&J), as one example, is a firm that takes pride in its credo, a series of statements about its values. Yet recently, J&J has been involved in a series of scandals that makes one question the extent to which these values are truly institutionalized.

Another exaggerated claim that some companies make is to state that they are truly global. If in fact more than 50 % of a company's sales are coming from outside of its home market, or if its strategy entails opening up businesses in different markets around the world, it might seem reasonable that a company would consider itself a global company.

Several years ago, Bartlett and Ghoshal (1999) coined the term "transnational" to refer to a type of management strategy that tries to resolve and integrate the tensions that arise in global companies between responding to local pressures to customize ("localization") and global pressures to standardize ("integration").

To be truly global, or transnational, is not just about having products and services sold outside your home country. Companies that have subsidiaries overseas in several countries, or where their overseas sales are approaching close to half their revenues, are not necessarily global or transnational companies. In their annual study of the global board capability of Standard & Poor's (S&P) 500 companies, Egon Zehnder reported that 72 % of all S&P 500 companies reported some amount of international income, and that international revenues represented 37 % of their revenues last year (up 5.5 percentage points since 2008).[34]

While these are indicators of the "globalness" of a company, disturbing gaps still exist. Only 7.2 % of all directors of US-based companies are foreign nationals (although this is up from 6.6 % in 2008), and only 14.1 % of these directors have international work experience (although again, this is up from 8 % in 2008). Even among companies that reported international revenue, the share of directors with international work experience is only 17 %. In fact, 45 % of these firms had no foreign nationals on their boards.[35] There do not appear to be studies that have looked at non-US corporations, but it is unlikely that the statistics will differ significantly. What is also interesting to consider is the percentage of C-suite executives in these companies who are non-US citizens. There should be a positive correlation between the number of foreign nationals on the executive team and the percentage of revenues from overseas, but this does not seem to be the case.

As others (Hill 2011; Bartlett and Beamish 2014) have pointed out, companies competing globally today face two types of competitive pressures: the need to integrate globally, and the need to respond locally. These competitive pressures have led companies to devise one of the following strategies:

- In industries where products are standardized (such as the semiconductor industry) and the need for local responsiveness is low, companies succeed with a *global standardization* strategy. Manufacturing and R&D tend to be highly centralized or concentrated in a few locations, with a focus on economies of scale, and product offerings tend not to be customized.
- In industries where national, cultural, and consumer differences dominate, and where standardization of product offerings is not as a big a concern relative to customization, companies succeed with a *localization or multinational* strategy. Traditionally, these companies have built strong local subsidiaries and country managers are like mini-CEOs, responsible for multiple functions and ultimately the profit and loss statement (P&L) of their subsidiary. These companies may sacrifice some scale efficiencies, but they more than make up for it by increased local acceptance and demand for their customized products. Such companies are typically fairly decentralized.
- In industries where pressures for integration and responsiveness are low, companies can succeed with an *international* strategy. This makes sense, according to Bartlett and Beamish, particularly in industries where technological forces are central; companies that are able to innovate, create new products, and quickly transfer these technologies overseas will succeed. Product development functions are typically based in the home country.
- Increasingly, industries are facing both pressures for integration and local responsiveness. Global integration has become easier due to new economies of scale, brand management, and greater product standardization (e.g., car platforms for different regions, common product formulations for consumer products). At the same time, company subsidiaries are becoming increasingly interdependent as they are realizing that they can learn from their local markets, as well as from each other, and continue to innovate. Under these conditions, companies that adopt a *transnational* strategy are more likely to succeed than other companies.

Becoming transnational therefore is a bit more complex than simply selling products or having subsidiaries in different markets. There is additional complexity because such organizations are both centralized and decentralized, which can be quite confusing to those who are used to thinking of this dimension as an either-or strategic choice. For example, in an increasing number of multinationals, functions such as marketing and sales (where local knowledge and quick adaptation are critical) tend to be decentralized, while functions such as Procurement (where scale and costs can be optimized), tend to be centralized at least at the regional level.

In a study to test the Bartlett and Ghoshal typology, Leong and Tan (1993) surveyed 131 senior executives and had them classify their organizations as multinational, global, international, or transnational. As expected, the transnational form received the fewest proportion of mentions (18 %). Harzing (2000) surveyed CEOs and human resource managers at the headquarters of 122 multinationals and the managing directors of 1650 wholly owned subsidiaries in 22 countries on this typology. Although the response rates were not very high (about 20 % at the subsidiary level and about 10 % at the headquarters level), Harzing found predicted relationships between companies' strategies and their responses to indicators for each of these strategies. For example, network structures and inter-subsidiary flows of products, people, and information were most common in transnational companies.

Bartlett and Ghoshal had proposed their typology based upon three variables: the configuration of assets and capabilities, the role of overseas operations, and the development and diffusion of knowledge. Although there have been other typologies, theirs has been the most influential (Rugman et al. 2011), despite some criticism. Devinney et al. (2000) have argued, among other things, that the typology does not adequately account for transactional pressures on the value chain and assumes that each subsidiary has an aggregate role spanning the entire value chain. Rugman et al. (2011) in fact propose examining four different value chain activities in subsidiaries: innovation, production, sales, and administrative functions. In addition, an organization may have different businesses with different roles within a subsidiary. At Merck & Co., for example, the company has a manufacturing facility in Singapore that plays more of a regional and global role for the company than its sales and marketing function in that city-state, which is strictly local.

Javidan and Bowen (2013, p. 146) have proposed a set of six statements to determine whether or not a company is globalizing:

- Over the next five years, the corporation's opportunities, in terms of markets and supplies, are mostly outside of its home country.
- Over the next five years, the firm will be hiring more people outside its home country.

- Over the next five years, managers at the firm will increasingly need to work with people from other parts of the world.
- Over the next five years, managers at the firm will increasingly need to work with direct reports who are located in different parts of the world.
- The top management and middle management in the company are not very experienced in leveraging global opportunities.
- A key to the company's competitive advantage resides in its capability to manage cross-cultural complexity in its value chain of suppliers, managers, employees, distributors, and customers better than its competitors.

Research and practice suggest that the transnational model will become the most viable strategy for global companies in the future (Hill 2011). Extrapolating from the various descriptions and analyses of transnational strategies (including an early article by Adler and Bartholomew 1992), the following are proposed key questions for assessing whether an organization is making progress toward implementing a transnational strategy:

1. How culturally diverse are the executives in the C-suite? Do they only come from the company's home country, or are other countries represented?
2. Do subsidiaries in the most important overseas markets have direct reporting relationships to the CEO or COO or do they tend to be buried in layers of reporting structures?
3. Do executives in key subsidiaries have meaningful global roles (e.g., chairing a global task force) or is their role restricted to delivering profits for their country of responsibility?
4. How frequently do headquarters executives meet with their subsidiary executives as a team? Do they fly out to the regions for meetings or do they expect their subsidiary heads to come to home office all the time?
5. How involved are subsidiary executives with key corporate initiatives? Do they sit on important corporate councils? Do headquarters executives seek their input on corporate initiatives before they are rolled out to their regions?
6. Has the company identified which parts of their value chain, functions, and activities are global and therefore should remain fairly

consistent and integrated across countries, and which can allow for localization?

7. Does the company have a global talent strategy which includes, among other things, the identification of high potentials globally and targeted development plans for these high potentials, no matter what their nationality or country of origin is? Does its talent strategy also include rotation of individuals from country to country, and not just from headquarters to subsidiaries?

8. When cross-functional teams are formed to tackle specific initiatives, to what extent are various subsidiaries represented?

9. Does the company have global leadership programs that are implemented across subsidiaries, and to what extent do their offerings include content on globalization, cross-cultural sensitivity and related subjects?

10. Are there mechanisms and processes for sharing information and leveraging expertise across borders? For example, if the company has centers of excellence, does it make sure that these centers have worldwide responsibility for sharing information?

11. Is global mindset a competency that the company is actively developing, both for its employees and for the firm as a whole?

In general, if a company can respond affirmatively to a majority of these questions, then it is well on its way to becoming a truly global or transnational company. Corporations can of course vary in their degree of transnationalism. However, to become truly global and respond effectively to some of the major trends described above, today's multinationals will need to address and begin implementing solutions suggested by these questions.

Ahmet Bozer, president of the Coca-Cola Company's Eurasia and Africa Group, echoes what many global executives have stated[36]: "We are still evolving in finding the best local and global combination that works for us." With Coca-Cola, he goes on to say, "When it comes to franchise relations with the bottlers, that is local ... Quality standards are both global and local ... But we take advantage of our global properties and collaborate as a global team, bringing the best resources to bear on a specific issue."

NOTES

1. Fortune Magazine, Fortune Global 500, August 1, 2015.
2. "The Gated Globe" in The Economist, October 12, 2013.
3. "The Pacific Age," November 15, 2014, The Economist.
4. Economic Intelligence Unit: Economic Intelligence Unit. http://www.eiu.com/Handlers/WhitepaperHandler.ashx?fi=Long-term_macroeconomic_Forecasting-upto-2050.pdf&mode=wp&campaignid=ForecastingTo2050
5. "Demystifying the Market for Executive Talent in Asia," Russell Reynolds Report, 2015: http://www.bain.com/publications/articles/eight-great-trillion-dollar-growth-trends-to-2020.aspx
6. http://www.ey.com/Publication/vwLUAssets/ey-megatrends-report-2015/$FILE/ey-megatrends-report-2015.pdf
7. "Megatrends 2015: Making Sense of a World in Motion," E&Y Report: http://www.ey.com/Publication/vwLUAssets/ey-megatrends-report-2015/$FILE/ey-megatrends-report-2015.pdf
8. "Deloitte Globalization Survey: Preparing for the Next Wave in Globalization" by Deloitte University Press: http://www2.deloitte.com/content/dam/Deloitte/es/Documents/estrategia/Deloitte_ES_Estrategia_Globalization-survey-overview-2014.pdf
9. Their web site (www.prb.org) contains very useful information on population statistics and trends.
10. "Hitting the Sweet Spot: The Growth of the Middle Class in Emerging Markets," E&Y Report: http://www.ey.com/Publication/vwLUAssets/Hitting_the_sweet_spot/$FILE/Hitting_the_sweet_spot.pdf
11. The Rise of the Middle Class, Word Bank document by Augosto de la Torre and Jammele Rigolini.
12. "Burgeoning Bourgeoisie" in The Economist, February 12, 2009.
13. "The Great Eight: Trillion-Dollar Growth Trends to 2020," Bain & Company, 2011: http://www.bain.com/publications/articles/eight-great-trillion-dollar-growth-trends-to-2020.aspx
14. "The New Demographics: How to Live with an Ageing Population," The Economist, November 1, 2001.
15. "World Population Ageing 2013," United Nations Report.
16. United Nations World Population Prospects (the 2004 revision).
17. http://esa.un.org/unpd/wup/FinalReport/WUP2014-Report.pdf
18. See http://www.russellreynolds.com/insights/thought-leadership/the-rise-of-the-chief-digital-officer
19. "The Pioneering Continent" in The Economist, April 25, 2015.
20. "The Gated Globe," in The Economist, October 12, 2013.
21. Carol Matlack, "Putin's Latest Target: More than 200 Russian McDonald's," Bloomberg Business Week, October 20, 2014.

22. Olga Razumovskaya, "McDonald's Extends Reach in Russia," The Wall Street Journal, August 24, 2015.
23. http://www.dhl.com/content/dam/Campaigns/gci2014/downloads/dhl_gci_2014 _study_high.pdf
24. http://abcnews.go.com/Business/story?id=4528213
25. http://jalopnik.com/5981170/volvos-chinese-parent-geely-swoops-in-to-save-the-london-taxi
26. http://www.wsj.com/articles/SB10001424052702304213904579095061880118346
27. See "The CEO Pay Circus of 2013." 2015. *Yahoo Finance*. Accessed August26.http://finance.yahoo.com/blogs/the-exchange/ceo-pay-circus-2013-214028626.html.
28. "Managing Complexity and Change in a New Landscape": http://www.ey.com/Publication/vwLUAssets/EY_-_7_big_changes_to_asset_management_operating_models/$FILE/EY-Managing-complexity-and-change-in-a-new-landscape.pdf
29. "Research on the Strategy-Execution Gap": http://www.strategyand.pwc.com/global/home/what-we-think/cds_home/the_concept/research-strategy-execution-gap
30. "Rethinking Emerging Market Strategies: From Offshoring to Strategic Expansion," Deloitte Review, 2009: http://www.strategyand.pwc.com/global/home/what-we-think/cds_home/the_concept/research-strategy-exe
31. Peter Vanham, "Skills for Global Business," March 11, 2013.
32. "McDonald's to Speed Refranchising, Cut Costs" in The Wall Street Journal, May 4, 2015.
33. See Robert's Hof's article in Forbes, February 19, 2015.
34. "2014 Egon Zehnder Global Board Index": http://www.egonzehnder.com/files/global_board_index_2014.pdf
35. Joann Lublin, "U.S. Businesses Get Global, But Boards Remain All-American," the Wall Street Journal, October 1, 2014.
36. From an interview with Mr. Bozer, "How Coca-Cola Manages 90 Emerging Markets" by William Holstein, published November 21, 2011: http://www.strategy-business.com/article/00093?gko=f3ca6

REFERENCES

Adler, Nancy J., and Susan Bartholomew. 1992. Managing Globally Competent People. *Academy of Management Executive* 6(3): 52–65.
Baliga, B. Rajaram, and Alfred Jaeger. 1984. Multinational Corporations, Control Systems and Delegation Issues. *Journal of International Business Studies* 10(1): 25–40.

Bartlett, Christopher, and Paul Beamish. 2014. *Transnational Management*, Seventh edn. New York: McGraw-Hill.

Bartlett, Christopher, and Sumantra Ghoshal. 1999. *Managing Across Borders: The Transnational Solution*. Boston, MA: Harvard Business School.

Beamish, Paul, Allen J. Morrison, Philip M. Rosenzweig, and Andrew Inkpen. 2003. *International Management: Text and Cases*. New York: McGraw-Hill.

Bernard, Andrew B., and J. Bradford Jensen. 1997. Exporters, Skill Upgrading, and the Wage Gap. *Journal of International Economics* 42(1): 3–31.

Black, J. Stewart, and Hal B. Gregersen. 1999. The Right Way to Manage Expats. *Harvard Business Review* 77(2): 52–63.

Chand, Masud, and Rosalie Tung. 2014. The Aging of the World's Population and Its Effect on Global Business. *The Academy of Management Perspectives* 28(4): 409–429.

Chandy, Lawrence, and Geoffrey Gertz. 2011. *Poverty in Numbers: The Changing State of Global Poverty from 2005 to 2015*. Washington, DC: The Brookings Institution.

Charan, Ram. 2013. *Global Tilt: Leading Your Business Through the Great Economic Power Shift*. New York: CrownBusiness.

Colakoglu, Saba, and Paula Caligiuri. 2008. Cultural Distance, Expatriate Staffing and Subsidiary Performance: The Case of US Subsidiaries of Multinational Corporations. *The International Journal of Human Resource Management* 19(2): 223–239.

Devinney, Timothy M., David F. Midgley, and Sunil Venaik. 2000. The Optimal Performance of the Global Firm: Formalizing and Extending the Integration-Responsiveness Framework. *Organization Science* 11(6): 674–695.

Dobbs, Richard, Anu Madgavkar, Dominic Barton, Eric Labaye, James Manyika, Charles Roxburgh, Susan Lund, and Siddarth Madhav. 2012. *The World at Work: Jobs, Pay, and Skills for 3.5 Billion People*. New York: McKinsey Global Institute.

Dobbs, Richard, James Manyika, and Jonathan Woetzel. 2015. *No Ordinary Disruption: The Four Global Forces Breaking All the Trends*. New York: PublicAffairs.

Dörrenbächer, Christoph, Jens Gammelgaard, Frank McDonald, Andreas Stephan, and Heinz Tüselmann. 2013. Staffing Foreign Subsidiaries with Parent Country Nationals or Host Country Nationals? Insights from European Subsidiaries. Working Paper No. 74. Berlin: IMB Institute of Management.

Dyson, Tim. 2010. *Population and Development: The Demographic Transition*. New York: Zed Books.

Erez, Miriam, and Gili Drori. 2009. Global Culture and Organizational Processes. In *Cambridge Handbook of Culture, Organization, and Work*, eds. Rabi Bhagat and Richard Steers, 148–173. New York: Cambridge University Press.

Goldman, Glenn, and Eammon Kelly. 2015. *Another Billion. In Business Trends 2014: Navigating the Next Wave of Globalization.* Deloitte Report. Deloitte University Press.

Govindarajan, Vijay, and Chris Trimble. 2012. Reverse Innovation: A Global Growth Strategy That Could Pre-empt Disruption at Home. *Strategy & Leadership* 40(5): 5–11.

Gupta, Anil, Vijay Govindarajan, and Haiyan Wang. 2008. *The Quest for Global Dominance.* San Francisco, CA: Jossey-Bass.

Hamel, Gary. 2007. *The Future of Management.* Boston: Harvard Business Review Press.

Harzing, Anne-Wil. 2000. An Empirical Analysis and Extension of the Bartlett and Ghoshal Typology of Multinational Companies. *Journal of International Business Studies* 31(1): 101–120.

Hill, Charles. 2011. *Global Business Today.* New York: McGraw-Hill.

Javidan, Mansour, and David Bowen. 2013. The 'Global Mindset' of Managers: What It Is, Why It Matters, and How to Develop It. *Organizational Dynamics* 42(2): 145–155.

Kharas, Homi, and Geoffrey Gertz. 2010. *China's Emerging Middle Class: Beyond Economic Transformation.* Washington, DC: Brookings Institution Press.

Leong, Siew Meng, and Chin Tiong Tan. 1993. Managing Across Borders : An Empirical Assessment of the Bartett and Ghoshal (1989) Organizational Typology. *Journal of International Business Studies* 24(3): 449–464.

Littler, Craig R., Retha Wiesner, and Richard Dunford. 2003. The Dynamics of Delayering: Changing Management Structures in Three Countries. *Journal of Management Studies* 40(2): 225–256.

McChrystal, General Stanley, Tantum Collins, David Silverman, and Chris Fussell. 2015. *Team of Teams: New Rules of Engagement for a Complex World.* New York: Penguin.

McKinsey Global Institute. 2015. Playing to Win: The New Global Competition for Corporate Profits. MGI Report. http://www.mckinsey.com/insights/corporate_finance/the_new_global_competition_for_corporate_profits

Moore, Fiona. 2005. *Transnational Business Cultures: Life and Work in a Multinational Corporation.* Burlington, VT: Ashgate Publishing.

Paul, Robert J., and James B. Townsend. 1993. Managing the Older Worker—Don't Just Rinse Away the Gray. *Academy of Management Executive* 7(3): 67–74.

Rugman, Alan, Alain Verbeke, and Wenlong Yuan. 2011. Re-conceptualizing Bartlett and Ghoshal's Classification of National Subsidiary Roles in the Multinational Enterprise. *Journal of Management Studies* 48(2): 253–277.

Schmidt, Eric, and Jonathan Rosenberg. 2014. *How Google Works.* New York: Grand Central Publishing.

Slater, Robert. 1998. *Jack Welch & The G.E. Way: Management Insights and Leadership Secrets of the Legendary CEO: Management Insights and Leadership Secrets of the Legendary CEO.* New York: McGraw Hill Professional.

Steers, Richard, Luciara Nardon, and Carlos J. Sanchez-Runde. 2014. *Management Across Cultures: Developing Global Competencies,* Second edn. New York: Cambridge University Press.

Subramanian, Arvind. 2011. *Eclipse: Living in the Shadow of China's Economic Dominance.* Washington, DC: Peterson Institute.

Wulf, Julie. 2012. The Flattened Firm: Not As Advertised. *California Management Review* 55(1): 5–23.

CHAPTER 3

The Context: What's Not Changing

The previous chapter documented some of the tremendous upheavals that are impacting organizations wherever they are doing business. Much has also been written about how organizations are changing, and that organizations of the future will be quite different from the ones we are familiar with today. Galbraith (1993) stated that "Today, the classic building blocks are becoming questionable. New competitive initiatives, such as total quality and competing in time, along with the new information technology, are leading to some fundamental changes in the functional organization." (p. 45)

Handy (1990) predicted that "institutions will be less important. More of us will spend more of our lives outside formal organizations." He then argues that the organization of the future will be like a shamrock, with the three leaves representing core workers (of whom there will be very few), contract workers (the vendors and suppliers that do the outsourced work), and the flexible work force (the part-time and temporary workers). Have Handy's predictions come true? Organizations have downsized and delayered, and have both outsourced and offshored work. And there is no question that these three "leaves" have become part of the organizational landscape. However, as to Handy's suggestion that the organization of the future will have very few "core" workers, it does not seem that this has come to pass.

© The Editor(s) (if applicable) and The Author(s) 2016
R. Henson, *Successful Global Leadership*,
DOI 10.1057/978-1-137-58990-3_3

As an example, Google's headcount has increased every year since 2003. In 2007, its headcount was 16,805; in 2008, 20,222. By 2014, its headcount had reached 53,600.[1] According to *USA Today* (August 22, 2013), the largest employers in America had the following numbers of employees in their headcount (note that these are global numbers):

Wal-Mart—2.2 million
Yum! Brands—523,000
McDonald's—440,000
IBM—434,246
UPS—399,000
Target—361,000
Kroger—343,000
Home Depot—340,000
H-P—331,800
GE—305,000

These headcount numbers have all grown in the past few years, despite the global recession, downsizing, and delayering. The continued survival and evolution of the modern organization attests to the endurance of its fundamental building blocks.

ORGANIZATIONAL BASICS

Over a century ago, Max Weber (1947) developed some of the basic concepts of the modern organization. He wrote about the principles of bureaucracy, and argued that every organization needed to have formal rules and regulations, a structure, and a division of labor. Weber wanted to professionalize organizations and counteract the tendencies toward autocratic rule and favoritism:

> Experience tends universally to show that the purely bureaucratic type of administrative organization ... is, from a purely technical point of view, capable of attaining the highest degree of efficiency and is in this sense formally the most rational known means of carrying out imperative control over human beings. It is superior to any other form in precision, in stability, in the stringency of its discipline, and in its reliability. (p. 337)

Even then, Weber was sensitive to the negative connotation of the word "bureaucracy." He acknowledged this, but wrote that this modern form of organization was still superior to any others because it was the most "rational."

Frederick Taylor would later expand on Weber's thinking by introducing what he called his principles of scientific management.[2] Weber's three elements and Taylor's principles continue to be among the building blocks of business organizations today. Every organization of course needs to have a strategy and objectives, a product or service that customers want, as well as customers to purchase these products or services. Every organization also needs to have resources—financial, physical, and human—in order to survive, gain competitive advantage, and grow. In addition, however, it needs three building blocks or "infrastructure" elements that will help it achieve its strategy and objectives: structures, rewards, and processes. The modern organization, despite criticisms, is arguably a great invention, and it will continue to evolve, but these building blocks of structure, rewards, and processes will remain essential to any organization.

Structure

According to Galbraith (1995), there are four dimensions to structure: specialization (similar to Weber's concept of division of labor), shape (which includes layers and span of control), distribution of power (where decision-making authority lies) the degree of centralization of the organization, and departmentalization (how groups within the organization are organized by function, customer segment, geography, etc.).

These four dimensions of structure are present in any organization today, large and small. In fact, while many large organizations have introduced innovations such as self-managing teams, matrix relationships, virtual teams, customer-centric organizations, and large spans of control, every organization uses variations on these four dimensions of structure.

Structures are important for the following reasons. One, they help define behaviors, roles and responsibilities, and tasks, thereby reducing ambiguity, providing clarity for individuals, and creating efficiency (Perrow 1970). Two, structures help to shape attitudes, and expected and desired behaviors (e.g., Schminke et al. 2000). Three, they reinforce and help employees align their behaviors with the organization's strategy (Lawrence and Lorsch 1967). Four, structures reflect hierarchy, which has been shown to be essential in social groups and especially in organizations (Chase 1980; Pfeffer 2010; Sidanius and Pratto 2001).

Note that while an organization's strategy should certainly influence its structure, national culture is also a potential source of influence for the structural choices that organizations make. For example, Hout and Michael (2014) found, in their research on management practices in Chinese private companies, that their organizational structures are simple and flat, but still hierarchical. Matrix management does not seem to exist in Chinese companies, and the head of the company has a large span of control. Business units and functions have a lot of autonomy and are allowed to operate independently, although Chinese executives are micromanagers. The impact of national culture on structural choices may be somewhat muted if the organization is part of a global organization, operating as a subsidiary. For example, a large company like Shell Oil will tend to have consistent organizational structures across the many countries where it has subsidiaries to make sure that these align with their strategy and the culture that they want to reinforce.

Many executives spend a great deal of time worrying about the right organizational structure or design for their organization with good reason, since designing an effective and aligned structure can help accelerate the company's progress toward its goals. Note the recent efforts by Microsoft and Google to redesign their structures.[3]

Rewards

Providing rewards is an important (although not the only) driver of motivating people in organizations. According to Erez (1994), there are three principles on which to base rewards: equity (based on one's contribution), equality, and need. Reward practices for many Western companies are based on the equity principle at least in theory—the concept of "pay for performance." Performance management systems are designed to help ensure that individual performance is linked to various extrinsic rewards. In other cultures, individual performance is less important than seniority. In fact, there is strong evidence to suggest that extrinsic reward preferences are to some extent culturally based. For example, rewards such as bonuses and incentives for employees in Japanese companies until recently have been based on division or company performance. In general, two Japanese graduates starting in the same company and in the same department would know each other's salary after 20 years because they would be exactly the same. In some industries where unions are strong, and/or in organizations where individual performance is difficult to measure, one may also find that the equity principle might not be applied as consistently. Nonetheless, equity is the basis of reward practices for the vast majority of private Western companies. In collectivist cultures, on the other hand, research has shown that at least within their in-group, individuals in these cultures tend to prefer equality over equity when it comes to reward allocation (Hui et al. 1991; Kim et al. 1990; Leung and Bond 1984).

Pay is not the only motivator in driving job satisfaction and performance; there are intrinsic rewards that employees strive for, which they may or may not find in the organizations where they are employed. For example, many Western organizations have been focusing on such practices as employee involvement, self-managing teams, and autonomous work groups. Pink (2011), based on Deci's pioneering work on intrinsic motivation (Deci 1975), has argued that work can be truly motivating when employees have jobs that enable them to gain mastery, autonomy, and purpose. There has been considerable research on how jobs can be designed to become intrinsically motivating (Hackman and Oldham 1976; Loher et al. 1985).

Even in Japanese companies, employees are encouraged to contribute their input, although the process (called *nemawashi*) is quite different from how it might work in a Western company. German companies have Works Councils where employees get to participate in many operational decisions. Regardless of culture, every organization needs to provide rewards to employees. This is part of the exchange relationship or contract that exists between an organization and an individual. This contract can be transactional, or it can be psychological (Rousseau and Tijoriwala 1998), and involves expectations that each party has with the other, with transactional contracts tending to be more explicit than psychological contracts.

Processes

Every organization needs to have processes, especially for determining how things get done, how problems get solved, how communication gets transmitted, and how decisions get made. In small organizations, where the output might be simple, processes tend to be informal and well understood. In large global organizations, on the other hand, too many informal processes can lead to unclear roles and responsibilities, lack of coordination across functions or units, inefficient decision-making, poor communication, and slow response times—which will ultimately have a negative impact on the customer and the firm's performance.

In the eighties, with the popularity of reengineering, delayering, and downsizing, process redesign was a significant focus for organizations.[4] This raised the awareness within and across organizations on the importance of defining, clarifying, and streamlining processes. "Lean" processes and Six Sigma are related approaches to making sure that processes are effective and add value to the customer (e.g., George 2002). Hence, processes are necessary for any organization in order to reduce variability, create some predictability in organizational behavior and in the quality of their products and services, and enable it to function more efficiently.

Human Behavior Basics

Anthropologists have shown that our species of humans called *Homo Sapiens* first surfaced about 200,000 years ago (Stringer and Andrews 1988), and that our ancestors survived through certain behaviors that became pretty much hard-wired into their brain circuitry. When agriculture was invented about 10,000 years ago, our ancestors no longer had to move around, live in small groups, and live a hand-to-mouth existence.

However, according to Nicholson (1997, 1998), all the environmental changes we have experienced since that time have not been significant enough to stimulate further human evolution. Evolutionary psychologists believe that 10,000 years is simply not enough time for significant genetic modifications to take place across populations. Nicholson (1998) states:

> there is a limit to how much the human mind can be remolded. Proponents of evolutional psychology assert that, because of natural selection, human beings living and working in today's modern civilization retain the hard-wired mentality—that is, the needs, drives, and biases—of Stone Age hunter-gatherers.

What are some of the behaviors that Nicholson believes are hard-wired? They include the following (paraphrased from Nicholson 1998):

1. Relying on emotion or instinct as the first filter for all information received. Stone Age people tended to rely on instinct so they could react quickly to predators or strangers outside their circle. More recent research by McClure et al. (2004) and Kahnemann (2013)

have pointed to the existence of two systems in the brain. As described by Mischel (2014), the emotional hot (limbic) system is impatient and is activated automatically by immediate rewards. Patience and the ability to choose between different delayed rewards on the other hand rely on the cool cognitive system, specifically in certain areas in the prefrontal cortex that developed later in the course of human evolution. Our reliance on our gut, and our tendency to form quick first impressions, seems to be a holdover from our ancestors.

2. Feeling more self-confident than reality justifies. Those who survived the conditions of the Stone Age had to project confidence so they could attract friends and mates. This overconfidence bias has spilled over to much of how we think and act today (Gino and Pisano 2011), and seems especially prevalent among executives.

3. Quickly classifying people, situations, and experiences into categories (e.g., good or bad, in or out). Without relying on "big data" or complex analyses, our ancestors had to make decisions quickly, whether they were about people to befriend or about certain types of food to avoid. As will be discussed later, this tendency to place people into categories quickly continues to be part of our present-day behavioral repertoire (Willis and Todorov 2006).

4. Participating in public competitions for status and boasting about their successes. Winning in contests and battles, as well as showing off, were important to impress others and to elevate the winners' status as well as making them more attractive to potential mates. In addition, our ancestors selected symbols of wealth to demonstrate their power and status, such as precious jewelry adorning their bodies or expensive apparel. We see some of this behavior among executives today as reflected in the outsized compensation packages of many CEOs and their ostentatious displays of wealth. When John Thain became CEO of Merrill Lynch in late 2007, he received a $15 million signing bonus, and a salary of at least $50 million annually. What was later revealed was that he spent more than $1.2 million of the firm's money to redecorate his office.[5] There were, for example, an area rug ($87,784), a nineteenth-century credenza ($68,179), and a commode on legs ($35,115). Interestingly, Davidson et al. (2012) found a negative correlation between the frugality of CEOs and a corporate culture that was associated with an increase in fraud

risk. They measured the lack of frugality by the ownership of luxury goods such as expensive cars, yachts, and houses.

5. Empathy and mind reading. Our ancestors realized that to survive, they also needed to build alliances as well as conquer their enemies. They needed to share food, and to barter and trade; those who learned how to be friendly and anticipate what others were thinking tended to be more successful. Empathy helped to address the demands of a complex social environment and motivate humans to behave altruistically toward others (Preston and De Waal 2002; Smith 2006). There is other evidence that suggests that empathy developed in humans early on to help us cooperate and make sure everyone was protected and had sufficient food (Hoffman 1981).

Not only have these human characteristics stayed relatively constant, but many of these are what in fact differentiate us from other species. In a fascinating set of experiments, Herrmann et al. (2007) administered a test battery called the primate cognitive test battery (PCTB) to 105 two-year-old children from a medium-sized German city, 106 chimpanzees living either in Uganda or Republic of Congo, and 32 orangutans in Indonesia. The PCTB measures both physical and social cognition—the former with such tasks as spatial memory and addition; the latter with social learning and gaze following. A human experimenter tested all participants three to five hours over the course of several days. They found that on tests of physical cognition, the children's scores did not differ significantly from the chimpanzees (although both scored higher than the orangutans). The big differences between children and apes came with the social cognition tests:

> Averaging across all the tasks in the social domain, the human children were correct on 75 percent of the trails, whereas the two ape species were correct about half as often (33–36 percent of the trials). Statistically, the humans were more skillful than either of the two ape species (P < 0.001 in both cases), which did not differ from one another. (p. 1362)

The researchers were attempting to tease out the differentiating role of social cognition in humans versus other species, calling this the cultural intelligence hypothesis. Even at two years old, our species already shows a superiority in being able to perform tasks that require some degree of social cognition. Interestingly, Herrmann et al. point out that domestic dogs, while not as good as the chimpanzees on tasks of physical cognition, outperform them on tasks of social cognition. We haven't changed that much, it seems. Fernandez-Araoz (2014) states that "Our brains now are not significantly different than those of the primitive hunters who chased deer in the savannah in prehistoric times."

Lawrence and Nohria (2002) propose that there are four drives through evolution that explain our behavior: the drive to acquire, the drive to bond, the drive to learn, and the drive to defend. The drive to acquire is fascinating because as the authors point out, there is a lot of evidence that even in primates there is a pecking order, and primates aspire to a higher social status. Higher social status is correlated with higher income and better wealth in humans. Also, humans with higher social status are likely to be more attractive to the opposite sex.

The second drive is the drive to bond. According to the authors, drawing on research by sociobiologists, this may also have evolved. The Pleistocene man sharing his meat and tools may have had more offspring than others. Another theory is that women tended to choose men who were more caring, since the women needed to be sure that they would not be abandoned. Over time, this drive to bond helped humans develop more complex forms of organization. The authors suggest that bonding extends to organizational life, and helps to explain why many of us exert extra effort to help the organizations we belong to succeed.

The third drive is the drive to learn. We seem to have an innate drive to satisfy our curiosity. We collect information and want to know how things work. Furthermore, as Golman and Lowenstein (2014) have argued in their information-gap theory, we have a need to remove a gap between something that is inconsistent between our observation and what we know because this creates an unpleasant sensation for us.

The fourth drive is the drive to defend. This drive to defend is essential for evolution because it has helped us to survive. We have alarm signals activated by chemical and electronic systems whenever we perceive threats to ourselves and to those whom we feel close. Our defenses, according to these researchers, include mechanisms such as resistance to change, caution, and anxiety. When these periods of stress are prolonged, we can slip into chronic defensive conditions such as passivity and helplessness. One of the key takeaways from Lawrence and Nohria's work is the need for organizations to make sure that they provide opportunities for employees to fulfill these drives: "More effective leadership is the kind that addresses to some degree the drive of humans to fulfill all four of the basic drives" (p. 256).

They argue that these four drives are universal: "They are the essence of what makes people human, regardless of where they were born or the circumstances in which they grew up ... In our reading of the anthropological literature, we could find no example of a society or culture where people did not display some measure of each of the drives" (pp. 259–260).

The evidence that these authors provide is quite strong. Nonetheless, different cultures seem to encourage or discourage these behaviors based on their cultural values. So while many of these behaviors may be universal, we are malleable enough that culture may trump or at least suppress some of these so-called hard-wired behaviors.

Let's examine how each of Nicholson's hard-wired behaviors can be seen through the filters of some cultural values, focusing especially on workplace behaviors. Organizations across the globe vary in the importance and emphasis they place on different organizational and management practices, in part as a function of their cultural values, and some preferred practices may in fact clash with these hard-wired behaviors.

Relying on Emotion

Organizations in some cultures like to pride themselves on being data driven, and to push for decisions that are based primarily on facts and air-tight logical reasoning. Yet like our ancestors, emotion plays a large part in our decision-making. Organizations with practices that place a high premium on rationality and logic (e.g., through the use of quantitative tools and a preponderance of data to drive decisions) may sometimes find it difficult to implement certain practices and initiatives in different cultural settings. Not only are we hard-wired to use emotion, but there are cultures where freedom of expression and spontaneity are encouraged (Hofstede 2001).

Feeling Self-confident

Many are familiar with cultures where this kind of behavior is encouraged. In fact, in countries like the USA, pointing out your accomplishments, doing a bit of self-promoting, and making sure that colleagues and bosses know about what you have done are in general acceptable behaviors (as long as they are not done excessively).In other cultures, individuals may let their accomplishments speak for themselves because of the cultural norms around humility. Ken, a very well-respected Japanese manager in a Tokyo-based financial services organization, is looked up to by all his colleagues. He has a quiet and calm style, is always prepared, and has developed a solid reputation for his research reports on the industry he is focusing. Yet he is very self-effacing, and to a Western manager, this may seem that Ken is diminishing his accomplishments constantly. This behavior is consistent with people who Zweig (2014) calls the "invisibles" in an organization, those who do not toot their own horn but are very valuable to an organization.

Classifying People into Categories Rapidly

Different cultures seem to make judgments about people based upon a narrow or wide scope. In some cultures, we look at someone's face, perhaps their attire and the way they speak, and quickly classify them accordingly. People from other cultures may cast a wider net in classifying people. They may also consider a person's family background, social status, and the way they follow the unwritten rules and the cultural code. For example, George, an Austrian manager who spent two years in Argentina on an overseas assignment with his company, made sure that while in that country, he was careful about his attire, his body language, the way he addressed people at different levels in the organization, and his deference to women. He knew that the Argentinians would be looking at all these cues in reaching conclusions about him.

Engaging in Competitive Behavior

Western capitalistic culture is based on the value and benefits of competition, and most organizations encourage some form of competitive behavior, whether it is through beating their rivals or competing for scarce resources within the organization. Yet in some cultures, such competitive behavior is downplayed; Hofstede (2001) refers to these cultures as more feminine, in that they place less emphasis on power, wealth, assertiveness, and "living to work." It's not that these cultures (which include Denmark and Norway) are uncompetitive; the competitive drive may still be there, but it is within the larger context of a culture that values family time, relationships, and "working to live."

Empathy and Mind Reading

It seems that even some of our ancestors had a degree of emotional intelligence that enhanced their chances of survival and success (Goleman 2005). Cultures that are high context (Hall 2013) have many people who are good at "reading between the lines," and who can communicate in different ways without offending others. These cultures have code words that people in that culture understand. For example, in Japan, a statement like "that might be difficult" really means "I don't agree with you." Similarly, in China, a statement like "it's not convenient" really means, "I don't want to do it."

While perhaps not as hard-wired as these other behaviors are, there is one other human characteristic that has been observed and researched in many studies: our tendency to affiliate with a group and have a social identity; Ahuja and Van Vugt (2010) refer to this as our tribal instinct. Not only do we seek social identity, but when we believe that a person is similar to or different from us in some ways, different parts of the brain get activated. Thinking about people who we believe are like us activates neurons in the ventral region of the medical prefrontal cortex, while thinking about people who are not like us activates neurons located in the dorsal region of the prefrontal cortex (Mitchell et al. 2006).There is no physical sensation connected with this activation, so we are not aware of these differences in brain activities. However, we very quickly make distinctions between "us" and "them."

The *Wall Street Journal* reported recently about an experiment at Zappos to move toward a "bossless" structure. Zappos, the successful online shoe company that Amazon acquired but operates quite independently from its parent, has moved quickly into this form of self-management by removing all managers from their roles.[6] Instead, teams are expected to manage themselves through a system called "holacracy." After only a few months, however, 210 out of 1500 employees (14 %) have left the company as a result of the switch to the boss-free workplace. Certainly, the research evidence for the effectiveness of self-managed teams and flat organizations is mixed, and it remains to be seen whether the Zappos experiment will work eventually. It may be that truly self-managed teams are going against the grain of the need for structure and the need to acquire. It is hard to imagine that such a setup would be embraced in cultures with strong "power distance" orientations.

Along with these organizational and human behavior basics are certain people management principles that seem to be accepted universally as key drivers of productivity and high performance. Pfeffer (1998), for example, suggests that there are seven such organizational behavior practices, including selective hiring, employment security, and self-managed teams.

When Stephen Covey passed away recently, I reread his book *The Seven Habits of Highly Effective People* (Covey 1989) for any additional insights. Over the years, I have always remembered to "begin with the end in mind" and to focus on the "important, and not necessarily the urgent" (although I have not always successfully followed his advice). Something different struck me in my rereading; this was Covey's insight that "Principles are not practices. A practice is a specific activity or action. A practice that works in one circumstance will not necessarily work in another ... While practices are situationally specific, principles are deep, fundamental truths that have universal application" (p. 35).

There are many so-called people management practices today that seem to work well for certain companies at certain times. Many of these practices are found in Fortune's annual Best Places to Work survey.[7] Who does not know about Google's free food, W.L. Gore's self-managing teams, and GE's Work-Out Programs (Ulrich et al. 2002), to name a few? But Covey is right. Practices, including people management practices, are situationally specific. Depending on the company's strategy, its organizational goals, its cultural context, and its industry (among other things), these practices may or may not work. For example, research by Fischer et al. (2014) demonstrates the impact of cultural dimensions on perceptions of organizational practices. In their study of a sample of 1239 employees from various organizations in six countries (Argentina, Brazil, Malaysia, New Zealand, Turkey, and the USA), they found significant effects of individualism and power distance (two of Hofstede's cultural dimensions) on the perceptions of the benefits of certain employee orientation practices (e.g., managers giving employees freedom to express their ideas, employees having a say in matters that directly involve them). Employees from individualistic and low-power-distance cultures, for example, reported that these practices were used more frequently versus employees from collectivistic and high-power-distance cultures. In general, cultural effects for their sample were significantly and consistently larger than any industry effects.

Are there people management principles with universal application that lead to high involvement and high performance? I propose five such principles, while also suggesting that the practices used to implement these principles may vary by culture. The first is to treat employees fairly and with respect. Whether it is a state-owned Chinese firm or a private enterprise in Brazil, research indicates that organizations upholding this principle will produce a higher level of commitment from employees than those that do not. However, the specific practices for implementing this principle will depend on culture, among other things. In Western cultures, for example, treating employees with respect might mean listening to their ideas. In Asian cultures, treating employees with respect might mean paying great attention to making sure employees do not lose face, and helping employees with some of their personal concerns. The latter, conceptualized by some as paternalistic leadership (e.g., Aycan et al. 2013) has been shown to have a positive impact on employee attitudes in collectivistic and high-power-distance cultures.

In an analysis of the global leadership and organizational behavior effectiveness (GLOBE) data[8] for the Middle East and North Africa (MENA) region, Kabasakal et al. (2012) found paternalistic leadership to be a preferred leadership prototype for the countries in this region. Such a leader gets involved in the personal lives of his/her subordinates, and creates a family-like atmosphere in the organization. For paternalistic leaders, consulting subordinates does not imply that they are empowering their subordinates but rather that they are showing that they care for them by asking for their opinion. This is a subtle but important difference. A Canadian expatriate interviewee who spent two years in Mexico learned that he had to set goals and targets for his Mexico team partly to show his strong leadership. Over time, he gradually created an "open platform" for them to engage in a collaborative approach on how to achieve these goals and targets.

A second principle is to create a positive and motivating environment. In Western cultures, this might include such practices as managers providing encouragement to employees, having an open-door policy, and conducting meetings where employees can express their opinions (Detert and Burris 2007). In Asian cultures, this might mean joining employees after work for karaoke, making sure they understand the history of the company, or even providing uniforms so employees can identify better with their company.

A third principle is to build self-confidence in employees. Berating employees may instill fear and compliance but more than likely will build resentment and counterproductive behavior. There is strong evidence from the research on "expectancy effects" between experimenters and their subjects (Rosenthal and Rubin 1978), teachers and students (Rosenthal and Jacobson 1968), as well as between managers and subordinates (Eden 1992). Expectations, or beliefs about the performance of subjects, students and subordinates, can have a powerful effect on their actual performance. Sports trainers and coaches spend considerable amounts of time working on the mental aspects of the sport with their pupils, even with world-class athletes. In Western cultures, building self-confidence practices might include giving some autonomy to employees or providing them with challenging assignments (Oldham et al. 1976). It might also include giving very specific individual feedback. Direct feedback is more valued in some cultures than in others. Reactions to negative versus positive feedback also differ across cultures. In Asian cultures, building self-confidence might include offering employees special titles or giving a team special recognition.

A fourth principle is to set high standards and expectations. There is strong evidence from the research on goal setting that setting moderately difficult goals can be motivating (Locke and Latham 2002).GE popularized the practice of "stretch" goals (Kerr and Landauer 2004). In Western cultures, setting high standards might involve meeting with subordinates to discuss goals and pointing to the alignment of these goals with department and company objectives. However, research has shown that some aspects of goal-setting may not necessarily work the same way across cultures. For example, Kurman et al. (2015) found that a country's "regulatory focus" tended to predict achievement-related behavior. In this concept, which is related to individualism/collectivism, promotion-oriented people strive for accomplishments and they emphasize gains while minimizing "non-gains." Prevention-oriented people, on the other hand, try to minimize losses. They are more concerned with fulfilling obligations and responsibilities to avoid possible social sanctions and criticism. Another example of a different cultural practice reflecting this principle would be to have a senior leader of a Middle Eastern company speaking to employees about the importance of meeting stretch goals for the good of the team and for the good of the company.

A fifth principle is to build collaboration and teamwork. While talented individuals will continue to come up with inventions and innovations, breakthroughs today are more often than not the product of teams of individuals working together. The image of the lone inventor or scientist toiling in isolation is somewhat exaggerated anyway; even Thomas Edison had a small team that worked with him to invent the light bulb (Pretzer et al. 2007). In Western cultures, building collaboration and teamwork might include focusing on the right incentives and rewards to reinforce the right behaviors. As another practice to build collaboration, many Western organizations emphasize empowerment, and some are experimenting with self-managed teams, a more extreme form of empowerment (Solansky 2008).Yet the research suggests that in high-power-distance cultures, empowerment may actually result in lower performance (Eylon and Au 1999).

Oloko and Ogutu (2012) for example surveyed employees of over 50 multinational companies in Kenya and found that power distance moderated the relationship between perceptions of empowerment and the multinational corporations' performance. Building collaboration and teamwork in some non-Western cultures might involve practices such as focusing on team building to create a strong sense of group and company identity for employees, or on redesigning the work to build interdependence.

These people management principles, interestingly enough, reflect attributes of leaders that both the GLOBE study and Kouzes and Posner (2007) claim are universally endorsed. As Table 3.1 shows, it would be expected that leaders who possess these specific attributes will more than likely adhere to these people management principles:

Other relevant research supports the effectiveness and the contextual application of these principles. For example, Denison et al. (2003) conducted research to determine whether there were cross-cultural dif-

Table 3.1 Implicit leadership attributes in people management principles

People management principle	Kouzes and Posner most admired leadership attributes	GLOBE leadership attributes
Treat people with respect	Honest	Integrity
Create a positive and motivating environment	Forward-looking, inspiring	Inspirational (encouraging, positive); visionary
Build self-confidence in employees		Inspirational (confidence builder)
Set high standards and expectations	Competent	Performance oriented (excellence oriented)
Build collaboration and teamwork		Team integrator

ferences in the relationship between organizational culture and effectiveness. They examined data from over 36,000 individuals working for 230 organizations across different industries. While the correlations between their organizational culture indices (such as involvement, consistently, and adaptability) and performance (such as measures of profitability and sales growth) were significant, they conclude (p. 17):

> we would not argue that this means that these traits are expressed in the same way in each of these contexts, or that the same meaning would be attached to the same behaviors in different national contexts. On the contrary, we would take these results to mean that a concept like empowerment is important around the world, but we would not argue that this means that the same behaviors would necessarily constitute empowerment in different national contexts.

Castaño et al. (2015) used data from the second phase of the GLOBE study to examine perceptions of leadership among 1886 middle managers in 11 Latin American countries in various industries. They found that both charismatic/value-based and team-oriented leadership styles were desired, but the attributes that distinguished Latin American charismatic managers included being inspiring, visionary, future-oriented, and anticipatory, while the attributes that distinguished Latin American team-oriented Latin American managers included being an integrator, good administrator, group-oriented, and collaborative. These were not necessarily the attributes viewed as effective leadership in other regions.

Since these people management principles are applied and implemented differently in various cultures, Covey's advice is worth heeding. Lonner (1980) refers to these as variform universals—where a general statement might hold across cultures, but where the implementation of that principle differs across cultures.

In an ethnographic research study, Chevrier and Pires (2013) interviewed employees of a French NGO in Madagascar on perceptions of formalization, collective work (or collaboration in our terms), decision-making, and delegation. To put their findings in cultural perspective, Chevrier and Pires first described certain key aspects of French culture:

> In French society, the basic fear is servility (i.e., the experience of being bent by fear or by interest) ... The path to salvation is resistance, in the name of something great, over fear and petty interests; this path is associated with

expressions such as 'to face' and to 'stand up to.' Courage is opposed to cowardice … Thus, many French myths glorify resistance. (p. 432)

French managers in Madagascar expected their Malagasy teams to take on initiatives, act independently, and be willing to make decisions autonomously and take risks:

> In the French context, decision-making is considered a matter of personal choice for which individuals should take responsibility. Some say that several responsible parties make as many irresponsible people … Because ideas prevail over relationships, individuals are expected to stand up for their opinions, even if these opinions are different from the leader's point of view. In this context, decisions are made and implemented because they are considered relevant, not simply because they were explicitly requested by leaders. Accordingly, once a decision has been made, it may be easily changed if another alternative is perceived to be better. (p. 437)

In the Malagasy context, however, expectations were somewhat different. In their interviews, the Malagasies mentioned their fear of making bad decisions and of incurring the wrath of their supervisors for this. They also were afraid of taking on responsibility unless their tasks and with whom they should communicate were clearly defined. They expected to have detailed reporting relationships so they could determine who was responsible for making decisions. For the French, this seemed like mere bureaucracy.

Furthermore, for the Malagasies, teamwork meant creating shared objectives to generate engagement and cohesion. They also saw this as an opportunity to help each other and to find solutions jointly. A Malagasy mentioned a local proverb to one of the interviewers: "Once shared, a burden becomes a feather." For the French, however, teamwork and meetings were places for debate and confrontation, and where people could disagree and even interrupt each other when arguing. The researchers' conclusion—that while delegation (which is related to collaboration) may be an ideal principle, specific practices will vary across cultures—is consistent with our own.

However, if practices are situationally specific, does it tend to lead to less useful advice for leaders? Dickson et al. (2009) argue that "Telling an expatriate manager from Finland that transformational leadership is universal, and so he or she should rely on it during his or her assignment to Bolivia, is unlikely to be useful advice if the behaviors that comprise transformational leadership differ drastically between the home culture and the host culture, especially if it is still unclear exactly what such behaviors would be."(p. 238)

To address this, researchers do offer frameworks for understanding different cultures. These will be discussed in greater detail in a later chapter. In addition, as the GLOBE study has done, there exist country clusters or categories so managers can identify the range of behaviors (or practices) most appropriate for different clusters.

The following are some implications for leaders managing individuals and teams across cultures. First, be aware that these hard-wired behaviors are part of what makes us "human" and it will be impossible to completely eliminate these behaviors in the work place. For example, while many organizations have hiring and promotional practices that emphasize objective qualifications and merit, individuals may still continue to show a bias toward relying on their initial impressions or judgments. In addition, cultural values (such as collectivism) may further reinforce these behaviors. Implementing systems and processes to reinforce specific management practices should help, but implementation may still be challenging.

Second, recognize that societies may differ in how the workers in these societies express these hard-wired behaviors. Understanding the cultural code will help leaders better manage and motivate individuals in different cultures. Third, our tendency to create distinctions between "us" and "them" may unconsciously make us favor one individual or one group over another in different cross-cultural settings, so we need to be aware of this bias. For example, a manager assigned to work in a subsidiary of a global company that is in another country may have a tendency to affiliate quickly with those local employees who he perceives to be similar to him in some ways. Perhaps that local employee has lived in the same part of the country where the manager is from, or perhaps the employee speaks the manager's native language somewhat fluently.

NOTES

1. See http://www.statista.com/statistics/273744/number-of-full-time-google-employees/
2. Taylor wrote his book *The Principles of Scientific Management* based on his experiments in steel plants in Pennsylvania.

3. Microsoft announced a restructuring prior to Steve Ballmer's retirement from the company. Google has restructured the company to create a new name called Alphabet.

4. Michael Hammer was one of the first management gurus to coin the term "re-engineering" and his personality and charisma went a long way to popularize this concept. He was constantly giving seminars and consulting to organizations and governments before he passed away prematurely.

5. "Thain's Overhaul Said to Cost $1.2 Million, January 22, 2009 from the Deal Book of the New York Times: http://dealbook.nytimes. com/2009/01/22/thains-office-overhaul-said-to-cost-12-million/?_r=0

6. Rachel EmmaSilverman, "At Zappos, Banishing the Bosses Brings Confusion," *Wall Street Journal*, May 21, sec. Business. http://www.wsj. com/articles/at-zappos-banishing-the-bosses-brings-confusion-1432175402.

7. http://www.greatplacetowork.com/best-companies/100-best-companies-to-work-for

8. GLOBE is an acronym for Global Leadership and Organizational Behavior Effectiveness, a 62-nation study involving many researchers over a period of 11 years.

REFERENCES

Ahuja, Anjana, and Mark Van Vugt. 2010. *Selected: Why Some People Lead, Why Others Follow, and Why It Matters*. London: Profile Books.

Aycan, Zeynep, Birgit Schyns, Jian-Min Sun, Jorg Felfe, and Noreen Saher. 2013. Convergence and Divergence of Paternalistic Leadership: A Cross-Cultural Investigation of Prototypes. *Journal of International Business Studies* 44(9): 962–969.

Castaño, Nathalie, M. Sully de Lugque, T. Wernsing, E. Ogliastri, R. Shemueli, R. Fuchs, and J. Robles-Flores. 2015. El Jefe: Differences in Expected Leadership Behaviors Across Latin American Countries. *Journal of World Business* 50(3): 584–597.

Chase, Ivan D. 1980. Social Process and Hierarchy Formation in Small Groups: A Comparative Perspective. *American Sociological Review* 45(6): 905–924.

Chevrier, Sylvie, and Michaël Viegas-Pires. 2013. Delegating Effectively Across Cultures. *Journal of World Business* 48(3): 431–439.

Covey, Stephen. 1989. *The Seven Habits of Highly Effective People*. New York: Simon and Schuster.

Davidson, Robert, Aiyesha Dey, and Abbie Smith. (2012). Executives' "Off-the-Job" Behavior, Corporate Culture, and Financial Reporting Risk. Working

Paper 18001. National Bureau of Economic Research. http://www.nber.org/papers/w18001.pdf

Deci, Edward. 1975. *Intrinsic Motivation*. New York: Plenum Press.

Denison, Daniel, Stephanie Haaland, and Paolo Goelzer. 2003. Corporate Culture and Organizational Effectiveness: Is There a Similar Pattern Around the World? http://www.denisonconsulting.com/resource-library/corporate-culture-and-organizational-effectiveness-there-similar-pattern-around

Detert, James R., and Ethan R. Burris. 2007. Leadership Behavior and Employee Voice: Is the Door Really Open? *Academy of Management Journal* 50(4): 869–884.

Dickson, Marcus, Deanne Den Hartog, and Nathalie Castaño. 2009. Understanding Leadership Across Cultures. In *Cambridge Handbook of Culture, Organization, and Work*, eds. Rabi Bhagat and Richard Steers, 219–244. New York: Cambridge University Press.

Eden, Dov. 1992. Leadership and Expectations: Pygmalion Effects and Other Self-Fulfilling Prophecies in Organizations. *The Leadership Quarterly* 3(4): 271–305.

Erez, Miriam. 1994. Toward a Model of Cross-Cultural Industrial and Organizational Psychology. In *Handbook of Industrial and Organizational Psychology*, vol 4, Second edn, eds. Harry Triandis, Marvin Dunnette, and Leaetta Hough 559–608. Palo Alto, CA: Consulting Psychologists' Press.

Eylon, Dafna, and Kevin Au. 1999. Exploring Empowerment Cross-Cultural Differences Along the Power Distance Dimension. *International Journal of Intercultural Relations* 23(3): 373–385.

Fernandez-Araoz, Claudio. 2014. *It's Not the How or the What But the Who*. Boston: Harvard Business Review Press.

Fischer, Ronald, et al. 2014. Organizational Practices Across Cultures: An Exploration in Six Cultural Contexts. *International Journal of Cross Cultural Management* 14(1): 101–125.

Galbraith, Jay. 1993. The Business Unit of the Future. In *Organizing for the Future: The New Logic for Managing Complex Organizations*, ed. Jay Galbraith. San Francisco, CA: Jossey-Bass.

———. 1995. *Designing Organizations*. San Francisco, CA: Jossey-Bass.

George, Michael. 2002. *Lean Six Sigma: Combining Six Sigma Quality with Lean Production Speed*. New York: McGraw Hill Professional.

Gino, Francesca, and Gary P. Pisano. 2011. Why Leaders Don't Learn from Success. *Harvard Business Review* 89(4): 68–74.

Goleman, Daniel. 2005. *Emotional Intelligence*. New York: Bantam Books.

Golman, R., and G. Loewenstein. 2014. Curiosity, Information Gaps, and the Utility of Knowledge. https://www.cmu.edu/dietrich/sds/docs/golman/Curiosity, percent20Information percent20Gaps, percent20and percent20the

percent20Utility   percent20of   percent20Knowledge   percent20Golman_
Loewenstein percent20April percent202015.pdf

Hackman, J. Richard, and Greg R. Oldham. 1976. Motivation through the Design of Work: Test of a Theory. *Organizational Behavior and Human Performance* 16(2): 250–279.

Hall, Edward. 2013. *The Silent Language*. Reissued. New York: Anchor Books.

Handy, Charles. 1990. *The Age of Unreason*. Boston: Harvard Business School Press.

Herrmann, Esther, Josep Call, María Victoria Hernàndez-Lloreda, Brian Hare, and Michael Tomasello. 2007. Humans Have Evolved Specialized Skills of Social Cognition: The Cultural Intelligence Hypothesis. *Science* 317(5843): 1360–1366.

Hoffman, Martin L. 1981. Is Altruism Part of Human Nature? *Journal of Personality and Social Psychology* 40(1): 121–137.

Hofstede, Geert. 2001. *Culture's Consequences*. New York: Sage Publications.

Hout, Thomas, and David Michael. 2014. A Chinese Approach to Management. *Harvard Business Review* 92(9): 103–107.

Hui, C. Harry, Harry C. Triandis, and Candice Yee. 1991. Cultural Differences in Reward Allocation: Is Collectivism the Explanation? *British Journal of Social Psychology* 30(2): 145–157.

Kabasakal, Hayat, Ali Dastmalchian, Gaye Karacay, and Secil Bayraktar. 2012. Leadership and Culture in the MENA Region: An Analysis of the GLOBE Project. *Journal of World Business* 47(4): 519–529.

Kahnemann, Daniel. 2013. *Thinking, Fast and Slow*. New York: Farar, Straus, and Giroux.

Kerr, Steven, and Steffen Landauer. 2004. Using Stretch Goals to Promote Organizational Effectiveness and Personal Growth: General Electric and Goldman Sachs. *Academy of Management Executive* 18(4): 134–138.

Kim, Ken I., Hun-Joon Park, and Nori Suzuki. 1990. Reward Allocations in the United States, Japan, and Korea: A Comparison of Individualistic and Collectivistic Cultures. *Academy of Management Journal* 33(1): 188–198.

Kouzes, Jim, and Barry Posner. 2007. *The Leadership Challenge*, Fourth edn. New York: Wiley.

Kurman, Jenny, Gregory Liem, Tal Ivancovsky, Hiroaki Morio, and Joo Lee. 2015. Regulatory Focus as an Explanatory Variable for Cross-Cultural Differences in Achievement-Related Behaviors. *Journal of Cross-Cultural Psychology* 46(2): 171–190.

Lawrence, Paul, and Jay Lorsch. 1967. *Organizations and Environment*. Boston: Harvard University.

Lawrence, Paul, and Nitin Nohria. 2002. *Driven: How Human Nature Shapes Our Choices*. San Francisco, CA: Jossey-Bass.

Leung, Kwok, and Michael H. Bond. 1984. The Impact of Cultural Collectivism on Reward Allocation. *Journal of Personality and Social Psychology* 47(4): 793–804.

Locke, Edwin A., and Gary P. Latham. 2002. Building a Practically Useful Theory of Goal Setting and Task Motivation: A 35-Year Odyssey. *American Psychologist* 57(9): 705–717.

Loher, Brian T., Raymond A. Noe, Nancy L. Moeller, and Michael P. Fitzgerald. 1985. A Meta-Analysis of the Relation of Job Characteristics to Job Satisfaction. *Journal of Applied Psychology* 70(2): 280–289.

Lonner, Walter J. 1980. The Search for Psychological Universals. In *Handbook of Cross-Cultural Psychology*, vol 1, eds., H. C. Triandis and W. W. Lambert. Boston: Allyn and Bacon. 143–204.

McClure, Sameul, David Laibson, George Lowenstein, and Jonathan Cohen. 2004. Separate Neural Systems Value Immediate and Delayed Monetary Rewards. *Science* 306(5695): 503–507.

Mischel, Walter. 2014. *The Marshmallow Effect*. New York: Little Brown and Company.

Mitchell, Jason P., C. Neil Macrae, and Mahzarin R. Banaji. 2006. Dissociable Medial Prefrontal Contributions to Judgments of Similar and Dissimilar Others. *Neuron* 50(4): 655–663.

Nicholson, Nigel. 1997. Evolutionary Psychology: Toward a New View of Human Nature and Organizational Society. *Human Relations* 50(9): 1053–1078.

———. 1998. How Hardwired Is Human Behavior? *Harvard Business Review* 76: 134–147.

Oldham, Greg R., J. Richard Hackman, and Jone L. Pearce. 1976. Conditions Under Which Employees Respond Positively to Enriched Work. *Journal of Applied Psychology* 61(4): 395–403.

Oloko, Margaret, and Martin Ogutu. 2012. Influence of Power Distance on Employee Empowerment and MNC Performance: A Study of Multinational Corporations in Kenya. *Education Research Journal* 2(2): 47–61.

Perrow, Charles. 1970. *Organizational Analysis: A Sociological View*. Belmont, CA: Wadsworth.

Pfeffer, Jeffrey. 1998. 7 Practices of Successful Organizations. *California Management Review* 40: 96–124.

———. 2010. *Power: Why Some People Have It and Others Don't*. New York: HarperBusiness.

Pink, Daniel H. 2011. *Drive: The Surprising Truth About What Motivates Us*. New York: Penguin.

Preston, Stephanie D., and B.M. Frans De Waal. 2002. Empathy: Its ultimate and proximate bases. *Behavioral and Brain Sciences* 25(1): 1–20.

Pretzer, William S., George E. Rogers, and Jeffery Bush. 2007. A Model Technology Educator: Thomas A. Edison: Recognizing Edison's Incorporation of Team-Based, Cooperative Learning into His Development Process Is Essential to Appreciating His Success and His Influence Today. *The Technology Teacher* 67(1): 27.

Rosenthal, Robert, and Lenore Jacobson. 1968. Pygmalion in the Classroom. *The Urban Review* 3(1): 16–20.

Rosenthal, Robert, and Donald B. Rubin. 1978. Interpersonal Expectancy Effects: The First 345 Studies. *Behavioral and Brain Sciences* 1(3): 377–386.

Rousseau, Denise M., and Snehal A. Tijoriwala. 1998. Assessing Psychological Contracts: Issues, Alternatives and Measures. *Journal of Organizational Behavior* 19(1): 679–695.

Schminke, Marshall, Maureen L. Ambrose, and Russell S. Cropanzano. 2000. The Effect of Organizational Structure on Perceptions of Procedural Fairness. *Journal of Applied Psychology* 85(2): 294–304.

Sidanius, Jim, and Felicia Pratto. 2001. *Social Dominance: An Intergroup Theory of Social Hierarchy and Oppression*. New York: Cambridge University Press.

Smith, Adam. 2006. Cognitive Empathy and Emotional Empathy in Human Behavior and Evolution. *The Psychological Record* 56(1): 3–21.

Solansky, Stephanie T. 2008. Leadership Style and Team Processes in Self-Managed Teams. *Journal of Leadership & Organizational Studies* 14(4): 332–341.

Stringer, C.B., and P. Andrews. 1988. Genetic and Fossil Evidence for the Origin of Modern Humans. *Science* 239(4845): 1263–1268.

Ulrich, Dave, Steve Kerr, and Ron Ashkenas. 2002. *The GE Work-Out: How to Implement GE's Revolutionary Method for Busting Bureaucracy & Attacking Organizational Problems*, First edn. New York: McGraw-Hill Education.

Weber, Max. 1947. *The Theory of Social and Economic Organization. (Translated by A. M. Hderson and T. Parsons)*. New York: The Free Press.

Willis, Janine, and Alexander Todorov. 2006. First Impressions: Making Up Your Mind After a 100-Ms Exposure to a Face. *Psychological Science* 17(7): 592–598.

Zweig, David. 2014. Managing the Invisibles. *Harvard Business Review.* 92(5): 96–103.

CHAPTER 4

Cultural Frameworks

In *Overwhelmed* (a book about the pressures of work–life balance, among other topics), Schulte (2014) described her trip to Denmark and her interviews with working couples there. Here's what she wrote about work life in that country:

> Danes don't live to work. Danes work hard … but they work in a very focused way. Lunch is usually no more than half an hour …Most Danes work the standard thirty-seven hours a week. Long hours are outlawed for most workers under the European Union's Working Time Directive … no European is allowed to work more than forty-eight hours a week … Workplaces tend to be flat, without a lot of layers of management … Most Danes don't feel obligated to check their smartphones and e-mail after hours … people who put in long hours and constantly check e-mail after hours are seen not as ideal worker warriors, as in America, but as inefficient.

And yet, Schulte points out:

> The Danish economy is one of the most competitive in the world, just a few rungs below the United States. And it's one of the most productive, ranking just behind the United States … Denmark has a low unemployment rate and one of the highest standards of living in the world. It has one of the smallest gaps between rich and poor of any country on earth … and only 6 percent

© The Editor(s) (if applicable) and The Author(s) 2016
R. Henson, *Successful Global Leadership*,
DOI 10.1057/978-1-137-58990-3_4

of Danes find it difficult or very difficult to live on their current income, compared to 21 percent of Americans.

Denmark is by no means unique among European nations. One of our interviewee managers, Beverly, was sent by her company to its German headquarters for a one-year assignment to support the launch of a new product that was successfully marketed in the USA. In the US subsidiary, she was used to working long days and, frequently, weekends. In Germany, when she started to pack her laptop to take it home with her, her colleagues would, as she described it, "give me the craziest looks." She learned that overtime was not allowed, and she even heard a rumor that people could get fired for working on a Sunday. She started out with 30 days of paid vacation a year, not including sick time and holidays.

In Switzerland, according to another of our interviewees, companies keep careful track of each employee's hours and any extra time beyond the standard work week of 40 hours could be taken as vacation. In addition, employees generally have 30 vacation days per year, plus an extra month of salary annually. In Belgium, yet another one of our interviewees assigned there recalled that Belgians left their workplace between 5:30 and 6:00 p.m. and completely disconnected in the evenings.

Those of us who have worked overseas are very well aware of the differences in workplace cultures. And scholars from Hofstede (2001) and House et al. (2004), to Trompenaars and Hampden-Turner (1998) have constructed outstanding frameworks to help us understand the underlying values or dimensions that account for variations in these workplace cultures. While there have been conceptual differences in the approaches these different researchers have taken, many of the dimensions these researchers have identified have remained remarkably similar.

In a study reviewing Hofstede's classification 25 years later, Fernandez et al. (1997) found some country shifts in dimension rankings partly as a result of environmental and social changes in these countries. For example, both China and Russia scored relatively high in uncertainty avoidance, a measure of concern for risk taking and accepting uncertainty. Were such a study conducted today, China would most likely show a greater tolerance for uncertainty avoidance than Russia. However, most of the dimensions have held up consistently. For example, the USA continues to have relatively high scores on individualism, while China and Japan continue to have relatively low scores on this dimension.

However, as Steers et al. (2009) have suggested, the dimensions underlying these different frameworks may not always be relevant to managers in the workplace; they refer to this proliferation of models as the "culture theory jungle." Adler (2008) emphasizes an important point: "We must recognize which differences are operating and learn to use them to our advantage, rather than ether attempting to ignore the differences or simply allowing them to cause problems" (p. 65).

The framework proposed here consists of eight cultural orientations relevant to the workplace. Some of these orientations reflect values and beliefs, while others reflect practices. I have integrated and synthesized these orientations based on the academic research, discussions with global executives over the years, as well as interviews we have conducted on which ones global managers believe are most relevant, keeping in mind what McCall and Hollenbeck (2002) stated: "Such classic distinctions as 'power distance' ... are no doubt real, but to the person on the front line, the experienced differences are finer-grained" (p. 83).

The eight are the following: formality, authoritarianism, structure, time orientation, assertiveness, individualism, directness, and expressiveness. They can be remembered with the acronym FASTAIDE.

1. Formality—How formal should I be? At the one extreme are cultures where people are very informal and quite casual. There are not a lot of rituals when meeting others, and people tend to treat each other in an egalitarian manner. In the workplace, people refer to each other, and even senior executives, by their first names, and there are few protocols involved in meetings and business discussions. At the other extreme are cultures that are quite formal, from their business attire to the way people address each other, and to the way meetings are conducted. Titles are important, and offices are designed to reflect this. One of the expatriates interviewed was initially surprised when, upon arriving in Thailand, he was assigned an office that would ordinarily be appropriate only for senior management in the USA. Furthermore, he was almost always addressed as "Sir" by everyone in the local subsidiary.

Similarly, Arlene, in her expatriate assignment in Switzerland for a pharmaceutical company, was told that she would have to address her boss by his last name in public, and was only allowed to address him by his first name when they were meeting privately. A global financial services firm that has a relatively flat structure learned, when it first opened a Bangalore office, that its Indian employees in Bangalore were concerned because they did not have the titles they felt they should have to indicate their status in the Indian work environment. Morale started to dip, and turnover began to increase until the firm decided to accommodate them to some extent by adding more titles especially in its larger units such as Finance.

By contrast, another interviewee described his surprise upon going to work for his first day of his international assignment in Belgium. He had dressed in his typical corporate attire, with wool trousers, dress shirt, and a tie. His formal attire clashed with the clothes worn by the local office staff, most of whom had actually biked to work and often biked from building to building in the company's large site. At lunch, he was surprised when he entered the company cafeteria where there were literally thousands of people all queuing up, and there were no special reserved seats for anyone, including senior management. And by 6 pm, the whole site was empty. Everyone was gone, and all employees disconnected for the evening. He found that on Wednesdays, elementary school children were dismissed at noon, so those employees especially with young children left early to meet them.

In general, in formal cultures, the higher the status or the older the person, the more formal and respectful you have to be. Based on Hofstede's and House et al.'s GLOBE study, countries that are typically formal include China, Mexico, Italy, the Philippines, and Portugal. Countries that are typically informal include Canada, Finland, Norway, Sweden, and the USA.

2. Authoritarianism—How directive should I be? Do employees believe in a strong hierarchy where managers are expected to lead in an authoritarian way, or are managers expected to be more egalitarian, where they get employees' input before making decisions, or empower them to make decisions? Do employees accept decisions that are made autocratically, or do they expect to participate in decisions? Is authority more or less accepted, or is challenging authority encouraged? When conflicts arise, do parties justify their position because of their status and/or try to defer to a high status person?

According to Altmeyer (1996), authoritarians adhere to conventional morality, emphasize hierarchy and deference to authority figures, and possess a "law and order" mindset especially against those who violate social norms and conventions. In a study that Tinsley (1998) conducted, she gave Japanese, German, and American managers conflict scenarios and found that Japanese, in contrast to the Germans and Americans, had a strong preference for the "deferring to status" model of conflict resolution. Some cultures such as France expect bosses to give orders and run a command-and-control type of organization, while other cultures such as Israel expect their bosses to be more participative, asking for input from others. From the Hofstede (2001) and GLOBE research, countries that are typically more authoritarian include India, Iran, Malaysia, South Korea, and United Arab Emirates. Countries that are typically more egalitarian include Australia, Denmark, Israel, Netherlands, and New Zealand.

In a cross-cultural study of employee perceptions of authority (cited by Steers et al. 2009), Laurent found the following percentages of managers who agreed with the statement, "Managers must have the answers to most questions asked by subordinates":

Japan	78 percent
China	74 percent
Indonesia	73 percent
Italy	66 percent
France	53 percent
Germany	46 percent
United Kingdom	27 percent
United States	18 percent
Sweden	10 percent

Reproduced from page 74 of Steers et al. (2009)

Jerry was an American naval lieutenant who was assigned recently to be an exchange officer aboard a French aircraft carrier. He had been responsible for the maintenance and safe operation of his former ship's catapults and arresting gear that launch and recover aircraft, as well as the 200 sailors who worked on these systems. Jerry got a call from the Naval Air Forces Command, asking him to serve as the Catapult and Arresting Gear Officer on board a French ship for three years. He would be the only American on the ship's crew of over a thousand sailors, and would be reporting to the ship's chief engineer who in turn reported to the captain of the vessel. Jerry did not speak French, so he immediately took French lessons and tried to read as much as he could about French culture.

From his previous experience as a Naval officer, Jerry believed in what he described as "leadership through presence." Whenever the French sailors were working on the arresting and catapult gear, Jerry was there—observing, explaining, rolling up his sleeves, and working alongside the sailors. For Jerry, a leader was someone who showed an interest in what his subordinates were doing and shared the hardship of long hours. After the first week, he noticed that the French sailors were uncomfortable with his continuous presence. One of the French officers suggested that he should go work out or go to his stateroom to read. In France, bosses were not expected to work side by side with subordinates but rather to stay a bit aloof and somewhat removed from the day-to-day work. Jerry was a bit taken aback by the French officer's suggestion, but realized that this was a cultural expectation that he had to take seriously. This also spilled over to the approach to humor he was accustomed to in US ships, where American sailors would make jokes and engage in "gallows humor" when some of the problems were challenging. In contrast, he learned that French sailors were "all business and long faces" until the problems were solved.

On the other hand, Brian, a Korean manager on his first expatriate assignment to the USA for a Korean company, struggled at first working with his American colleagues. He was used to being given direct orders without much information by his Korean boss, and was expected to simply follow orders. In Korea, as he explained it, subordinates might privately question what they are asked to do, but would not dream of publicly questioning their manager. Over time, he learned to manage not only his US management, but also how to deal with requests he was receiving from his Korean management. As a manager based in Hong Kong told one of our interviewers:

> In some countries in Asia, in the work environment, you may have people who will only talk when they are asked. You may have a bit of hierarchy. That's clearly not what we're used to in the Western world, (where) everyone jumps in when they have questions or comments. Here you may want to ask people if they have any comments at the end of the meeting because if they haven't spoken but have some thoughts they are actually just waiting for you to ask them. It's not obvious but it's useful to know as a manager of a team.

Awareness of this is important in countries such as Vietnam, where a manager might be dealing with a local team or with a local vendor.

Although you might be meeting with groups of people, it is important to
show respect by not bypassing the leader and making sure you work with
the local leader and negotiate with him or her directly.

3. Structure—How much detail should I provide; how explicit should
   I be? Do employees expect to have sets of rules and social norms to
   be able to anticipate different contingencies? Is ambiguity very
   uncomfortable, or tolerated and even accepted? In some cultures,
   being explicit is important as a means to mitigate the risks of ambiguity. For example, job descriptions are essential, and employees
   have handbooks that describe the company's procedures in detail.

Kevin was an American expatriate in Hungary who was very frustrated
initially with managing Hungarians. As he described it, "In the U.S., we're
not used to having to micro-manage every task and issue. We look for people with initiative, and expect them to make decisions about how to complete tasks." While he found Hungarians to be very task-oriented, they
also asked a lot of questions and wanted to have their tasks fully explained.

In other cultures such as Jamaica and Sweden, employees have a higher
tolerance for ambiguity. This orientation is related to Hofstede's concept
of uncertainty avoidance. In Hofstede's original definition, however, he
included concerns about job security and work stress, which are not strictly
part of this orientation (although these aspects may indeed be correlated).
In a later study, Minkov and Hofstede (2014) found that countries with
high uncertainty avoidance scores (which included the three aspects origi-
nally defined by Hofstede) include Bulgaria, Greece, and Ukraine; countries with low uncertainty avoidance scores include Denmark, Ireland, and
the Netherlands.

This orientation is also related to cultures that are characterized as tight
or loose (Gelfand et al. 2006). In tight cultures, social norms are clearly
defined, while in loose cultures, social norms are relatively flexible and
informal. As Triandis (1994) has written, "In cultures high in Uncertainty
Avoidance, people want to have structure, to know precisely how they
are supposed to behave and what is going to happen next. Predictability
of events is highly valued." In tight cultures, there is a higher degree of
situational constraint that restricts the types of behavior that might be
considered acceptable or appropriate. There are clear norms, and devia-
tions from these norms are not lightly tolerated. Loose cultures have lower
degrees of situational constraint, and there is a greater range of what is

considered permissible behavior. Uz's model (2015) proposes that threats to survival and the socio-political context (such as institutional repression) are prerequisites to the cultural tightness of a society, and that tightness can be measured in part by a society's homogeneity in values, norms, and behaviors.

Gelfand et al. (2011) gathered data from over 6000 respondents across 33 countries. She measured tightness–looseness with a set of items on a six-item agree–disagree Likert scale. These items included the following:

- There are many social norms that people are supposed to abide by in this country.
- In this country, if someone acts in an inappropriate way, others will strongly disapprove.

They then measured the degree of constraint across a wide range of social situations by having participants rate the appropriateness of 12 behaviors (e.g., arguing, laughing) across 15 situations (e.g., job interview, party, workplace). Tightness scores were highest for Malaysia, Singapore, South Korea, and India. They were lowest for Hungary, Brazil, and Netherlands. As predicted, there was much higher constraint across everyday situations in tight nations versus loose nations.

There's an intriguing connection between the tightness and looseness of cultures and trust, as suggested by Yamagishi et al. (1998). In tight cultures, where norms are clearly defined, individuals tend to rely more on institutional trust versus interpersonal trust to shape and control behavior. On the other hand, in loose cultures, where norms are more flexible, people tend to rely more on interpersonal trust as well as personal characteristics of the person such as their competence to develop trust. Cultures that are tight tend to trust people less than cultures that are loose; specifically, the basis of their trust will depend on the other person's social network, and the way to build trust therefore is to invest time and effort in developing and building these networks.

Gunia et al. (2011) have taken this research and extended it to studies of negotiation, where they found that negotiators from tight cultures tend to trust less, since many negotiation situations tend to have little if any clear norms and sanctions. They also tend to use negotiation strategies that assume low levels of trust (i.e., substantiation tactics such as threats and power plays) versus strategies that assume higher levels of trust (i.e., question-and-answer tactics).

One interviewee, a German expatriate, found it difficult to adjust to the decision-making process in the American subsidiary where she was assigned. As she reflected on this, she commented that Germans typically employ a more deliberate and cautious approach, explaining that this did not mean that things were done slower, only that colleagues were more willing to talk issues through at length before making a final decision. On the other hand, she felt business decisions in the USA were too rushed.

Another interviewee working in Slovakia had a similar experience. As she recalled, decision making with her Slovakian team took several stages. Her team would first want to learn the problem, and if there was no obvious answer, they would all part ways, with no specific clear path forward. They would work individually and then bring their results together, discuss them, and present their answer. She had to learn to adjust to this more methodical approach.

As a third example, an American expatriate we interviewed who was assigned to his company's Belgian subsidiary commented that he needed to slow down decision making to make sure that he involved his Belgian team members, who seemed to have a strong desire" … to understand how and why they were going from point A to point B."

Other countries that typically value structure and clear sets of rules include Czech Republic, Indonesia, Mexico, the Philippines, and Russia. Countries that typically place less value on organization and structure include France, Hong Kong, Israel, New Zealand, and the UK.

4. Time Orientation—Do people in the culture have a preference for dealing with multiple tasks and relationships rather than adhering strictly to deadlines, or do they prefer a more sequential approach and a strong commitment to meeting deadlines? Is there a high value placed on tradition and on long-term results versus getting quick results? The two sub-orientations of this orientation are the monochronic/polychronic distinction and the past–present–future time orientation (Hall 2013). When Hall introduced this distinction, he was referring to the priority some cultures have toward schedules and deadlines as well as a preference for sequencing of activities (monochronic), versus loose attention to schedules and a tendency to attend to different activities at the same time. Some cultures such as Switzerland and Germany are very strict on time, whether it's when meetings start and end, or on deadlines for projects. Hall describes this as linear or monochronic time. Other cul-

tures such as Central and South American countries are more fluid and flexible about time. An expatriate working in India told us that us that he operates on "Indian Standard Time," which implies being about 30 minutes late for everything. Schedules are not adhered to strictly and interruptions are welcome. It's not that these cultures are uninterested in meeting deadlines, but their attitude toward time is more fluid.

A Japanese executive we interviewed who manages a team in several countries describes her approach to working with her Indian team members. She says that she sets "pretend deadlines" with the expectation that deliverables will most likely not be met by these deadlines. On the other hand, an Indian expatriate working for a global financial services firm in New Zealand found that, while his "Kiwi" colleagues were friendly, they were very strict on punctuality. He had to adjust his own working style to make sure that he started meetings on time and adhered to deadlines strictly.

Countries that have typically high concerns about managing time include Germany, Hong Kong, Japan, Switzerland, New Zealand, and the USA. Countries that have typically lower concerns about punctuality include Chile, Pakistan, Spain, United Arab Emirates, and Vietnam.

Kemp and Williams (2013) studied meeting behavior of participants in three large organizations (one public, one private, and the third semi-private) in United Arab Emirates over a period of three years. They studied organizational rituals through an analysis of various themes such as space (e.g., seating arrangements), time (e.g., lateness), formality (e.g., interruptions), and communication (e.g., side conversations).Their conclusions, based on extensive observations and content analyses of meetings, include the following:

> A lack of respect for meeting business and meeting colleagues is suggested in the behavior at meetings when looked at with a western cultural perspective. It would seem that these meetings are not being held in accordance with 'traditional' rules, under which many western meetings take place. There also appears to be differences in cultural interpretation attached to the time and space components of a meeting. In a meeting situation, these different approaches are commonplace in the Arab world. Formal meetings are conducted in a more unstructured, flexible way. For example, there is often flexible rather than explicit work agendas for meetings, and when they do meet, the participants may not follow the agenda closely. Meetings

sometimes appear to be social occasions with oblique reference to the task at hand. Such facets of cultural behavior can be frustrating for westerners conducting meetings in this Arab context. (pp. 227–228)

5. Assertiveness—This orientation is similar to the GLOBE dimension of assertiveness, and we use a similar definition: the degree to which individuals are assertive, dominant, and demanding in their relations with others. This is also related the vertical aspect of individualism, which values competition and outperforming others. How competitively should I behave? Are employees' mindset around taking control of their environment, or more around accepting and living in harmony with it? Do employees approach negotiations, for example, as distributive versus integrative (McKersie and Walton 1992)?

   In their study of 1000 business people and university students in Finland, Mexico, Turkey, and the USA, Metcalf et al. (2007) found that while integrative approaches were generally favored, there were significant differences across cultures, with US and Mexican managers generally favoring a distributive approach. Assertive cultures tend to be competitive and encourage people to be opportunistic. Countries where high assertiveness is valued include Austria, Germany, Greece, and Israel, while countries where lesser assertiveness is valued include Japan, India, Portugal, and Thailand.

6. Individualism—How much should I focus on individual goals versus group goals? How valued is independence or individual interests versus group interests? Do employees see themselves primarily as members of specific groups, or do they see themselves primarily as individuals with a "self" that is stable and not dependent on whatever group they are with? In some cultures, such as the USA and Australia, the emphasis is on "I" and self-reliance. These cultures value individual over group identity, and individual rights are very important. This individualism–collectivism dimension of culture is probably the most researched of all the orientations, with some researchers stating that this is perhaps the most relevant cultural value in explaining workplace behavior (Triandis et al. 1988). As Kagitcibasi (1997) has pointed out in his excellent historical overview of the concept, the roots of individualism in Western society have existed since the time of the ancient Greeks, and this concept found expression in Britain and then the USA. At the same time, collectivist themes also existed in European philosophy. He con-

cludes that while individualism is more widespread in the Western countries, these countries represent less than 30 % of the world's population.

Brewer and Venaik (2011) reanalyzed the Hofstede and GLOBE data on this dimension, and concluded that there were some discrepancies in the definitions of individualism and collectivism. Their concept of "in-group collectivism" comes closest to the definition offered here. In their classic article, Markus and Kitayama (1991) explain this concept as follows:

> In some cultures, on certain occasions, the individual, in the sense of a set of significant inner attributes of the person, may cease to be the primary unit of consciousness. Instead, the sense of belongingness to a social relation may become so strong that it makes better sense to think of the relationship as the functional unit of conscious reflection. (p. 226)

Other research (Singelis et al. 1995; Triandis and Gelfand 1998) has shown that there are actually two aspects of individualism, vertical and horizontal; we focus on the horizontal aspect here, that is, the desire to be unique and different from equal others. Earley (1993) for example has conducted studies on the impact of this cultural influence on task performance. In one study, in which subjects participated in an in-basket exercise (a simulated management activity), subjects were told that they were members of a group of ten, and that their groups were either from the same region of the country or a different region (nationalities of the subjects were Israeli, Chinese, and American). Despite the somewhat superficial nature of the experimental design, Earley found that collectivists (the Israeli and Chinese subjects) had lower performance working alone or in an out-group (i.e., other members from different countries than the subject) than the individualists (the American subjects). He attributes this to "individual loafing" by collectivists (i.e., a tendency to reduce their performance while working alone versus while working in a group).

Intriguingly, there is even research cited by Alter (2013) that the origins of individualism and collectivism might have come from the various concentrations of disease-causing microbes. Since collectivistic cultures fear outsiders more than individualists, they were at one point protected from alien diseases that their bodies could have not have fought. Over time, according to this research, collectivists emerged in pathogen-rich areas of the world, while individualists thrived in areas with fewer dangerous pathogens. This research shows that "regions with historically higher pathogen levels tended to be far more collectivistic, historically, than the areas with lower pathogen levels" (p. 134).

Other researchers, such as Sanchez-Burks and Uhlmann (2014), point to the ideological underpinnings in America of the Protestant ethic and the influence of Calvin. This has led, according to these researchers, to the "valorization" of work in America, and is in stark contrast to countries such as France and Germany, which restrict the number of work hours and have generous vacation policies mandated by the state. Of course, this commitment to working hard is also found in many Asian countries, but the reasons may have more to do with family obligations and duty versus ideology. This valorization of work has also led to the "ethic of individual merit" and the value of meritocracy in organizations. Managers in individualistic cultures will tend to hold individuals personally accountable. In other cultures, such as China and some Latin American countries, the emphasis is on a larger entity, such as the group, organization, or tribe. The good of the group often trumps the individual rights of individuals. As Triandis (1995) points out, "Managers in collectivist cultures are not as concerned with performance as managers in individualist cultures are, but they are more concerned with interpersonal relationships than managers in individualist cultures are."

In collectivist cultures, perhaps, managers are more concerned with group performance rather than individual performance. One of the reasons why Deming's approach to quality resonated very well in Japan was because of his assumptions about the root causes of quality problems being in systemic rather than individual factors. Pritchard and Youngcourt (2008) suggest that various cultures differ not only in how they give feedback, but also on what type of feedback they provide. Individualistic cultures are likely to emphasize personal goals and outcomes, while collectivistic cultures are more likely to emphasize group-oriented goals and outcomes. Their point is that the more congruent the feedback is with the cultural values of the person receiving the feedback, the more likely it is to be accepted.

It should be noted that individualism does not necessarily suggest anti-authoritarian preferences. As Kemmelmeier et al. (2003) have pointed out, strong individualists may still be quite authoritarian. Countries that are typically individualistic include Australia, Belgium, New Zealand, Netherlands, and the USA. Countries that are typically group-oriented include Ecuador, Egypt, Indonesia, the Philippines, and South Korea.

7. Directness—How straightforward should I be? Do employees expect communication to be very clear and straightforward, or is communication more indirect? Some cultures such as Australia and Israel encourage managers to get straight to the point. Earley and Erez (1997), for example, state that "Israelis are most likely to tell each other directly, and very explicitly, what they have in mind, even when it may lead to a confrontation." Alan Dershowitz, the renowned attorney, in discussing his belief that Jewish culture has helped Jews finding success in the legal profession, stated: "Why are there so many Jewish lawyers? Why not? ... Jews are quarrelsome people ... We argue with everybody. And why shouldn't we, considering our heritage?"[1]

In other cultures such as in several East Asian countries, the message is more subtle and indirect. What is implied is more important than what is actually stated. People in these cultures place a great deal of emphasis on nonverbal communication. This is similar to Hall's concept of high and low context cultures. Hall (2013) refers to context as "the nature of how meaning is constructed differently across cultures using different ratios of context and information." Studies on this concept have yielded clear results for some countries and mixed results for others (Kittler et al. 2011). There is general agreement in the research, however, that indirect/high-context cultures include Argentina, Brazil, Italy, Japan; while direct/low-context cultures include Australia, Belgium, Denmark, and Germany.

Luc Minguet, a French national who is head of Group Purchasing for Michelin, described his observations while he was in the USA as COO of Michelin's truck business unit (Minguet 2014):

In France, we focus on identifying what's wrong with someone's performance. It's considered unnecessary to mention what's right. What's good is taken as given. A French employee knows this and reacts accordingly. But for a U.S. employee, as I discovered, it is devastating, because Americans tend to sugarcoat one negative with a lot of positives. French managers get their wires crossed. When they get what sounds like glowing feedback from an American boss, they think they're superstars. Of course, when they don't get the big pay raise they expected after the great review, they're bitterly disappointed!

Daniel, a Brazilian expatriate working in Thailand, remembers a time when his project team was late on a key project milestone. He sent an e-mail to the team in what he thought was a polite message, reminding them that the project was at risk of falling behind schedule, and asking everyone to pay increased attention. He later learned that his e-mail was perceived as both "rude and pushy." He learned to soften his approach, for example, by asking questions such as "Will you help me with …?"

Another interviewee, Julia, an American expatriate assigned to Germany, noticed this when she gave her first presentation to her German boss. He said to her very directly, "Don't take it personal; this report isn't organized well. Talk to me again when it's ready." In the USA, according to her, she would have received very polite feedback, and would probably have heard something like this: "Here are the ten things that are good about this report; however, it would make me more comfortable if you added this." The bluntness of the Germans, in contrast to the watered-down feedback from Americans, was a difficult adjustment for Julia to make. A French interviewee assigned to his American subsidiary recalled that his American team was taken aback by his candor, and he had to learn to "tone down" his comments.

Sanchez-Burks and his colleagues (2003) have suggested that this directness is related to "relational concerns," and in a series of experiments, have shown cultural variations on this variable, although the magnitude may vary across work and social settings. They explain the relative absence of relational concerns (at least historically) in America to the influence of Calvinist theology, which tended to stress the importance of limiting social–emotional and interpersonal concerns at work. In one of their studies, they examined how Americans and East Asians interpreted indirect messages in work versus non-work settings. They expected Americans to make more errors in indirect cues at work than non-work settings, unlike East Asians. In the work-setting condition, European Americans, Chinese and South Korean students were told that they were working for a large company and were in charge of compiling and organizing information from employee performance evaluations. They were then told that the original form was lost, and that they were reading a transcript of a discussion between the reviewer and the person being evaluated. The transcript read:

> This is your interim evaluation summary. Overall the evaluation indicates that your strengths are in communication skills, anticipating events and

creativity. The other areas are not as strong as these—some are poor, but frankly it's difficult to evaluate those areas. Good job!

Next, the participants were asked to estimate the actual ratings given to the employee being evaluated. In the non-work condition, participants were asked to imagine overhearing friends talking about the results of a personality test, and were given a transcript of what one friend said to the other. Participants were asked to reproduce the ratings of this test. The transcript and rating used were the same as in the work condition. As predicted, Americans made more errors of interpretation (i.e., they were less sensitive to indirect cues) than the East Asian participants in the work condition compared to the non-work condition; specifically, they overestimated the actual rating more in the work versus the non-work condition.

In another study, Sanchez-Burks and his colleague (2003) modified Holtgraves' (1997) indirectness scale so that participants would respond to the statements with a specific person in mind at work. As an example, an item from the original scale read, "I try to consider all interpretations of others' remarks before deciding what they really meant." In the modified version, this statement read, "When interacting with X at work, I try to consider all interpretations of X's remarks before deciding what he or she really meant." Again, Americans were significantly less indirect than East Asians. If they had conducted their research among cultures known to be relatively more direct (such as France and Germany), they would probably have found even greater differences with their East African subjects.

Steve Jobs was known for being not only direct, but even extremely blunt. He was criticized by some for his withering and no-holds-barred comments as being too insensitive to others. In a story about his chief industrial designer at Apple Jonathan Ive,[2] Ive recalls that when he protested to Jobs, Steve replied: "Why would you be vague?" He actually argued that ambiguity (or indirectness) was a form of selfishness: "You don't care how they feel! You're being vain, you want them to like you" (p. 126). Ive finally concluded that Jobs did not mean to be hurtful and just wanted to make sure he gave clear, unambiguous feedback. The assumption that Jobs had, like many in the Western world, is that the best way to communicate clearly is by being direct.

Yannick, a French expatriate from a Paris-based consumer products company, realized when he first moved to the USA that his subordinates thought he was too "rough and direct," and even though he explained to his team that this is the way the French manage, he realized that he had to modulate his management style to adapt to the American work environment. At times, he found his staff shocked by his candor. Yannick modified his approach in part by quantifying and creating metrics for his subordinates' key objectives so that they got feedback about their performance by comparing their results with the quantitative standards.

Bridget, a German manager for a multinational company assigned to the USA, also found that she had to adapt her style of giving feedback to four Americans who were reporting to her. Bridget explained that Germans are more inclined to point out what was wrong or to focus on areas for improvement when debriefing a project or delivering feedback. During her first round of performance reviews, she noticed that her team seemed to be losing enthusiasm. She realized that the feedback she had given her team was perceived as too harsh. After attending a training session and getting some coaching on giving performance reviews, she began to change her approach and provide more balanced feedback.

In other cultures, where loss of face is very important, managers may need to be more indirect especially when giving feedback in order to preserve harmony. Comfort and Franklin (2014) refer to "blurring techniques" that managers can use to soften the harshness of providing negative feedback. For example, they suggest talking about a hypothetical case to direct the feedback receiver's attention to the problem rather than confronting the individual directly.

Countries that are typically direct include Austria, Germany, Israel, Norway, and Sweden. Countries that are typically indirect include China, Ghana, Japan, Singapore, and Thailand.

8. Expressiveness—How transparent and spontaneous can I be? How open should I be about expressing my feelings? In Fig. 4.1, Trompenaars and Hampden-Turner (1998), for example, have shown a large variability in countries among respondents who say they would not show their emotions openly:

In Russia and Hungary, you will find it difficult to "read" others because they typically will not show much emotion, at least initially. Countries that are typically more expressive (as indicated in Fig. 4.1) include Argentina, Egypt, Ireland, and Spain. Countries that are typically less expressive include Austria, China, Japan, and Ethiopia.

In her expatriate assignment to London, Samantha expected the business cultures of the USA and England to be very similar. What she learned,

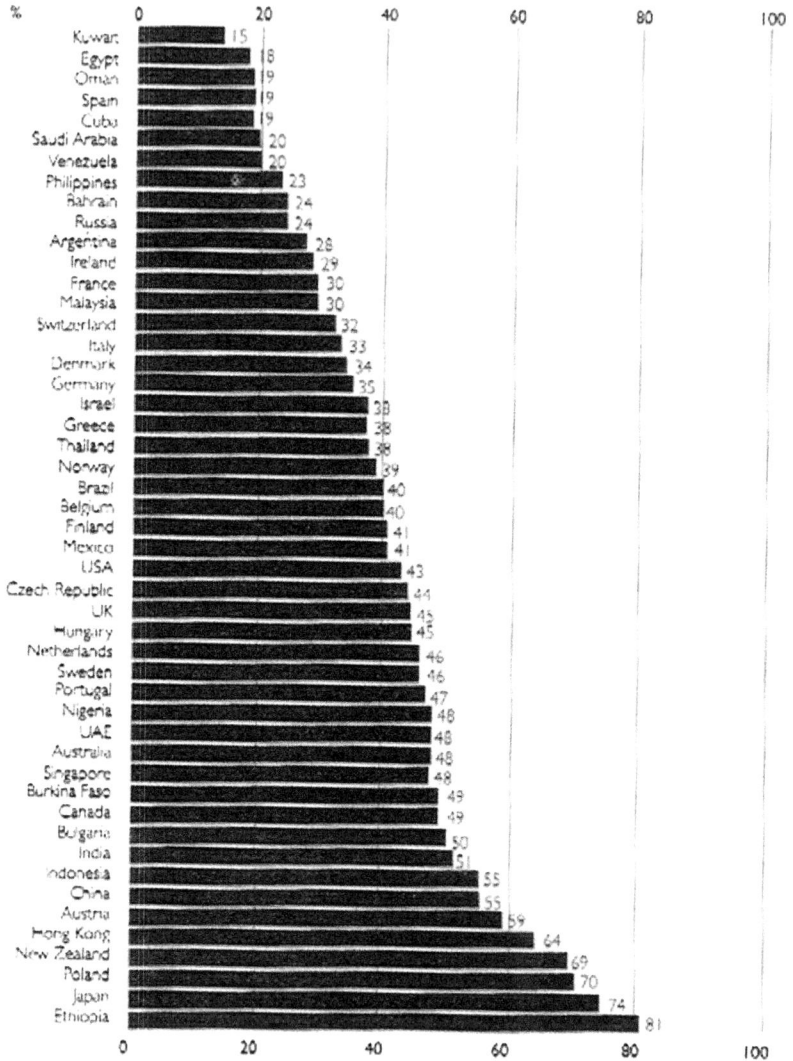

Fig. 4.1 Percentage of employees not showing emotions openly (From least to most)

Table 4.1 Influence of cultural orientations on organization basics

Cultural orientation (Preference)	Structure	Rewards	Processes
Formality (Formal)	There is an emphasis on titles to reflect status, and reporting relationships are clearly defined	There is a greater emphasis on ascribed rather than achieved status in who gets ahead	Rules and procedures are spelled out and communicated
Authoritarianism (Authoritarian)	Chain of command is clear, with decision-making centralized	Rewards are based on loyalty and seniority	Decision-making tends to be centralized, and there are few mechanisms for employees to voice their input or give their opinions
Structure (Strong need for structure)	Matrix types of organization designs are disliked and/or avoided	Advancing within a functional area and developing expertise in a set of tasks is more valued than mobility across functions	Rules and procedures are spelled out and communicated
Time orientation (Short term)	No specific design preferred over another	Rewards tend to be frequent and immediate, typically for short-term results	Decision-making tends to be quick
Assertiveness (Highly assertive)	Clearly defined reporting relationships	Top performers are very visible and publicly recognized	Competitiveness is strongly encouraged within the organization
Individualism (Highly individualistic)	Organization design is focused on making sure that the structure clarifies accountability, for example, through individual P&L responsibility	There is a strong emphasis on individual accountability and on extrinsic rewards. Advancement and promotional opportunities are clear	Roles and responsibilities are defined so individual accountability can be pinpointed

(*continued*)

Table 4.1   (continued)

Cultural orientation (Preference)	Structure	Rewards	Processes
Directness (Very direct)	Structures tend to be flatter, with fewer levels	Rewards are individually based, with recognition of individuals in public	Projects and tasks are well defined, with clear deadlines and milestones
Expressiveness (Highly expressive)	No specific design preferred over another	Spontaneous rewards are given and appreciated	Meetings and discussions tend to take longer than usual to make sure everyone is heard and to reach consensus

after a month on the job, was that her British colleagues valued polite-ness and courtesy, and that interactions tended to be quite cordial. At the same time, she learned that her communications needed to be clear and as unambiguous as possible; there was a great deal of documentation to confirm and maintain a record of discussions and decisions. Vromans et al. (2013) describe experiences like Samantha's with the term, "presumed cultural similarity paradox," suggesting that expatriates' adjustments may be more difficult with apparently similar cultures because of, among other things, different and unmet expectations.

An American expatriate interviewee who worked in Greece com-mented that in that country, the spoken word is held in much higher regard than written communication, and so most business is done face-to-face. Office doors typically remain open, and people interact continuously with colleagues throughout the day. He described Greek business culture as "fluid," where conversations can include discussions around family, romance, and finance along with business topics.

Earlier, we made the point that national cultures can influence the structural choices an organization makes. Expanding on this, Table 4.1 is a conceptual overview of how each of these cultural orientations might influence the three infrastructure elements of organizations: structure, rewards, and processes. For illustrative purposes, one extreme of each of these orientations is used.

Research and practice have shown that having a framework to under-stand differences in workplace cultures is extremely important for global leaders. For this and other frameworks, however, a few caveats are in order. First, each of these orientations is on a continuum and, while cultures can be arrayed along this continuum, it is important to consider the relative standing of cultures on each orientation rather than their absolute position. For example, while many would consider the USA to be direct relative to say, China, it is relatively less direct than other countries like Germany. Second, as Hofstede has indicated, these orientations tend to be relatively independent of each other although there may be some natural clusters. Third, these are averages or central tendencies. It does not mean that everyone in that culture behaves in accordance with these orientations. Individuals within a culture will tend to fall along a distribution, although the shape of the distribution (e.g., tall or flat) may vary depending on the specific cultural orientation. For example, you may meet a Chinese executive in Beijing who you might expect to behave a certain way based on your expectations of how Chinese managers might behave along these orientations. However, when you find out that the Chinese executive actually went to college in America, worked for a Swiss company in Lucerne, and got his MBA at Insead, this individual will be an outlier compared to the typical Chinese.

Fourth, because cultures can evolve over time, these orientations should be considered as a starting point in analyzing countries' workplace cultural orientations. Technology and globalization have created a "flatter" world, and managers everywhere are increasingly exposed to management practices from all over the world. It is understandable that these external factors will have an influence on employees' beliefs and values around these orientations. For example, Migliore (2011) found relatively low power distance scores in her study of young Indian managers, which she attributes in part to the greater exposure of Indian mangers to technology and interactions with global companies. Fifth, some of these orientations may be multidimensional, so it is possible to have a culture that may be on both sides of an orientation, depending on the specific sub-dimension. Gannon (2007) makes this point well in his discussion of paradoxes around monochronic versus polychronic time and with low and high context. Hall's original formulation had several interpretations of these dimensions so it is possible that the two can co-exist. Gannon gives the example of the karaoke bar that allows for the expression of low-context behavior and in fact serves as an emotional outlet for people in high-context cultures. Gannon states: "While it is possible to describe the dominant profile of a culture as either low context or high context, we must realize that cultures can be both low context and high context but in different situations and contexts" (p. 87).

Sixth, not all these orientations are relevant in particular cross-cultural situations. This is especially the case when there is close cultural distance between the national culture of one manager and the national culture of a target individual. Seventh, as Triandis (1995) has suggested, the polar opposites in each of these orientations can co-exist. For example, he states: "All of us carry both individualist and collectivist tendencies; the difference is that in some cultures the probability that individualist selves, attitudes, norms, values and behaviors will be sampled or used is higher than in others" (p. 42). There may indeed be situations when individuals may behave contrary to the general expectations of the culture. However, in most situations, cultural values and expectations will tend to drive people toward preferring one side of the orientation over the other side.

An explanation for this is that some of these cultural values have survived over the years (and in some countries, over many centuries), so change may come slowly, especially for these cultures. Take the collectivistic belief around the importance of family, and specifically beliefs around obligations toward one's parents. In many individualistic societies, children are not expected to take care of their parents as they age; placing the elderly in assisted living and nursing home facilities is fairly common in these countries. Yet in describing this practice even to well-educated and well-traveled managers in collectivistic cultures, some express disbelief that adult children would even consider placing their parents in nursing homes as opposed to having their parents come and live with them in their homes. The sense of obligation and family ties are very strong despite their exposure to the outside world and global trends.

Nisbett (2010) provides an excellent discussion of some of the fundamental differences between East Asians and Westerners in his book *The Geography of Thought*. Two specific examples he gives are particularly striking. First, he cites a primer that Americans of a certain age will remember. In this early childhood book, Dick and Jane along with their dog Spot are the main characters. In one of these books, a pre-primer, there are pictures of Dick and Jane respectively and the captions, "See Dick. See Dick run" and "See Jane. See Jane run. Run, Jane, run." Nisbett compared this primer with the first page of a Chinese primer in the same time period showing a picture of a little boy on the shoulders of a bigger boy. The caption, according to Nisbett, reads "Big brother takes care of little brother.

Big brother loves little brother. Little brother loves big brother." Note the emphasis on relationships versus individual action, as Nisbett observes.

The second example is even more directly relevant to the workplace. A typical statement or probe from a person who might be interviewing someone for a position for which he/she is applying for is the following: "Tell me about yourself." According to Nisbett, Americans tend to respond to this question by focusing on their personality traits, role categories, and activities. I might also add that in an interview setting, Americans might talk about their job history and some of their individual accomplishments. Chinese, Japanese and Koreans, on the other hand, describe themselves invariably in terms of context. In one study that he cites, "Japanese found it very difficult to describe themselves without specifying a particular kind of situation—at work at home, with friends, etc. Americans, in contrast, tended to be stumped when the investigator specified a context, reflecting a belief that 'I am what I am'" (p. 53). Such cultural differences are deeply rooted, and in the case of Asians in particular, go back many centuries.

Na et al. (2015) did an interesting study in which they examined cultural differences in the use of Facebook. They looked at what they called ego networks, defined as networks:

> including a single actor (ego), the actors who are directly connected to the ego (first-order neighborhoods), and all the links among them. That is to say, we looked at how one's friends on Facebook are connected both to the person and to his or her other friends. Our hypothesis was that social networks on Facebook would be more ego-centric in individualistic cultures (e.g., Americans) than in collectivistic cultures (e.g., East Asians). In other words, Facebook users in individualistic cultures would have social networks with relatively fewer connections between friends, resulting in the increased importance of the ego's position in the network. (p. 359)

In examining over 26,000 Facebook users from 49 countries, they looked at the relationships between ego-centrality and individualism–collectivism based on their country of origin, and found significant correlations. They found that users in individualistic cultures had more ego-centric networks (i.e., members of networks were connected via the self) than users in collectivistic cultures. Despite the introduction of new technologies which some might have expected would shrink cultural differences, national cultural differences continue to play a key role.

In an unrelated study, Alter (2013) cites research analyzing Facebook profile pictures, where "12 percent of a sample of Texan and Californian users displayed photos of their faces without any background, while fewer than 1 percent of a sample from Hong Kong, Singapore and Taipei chose similar close-ups that focused on their faces and excluded the background" (p. 137).

Another study conducted recently examined cross-cultural differences on the endorsement of various self-presentation tactics (Sandal et al. 2014). Over 3500 students from ten countries (including Germany, Ghana, Hong Kong, Iran, Italy, Malaysia, Norway, Russia, Turkey, and the USA) were given a set of 32 items describing job applicants' behavior during interviews. They were told to imagine that they were applying for an attractive position and had been invited for an interview. They were then asked to rate the importance of behaving in each of the ways described in the items. The self-presentation tactics they identified were grouped into several categories: assertiveness, emphasizing individual excellence, accommodation, and pointing out obstacles (i.e., describing how they overcame obstacles in the pursuit of a goal). They found correlations between prevailing cultural values and the preference for these different self-presentation tactics. For example, individuals in countries with a strong cultural hierarchy orientation tended to score higher in self-presentation, accommodation, and individual excellence. Individuals in countries with a strong cultural harmony orientation tended to score lower on individual excellence and assertiveness.

Trompenaars (Digden 2011) has suggested that at a greatly simplified level, one can make a distinction between cultures that are more "peach" and cultures that are more "coconut." According to him, "… Peaches have soft outsides which are easy to bite into. Coconuts have hard outsides which are difficult to crack" (Comfort and Franklin 2014, p. 142). People in coconut cultures like Germany may seem unfriendly and unapproachable to peaches, since coconuts are unwilling to violate your personal space and respect your privacy. People from coconut cultures tend to separate their work from their non-work lives, while people from peach cultures tend to blend the two, so, for example, people are expected to socialize after work. Peaches willingly share personal information about themselves, and expect you to do the same. Coconuts are uncomfortable making small talk, while peaches are quite good at this. However, peaches do not necessarily want to develop deep and long-lasting relationships, and coconuts may misunderstand a peach's intentions when he/she is acting in a very friendly manner. Coconuts on the other hand tend to have long-lasting relationships with friends.

Philippa was a British manager who was assigned to New York who sought the advice of a colleague who had lived for a few months in America. Her colleague warned Philippa about Americans, who he felt were not genuine with people because they would be overtly friendly but yet would not really be interested in getting to know you better. Only when someone else explained to Philippa the distinction between peach and coconut cultures did she begin to understand and not resent Americans for their seeming superficiality.

Since North American and European researchers were instrumental in introducing many of these cultural models, there have been questions raised on their universality, and whether models developed "indigenously" might have different concepts and dimensions (Sinha 1997). For example, Smith et al. (2011) investigated three approaches to social influence that have been identified as indigenous: *guanxi* (in China), *wasta* (in Lebanon), and *jeitinho* (in Brazil). As a comparison, they also included a form of social influence used in the UK (and other Western cultures, we might add): pulling strings. All these concepts share some similarities yet are said to be indigenously developed.

The researchers developed different scenarios of influence attempts in two to five sentences that were judged by pilot test respondents to be representative of the local cultures of the participants (Chinese, Lebanese, Brazilian, and British). Here is an example from China:

> Ting took the university entry exam this year. As her exam result was not good enough, she was not accepted for her preferred course. Her father and Dr. Zhang, who works in that university, were schoolmates many years ago. Her father asks Dr. Zhang to convince the head of the department to transfer his daughter to the desired course. (p. 147)

Participants rated (either yes, not sure, or no) the extent to which each scenario was perceived as representative of the relevant locally named process. All scenarios were rated in China as instances of *guanxi*, in Lebanon as instances of *wasta*, and so on. Then the scenarios were modified to disguise their place of origin. Despite the conceptual differences based on culture, participants rated all these influence attempts as both representative of their locally indigenous designation and typical of what occurs within their local cultural contexts. The researchers conclude that "...

influence processes characterized as indigenous to local cultures are perceived as typical in a broader range of locations. There is evidently an element in common between informal modes of influence in widely varying cultural contexts. Informal influence processes may vary between cultures in frequency more than in quality"(p. 145).

While this was a lab study of student participants, and the topic was defined narrowly to social processes, the concerns about the lack of universality of some of these cultural models may be a bit overblown. Arguably, with the world's managers become more exposed to different cultures as well as the common language of business, indigenous models could blend more easily into general cultural concepts.

Smith et al. (2014), in focusing on relationships within an organization, proposed that there are three related attributes that characterize a *guanxi* relationship between subordinates and their supervisors: strong affective attachment (an emotional connection to care for one another), inclusion of one's personal life within the relationship (the degree to which supervisors and subordinates include each other in their private or family lives), and deference to the supervisor. They developed measures for each of these attributes, and collected data from managers in eight nations, including two Chinese cultures. Their results indicate that both affective attachment and deference demonstrated "metric invariance" across the eight nations sampled, while the personal-life inclusion scale (as they predicted) did not. While *guanxi* is indigenous, aspects of it do indeed exist in other cultures and relevant comparisons can be made.

Goldsmith (2007) lists 20 habits that he claims often prevent successful people from becoming more successful. The twentieth habit he calls "an excessive need to be me." Here is his explanation of this habit:

> Each of us has a pile of behavior that we define as "me." It's the chronic behavior, both positive and negative, that we think of as our inalterable essence … If we are incorrigible procrastinators who habitually ruin other people's timetables, we do so because we're being true to "me" … If we always express our opinion, no matter how hurtful or noncontributory it may be, we are exercising our right to be "me."

You may recognize this as a variation of the old cartoon character Popeye, who said, "I yam what I yam and that's all what I yam.[3]" There was a popular song many years ago called "I've Gotta Be Me" that had a similar theme. Kerry was an Australian manager of a global medical devices company when she was sent to Japan to open a sales and marketing office in Tokyo. Smart, ambitious, and highly driven, Kerry saw this as an opportunity to prove herself while acquiring skills and knowledge by working in another country. She had never been to Tokyo before, although two years ago she had completed a successful six-month assignment in the Philippines to help develop a marketing campaign for one of her company's products.

Needless to say, Kerry experienced a series of culture shocks in her first three weeks on the job. Her new boss, a Japanese who was head of the subsidiary, kept on bowing and apologizing to her, which she found very annoying. When she met her team of six direct reports, she was surprised at how formal they seemed to be. In meetings, they would sit quietly in their navy blue business suits (they were all male), and hardly spoke up. She knew a little bit about Japanese culture, and the head of HR, another Japanese, explained to her about some of the differences between the way business gets done in Japan versus Australia. I get it, she thought to herself. But this is not the way I do things, and I know that I have been successful doing things a certain way. Why change now? Besides, this is not me. All this bowing and politeness and talking so indirectly! I would go crazy if I were to adjust my style just because I am in Japan. Besides, I am not Japanese, and they should understand and adapt to me.

Eventually, Kerry's frustration got the better of her and after three months, she asked head office for a change of assignment. What happened to Kerry, and what could she have done differently? First, let's go back to what Marshall Goldsmith points out as an excessive need to be me. For Goldsmith, the solution to this is for the person to focus less on himself (or herself) and more on other people. For example, in Goldsmith's case study as described in his book, a manager who does not like to give recognition and praise to people because "that's not me" could improve by focusing more on what her people wanted (in this case, a little more praise and recognition) and less on the notion of "me."

This is easier said than done. What makes this difficult for many are two underlying issues. First, this mindset of "being me" is especially prevalent in individualistic cultures. When Kerry (and Goldsmith's example) clings to this notion, her behavior is in part culturally determined. This is what she and others have learned by growing up in a highly individualistic culture.

The second issue is the apparent dilemma that is created when people frame the problem as having to choose between being authentic and adapting (i.e., not being authentic). I have worked with a number of executives who believe that they are somehow compromising themselves if they were to change their management style. As Ibarra (2015a, b) stated, " … in global business, many of us work with people who don't share our cultural norms and have different expectations for how we should behave. It can often seem as if we have to choose between what is expected—and therefore effective—and what feels authentic"(p. 55).

The following are recommended strategies for avoiding this tendency. First, define the handful of values or qualities about yourself that are core to you and that you believe reflect best who you are. For example: honest, reliable, hardworking, assertive, and self-confident. Then as you work with people and teams from other cultures, consider how these values might be expressed in these different cultures. These are behaviors (or practices, as per the Covey discussion) that can be situationally specific (see Fig. 4.2):

For example, in Thailand, being honest might mean: keeping your word, being fair, and not cheating. In America, this might mean: being direct, speaking your mind. It may turn out that your Thai colleagues share some of your values (principles), but just express them in different ways (practices). The key point here is to recognize that the behaviors that demonstrate a quality or value that you feel strongly about because they mean "being you" may differ by culture. Therefore, what you might have to do to work effectively in these cultures is to adapt behaviors that are more appropriate for that culture but are still consistent with your underlying values.

The second strategy is to expand your comfort zone so you can begin to develop what Molinsky (2013) calls global dexterity. Every one of us has a style of behavior that we are comfortable with, or that comes naturally for us. Most of the time, we would rather not change our style either because we believe that this works well for us, or because it is too much trouble to

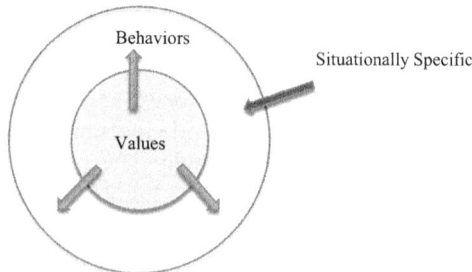

Fig. 4.2 Values and behaviors

learn a different style. When working across different cultures, there will be a range of behaviors and styles that will be different from what you are used to. Some will be easier to adapt to than others. For example, learning how to bow slightly in Japan, or learning how to greet someone in a different language are relatively easy behaviors to learn, and will not require much difficulty in getting you out of your comfort zone. However, other behaviors (e.g., learning how to be more patient rather than being your normal assertive self, learning to read nonverbals in high-context cultures) are more difficult to adapt especially if you are coming from a low-context culture. Expand your comfort zone by practicing some behaviors that may at first not feel too comfortable for you. Molinsky (2007) refers to this concept as "cultural code switching," which is "the act of purposefully modifying one's behavior, in a specific interaction in a foreign setting, to accommodate different cultural norms for different behavior." Watkins (2013) suggests finding some "cultural interpreters," for example, expatriates who have had experience in the culture and/or locals who have had a lot of experience working with expatriates or who have spent time living in the country you are from. One of our interviewees recalled this piece of advice he was given: "Don't go into a country with an idea of doing something a certain way; instead, go into the country and ask how can I make my idea work in this country?"

As Nathan (who has had assignments in three different countries) suggested, "Try to avoid an ethnocentric mindset, that the culture you grew up in is always right. Whether in Mexico, Japan or Wisconsin, if you stay within your comfort zone, you will be ineffective at establishing new relationships."

Ibarra (2015b) argues that we need to be careful in becoming so true to ourselves that we get stuck with the behaviors and styles that have served as well in the past. When situations change, some of us find it difficult to adapt and to put on a different self. She advocates becoming more playful with our different selves and recommends that you "... find a context or situation that makes you uncomfortable. This could be giving a presentation, speaking at an industry forum, or even speaking out at important meetings. Set learning goals. Act as radically different from your normal behavior as you can" (p. 155).

Sanchez-Runde et al. (2011) suggest:

> "the challenge for global managers is not to capriciously try to imitate local behavior ... it is to try to understand local conditions and then act in authentic ways that are compatible, but not necessarily synonymous, with local expectations. Being unique can often prove to be a successful behav-

ioral strategy, so long as such behavior is clearly understood by others to be supportive of local goals and objectives and not contradictory to cultural values and expectations"(p. 212).

Keeping these eight orientations in mind when trying to understand workplace cultures in different countries will help you become a more effective global leader. More fundamentally, however, becoming a global leader means first of all, examining your own self and then examining your interactions with others.

In working globally, the question of whether, and how much, to stereotype inevitably comes up. One executive I interviewed claims that he never stereotypes, nor does he believe in doing this. His approach is to learn as little as possible about his global colleagues' cultures so he does not get to judge them prematurely. Yet, according to Banaji and Greenwald (2013), "it is not possible to be human and to avoid making use of stereotypes" (p. 91). They cite Gordon Allport (1979) who wrote:

> The human mind must think with the aid of categories … Once formed, categories are the basis for normal prejudgment. We cannot possibly avoid this process. Orderly living depends on it.

In fact, Banaji and Greenwald take this one step further when they write that "stereotyping allows us to perceive strangers as distinctive individuals." The authors explain that we generally can use around six dimensions of people to create our unique mental images. When we meet someone from another culture, there is a set of dimensions by which we make some quick "stereotypes" about that person.

Banaji and Greenwald suggest that we all have stereotypes based on different categories (e.g., gender, doctor, old person, German), and that we rarely stereotype persons on one category alone. It is the combination of these categories that actually allows us to form an impression that makes this person unique. Little (2014) also endorses the idea of carrying multiple categories, although he phrases it somewhat differently. What he argues is that we also create quick impressions of others but we use it by applying one or more of three different approaches. One, we look at others and infer some personality traits, such as assertive, obnoxious, and friendly. Second, we may also look at them and imagine what he calls "personal projects"; these are the activities we perform that can range from routine actions to long-term commitments. Third, we may also create "narratives" to explain others' actions. Lane et al. (2009) use the term "mapping" or "sophisticated stereotyping" as a tool to help us describe characteristics of others in a systematic and objective way. As they describe it, "The most useful Mapping uses data and summaries of facts, organized with frameworks that help compare the data and facts across groups and individuals" (p. 67).

Recently, while I was in Tokyo, there were several instances when I became lost in the subway. As the crowds surged past me, I had to sort out who I should approach who spoke English well enough to be able to give me directions. Not surprisingly, I was successful three times out of four in general in figuring out the English-speaking Japanese from the hundreds of people walking down the halls of Shinjuku and Tokyo stations. It took me a brief second or two to figure out a constellation of characteristics that predicted English-speaking ability, for example, professionally dressed, a branded business brief case, a confident look, and so on.

As Little points out, "in our everyday lives we often make inferences and construct narratives about strangers on the basis of very little information" (p. 3). And, he argues, "the more numerous the lenses or frames through which you can make sense of the world, the more adaptive it is" (p. 4).

This applies directly to our recommended approach when meeting someone from another culture. Rather than looking at one dimension of culture alone (e.g., she is Italian, he is German, etc.), expand your impression-seeking sense to cover more than one or two dimensions. The danger for many, especially cross culturally, is that they will allow the cultural dimension to creep in and overpower all the other dimensions. As a result, some individuals will hold stereotypes of, say, an Italian or an Indian executive based primarily on his nation of origin. The challenges for cross-cultural managers are first, to consider multiple categories or dimensions in addition to culture and second, to continually adapt and evolve their impression based on new information.

What this also does is help to defuse a phenomenon that happens when people are made aware that a stereotype or a bias is widespread. Grant and Sandberg[4] write that:

> research suggests that if we're not careful, making people aware of bias can backfire, leading them to discriminate more rather than less.

They suggest that the reason this is so is because people may realize that their stereotype is common and that to act biased may be socially acceptable. In other words, "If everyone else is biased, we don't need to worry as much about censoring ourselves." Their conclusion is that awareness alone is not enough; one has to then point out that such stereotypes or biases are undesirable and unacceptable.

Similar "warnings" can be placed when considering stereotypes of different cultural groups. First, don't jump to conclusions about a person you are about to meet based on the stereotype of that person's culture alone. Second, make sure you take into account other aspects of the person (e.g., their educational level, their professional experience, their occupation, and their exposure to different cultures) while forming your impressions about that person.

This approach to culture is similar to what Zellmer-Bruhn and Gibson (2006) describe as a constructivist view, where "culture consists of bundles of knowledge, or a repertoire for 'strategies of action'" (p. 173). They also suggest viewing intercultural interactions as a dynamic process: "… the expectation is that individuals do not have one predisposed cultural content based on national origin or location (e.g., individualism) but rather hold (and can apprehend) multiple contents that can be elicited and applied differentially (e.g., individualism in one situation and collectivism in another)" (p. 175).

Notes

1. Alexandra Wolfe, "Weekend Confidential: Alan Dershowitz," the Wall Street Journal, September 19–20, 2015.
2. Ian Parker, "Jonathan Ive and the Future of Apple," The New Yorker, February 23, 2015.
3. http://www.buzzle.com/articles/famous-quotes-from-popeye-the-sailor-man.html
4. Adam Grant and Sheryl Sandberg, "When Talking About Bias Backfires," The New York Times, December 6, 2014.

References

Adler, Nancy J. 2008. *International Dimensions of Organizational Behavior*, Fifth edn. Mason, OH: South-Western Publishing.
Allport, Gordon. 1979. *The Nature of Prejudice*. New York: Basic Books.

Alter, Adam. 2013. *Drunk Tank Pink*. New York: The Penguin Press.

Altmeyer, Robert. 1996. *The Authoritarian Specter*. Cambridge, MA: Harvard University Press.

Banaji, Mahzarin, and Anthony Greenwald. 2013. *Blindspot*. New York: Delacorte Press.

Brewer, Paul, and Sunil Venaik. 2011. Individualism–Collectivism in Hofstede and GLOBE. *Journal of International Business Studies* 42(3): 436–445.

Comfort, Jeremy, and Peter Franklin. 2014. *The Mindful International Manager: How to Work Effectively Across Cultures*. London: Kogan Page.

Digden, Bob. 2011. *Communicating Across Cultures*. Cambridge, UK: Cambridge University Press.

Earley, Christopher. 1993. East Meets West Meets Mideast: Further Explorations of Collectivistic and Individualistic Work Groups. *Academy of Management Journal* 36(2): 319–348.

Earley, Christopher, and Miriam Erez. 1997. *The Transplanted Executive*. New York: Oxford University Press.

Fernandez, Denise Rotondo, Dawn S. Carlson, Lee P. Stepina, and Joel D. Nicholson. 1997. Hofstede's Country Classification 25 Years Later. *The Journal of Social Psychology* 137(1): 43–54.

Gannon, Martin J. 2007. *Paradoxes of Culture and Globalization*. Thousand Oaks, CA: Sage Publications.

Gelfand, Michele, Lisa Nishii, and Jana Raver. 2006. On the Nature and Importance of Cultural Tightness-Looseness. *Journal of Applied Psychology* 91: 1225–1244.

Gelfand, Michele, et al. 2011. Differences Between Tight and Loose Societies: A 33-Nation Study. *Science* 33: 1100–1104.

Goldsmith, Marshall. 2007. *What Got You Here Won't Get You There: How Successful People Become Even More Successful*. New York: Profile Books.

Gunia, Brian C., Jeanne M. Brett, Amit K. Nandkeolyar, and Dishan Kamdar. 2011. Paying a Price: Culture, Trust, and Negotiation Consequences. *Journal of Applied Psychology* 96(4): 774–789.

Hall, Edward. 2013. *The Silent Language*. Reissued. New York: Anchor Books.

Hofstede, Geert. 2001. *Culture's Consequences*. New York: Sage Publications.

Holtgraves, Thomas. 1997. Styles of Language Use: Individual and Cultural Variability in Conversational Indirectness. *Journal of Personality and Social Psychology* 73: 624–637.

House, Robert J., Paul J. Hanges, Mansour Javidan, Peter W. Dorfman, and Vipin Gupta. 2004. *Culture, Leadership, and Organizations: The GLOBE Study of 62 Societies*. Thousand Oaks, CA: SAGE Publications.

Ibarra, Herminia. 2015a. The Authenticity Paradox. *Harvard Business Review* 93(1/2): 53–59.

————. 2015b. *Act Like a Leader, Think Like a Leader.* Boston: Harvard Business Review Press.

Kagitcibasi, Cigdem. 1997. Individualism and Collectivism. In Berry, John, Marshall Segall, and Cigdem Kagitcibasi (Eds.). *Handbook of Cross-Cultural Psychology*, vol. 3, Second edn, 1–49. Boston: Allyn and Bacon.

Kemmelmeier, Markus, Eugene Burstein, Krum Krumov, Petia Genkova, Chie Kanagawa, Matthew Hirshberg, Hans-Peter Erb, Grzyna Wieczorkowska, and Kimberly Noels. 2003. Individualism, Collectivism and Authoritarianism in Seven Societies. *Journal of Cross-Cultural Psychology* 34: 304–322.

Kemp, Linzi J., and Paul Williams. 2013. In Their Own Time and Space: Meeting Behaviour in the Gulf Arab Workplace. *International Journal of Cross Cultural Management* 13(2): 215–235.

Kittler, Markus, David Rygl, and Alex Mackinnon. 2011. Beyond Culture or Beyond Control? Reviewing the Use of Hall's High-/Low-Context Concept. *International Journal of Cross Cultural Management* 11(1): 63–82.

Lane, Henry, Martha Maznevski, Joseph DiStefano, and Joerg Dietz. 2009. *International Management Behavior: Leading with a Global Mindset*, Sixth edn. Great Britain: Wiley.

Little, Brian. 2014. *Me, Myself and Us: The Science of Personality and the Art of Well-Being.* New York: Public Affairs.

Markus, Hazel and Shinobu Kitayama. 1991. Culture and the Self: Implications for Cognition, Emotion, and Motivation. *Psychological Review* 98: 224–253.

McCall, Morgan, and George Hollenbeck. 2002. *Developing Global Executives: The Lessons of International Experience.* Boston, MA: Harvard Business School Press.

McKersie, Robert, and Richard Walton. 1992. A Retrospective on the Behavioral Theory of Labor Negotiations. *Journal of Organizational Behavior* 13(3): 277–285.

Metcalf, Lynn E., Allan Bird, Mark F. Peterson, Mahesh Shankarmahesh, and Terri R. Lituchy. 2007. Cultural Influences in Negotiations A Four Country Comparative Analysis. *International Journal of Cross Cultural Management* 7(2): 147–168.

Migliore, Laura. 2011. Relation Between Big Five Personality Traits and Hofstede's Cultural Dimensions: Samples from the USA and India. *Cross-Cultural Management: An International Journal* 18(1): 38–54.

Minguet, Luc. 2014. Creating a Culturally Sensitive Corporation. *Harvard Business Review* 92(9): 78.

Minkov, Michael, and Geert Hofstede. 2014. A Replication of Hofstede's Uncertainty Avoidance Dimension across Nationally Representative Samples from Europe. *International Journal of Cross Cultural Management* 14(2): 161–171.

Molinsky, Andrew. 2007. Cross-Cultural Code-Switching: The Psychological Challenges of Adapting Behavior in Foreign Cultural Interactions. *Academy of Management Review* 32(2): 622–640.

Molinsky, Andy. 2013. *Global Dexterity: How to Adapt Your Behavior Across Cultures Without Losing Yourself in the Process*. Boston: Harvard Business Review Press.

Na, Jinkyung, Michal Kosinski, and David J. Stillwell. 2015. When a New Tool Is Introduced in Different Cultural Contexts: Individualism–Collectivism and Social Network on Facebook. *Journal of Cross-Cultural Psychology* 46(3): 355–370.

Nisbett, Richard. 2010. *The Geography of Thought: How Asians and Westerners Think Differently ... and Why*. New York: Simon and Schuster.

Pritchard, Robert, and Satoris Youngcourt. 2008. Culture, Feedback, and Motivation. In *The Influence of Culture on Human Resource Management Processes and Practices*, eds. Dianna Stone and Eugene Stone-Romero, 157–180. New York: Lawrence Erlbaum Associates.

Sanchez-Burks, Jeffery and Eric Uhlmann. 2014. Outlier Nation: In *The Cultural Psychology of American Workways*, eds. Masaki Yuki and Marilynn Brewer, 121–142. New York: Oxford Press.

Sanchez-Burks, Jeffrey, Fiona Lee, Incheol Choi, Richard Nisbett, Shuming Zhao, and Jasook Koo. 2003. Conversing Across Cultures: East-West Communication Styles in Work and Nonwork Contexts. *Journal of Personality and Social Psychology* 85(2): 363–372.

Sanchez-Runde, Carlos, Luciara Nardon, and Richard M. Steers. 2011. Looking Beyond Western Leadership Models: Implications for Global Managers. *Organizational Dynamics* 40(3): 207–213.

Sandal, Gro M., et al. 2014. Intended Self-Presentation Tactics in Job Interviews: A 10-Country Study. *Journal of Cross-Cultural Psychology* 45(6): 939–958.

Schulte, Brigid. 2014. *Overwhelmed: How to Work, Love, and Play When No One Has the Time*. New York: Farrar, Straus and Giroux.

Singelis, Theodore, Harry Triandis, Dharm Bhawuk, and M. Michele Gelfand. 1995. Horizontal and Vertical Dimensions of Individualism and Collectivism: A Theoretical and Measurement Refinement. *Cross-Cultural Research* 29(3): 240–275.

Sinha, Durganand. 1997. Indigenizing Psychology. In *Handbook of Cross-Cultural Psychology*, vol 1, Second edn, eds. John Berry, Ype Poortinga, and Janek Pandey, 129–170. Needham Heights, MA: Allyn & Bacon.

Smith, Peter B., Hai Juan Huang, Charles Harb, and Claudio Torres. 2011. How Distinctive Are Indigenous Ways of Achieving Influence? A Comparative Study of Guanxi, Wasta, Jeitinho, and 'Pulling Strings.' *Journal of Cross-Cultural Psychology* 43(1): 135–150.

Smith, Peter B., S. Arzu Wasti, Lusine Grigoryan, Mustafa Achoui, Olwen Bedford, Pawan Budhwar, Nadya Lebedeva, Chan Hoong Leong, and Claudio Torres. 2014. Are Guanxi-Type Supervisor–Subordinate Relationships Culture-General? An Eight-Nation Test of Measurement Invariance. *Journal of Cross-Cultural Psychology* 45(6): 921–938.

Steers, Richard, Luciara Nardon, and Carlos Sanchez-Runde. 2009. Culture and Organization Design: Strategy, Structure, and Decision-Making. In *Cambridge Handbook of Culture, Organizations, and Work*, eds. Rabi Bhagat and Richard Steers. New York: Cambridge University Press.

Tinsley, Catherine. 1998. Models of Conflict Resolution in Japanese, German and American Cultures. *Journal of Applied Psychology* 83(2): 316–323.

Triandis, Harry. 1994. Theoretical and Methodological Approaches to the Study of Collectivism and Individualism. In *Individualism and Collectivism: Theory, Method, and Applications*, eds. Uichol Kim, Harry Triandis, Cigdem Kagitcibasi, Sang-Chin Choi, and Gene Yoon. Thousand Oaks CA: Sage Publications.

———. 1995. *Individualism and Collectivism*. Boulder, CO: Westview Press.

Triandis, Harry, and Michele Gelfand. 1998. Converging Measurement of Horizontal and Vertical Individualism and Collectivism. *Journal of Personality and Social Psychology* 74: 118–128.

Triandis, Harry, Richard Brislin, and C. Harry Hui. 1988. Cross-Cultural Training Across the Individualism-Collectivism Divide. *International Journal of Intercultural Relations* 12(3): 269–289.

Trompenaars, Frans, and Charles Hampden-Turner. 1998. *Riding the Waves of Culture: Understanding Diversity in Global Business*, Second edn. New York: McGraw-Hill.

Uz, Irem. 2015. The Index of Cultural Tightness and Looseness Among 68 Countries. *Journal of Cross-Cultural Psychology* 46(3): 319–335.

Vromans, Pauline, van Engen Marloes, and Stefan Mol. 2013. Presumed Cultural Similarity Paradox. *Journal of Global Mobility* 1(2): 219–238.

Watkins, Michael. 2013. *Your Next Move: The Leader's Guide to Navigating Major Career Transitions*. Boston: Harvard Business Press.

Yamagishi, Toshio, Karen Cook, and Motoki Watabe. 1998. Uncertainty, Trust, and Commitment Formation in the United States and Japan. *American Journal of Sociology* 104(1): 165–194.

Zellmer-Bruhn, Mary, and Cristina Gibson. 2006. Multinational Organization Context: Implications for Team Learning and Performance. *Academy of Management Journal* 49(3): 501–518.

CHAPTER 5

The Challenges of Global Leadership

Larry was a marketing executive for the Asia Pacific division of a multinational company. Based in the USA, he would hold regular teleconferences with his marketing directors in Asia, but he found it difficult to make much progress with them. Asking for my advice, he commented, "Why is it that when I tell them that they need to meet a deliverable by a certain time, they all say they will do it, and yet nothing happens by the deadline? I can never tell if they have agreed to do something or not. Why can't they just be straight with me?"

When I asked Larry (a Midwesterner who had only begun to travel to Asia) what he thought was going on, he said that it was either because Asians don't have the same sense of urgency as Westerners, and/or that they are not as candid. Six months later, Larry requested a transfer from his position and eventually moved to a staff job in HQs.

In lectures and workshops I have given on global leadership, there are usually some participants in the audience who question the importance of leading globally, especially if individuals do not have much contact with others outside their home country in the course of their day-to-day work. In these discussions, I ask participants the following questions:

- Do you work for a company with customers from different cultures or countries?
- Do you manage or are you managed by someone from another nationality, country, or culture?

© The Editor(s) (if applicable) and The Author(s) 2016
R. Henson, *Successful Global Leadership*,
DOI 10.1057/978-1-137-58990-3_5

- Do you lead, manage, or work with team members from more than one country or culture where some are located in different countries?
- Does your work have an important impact in more than one country, culture, or market?
- When doing business for your company, do you interact or negotiate with vendors, suppliers, or other outside stakeholders on a regular basis?

If they answer "yes" to at least three of these questions, I suggest to them that they will invariably have a global leadership role. The skills they need will vary depending on their specific role. As an example, IBM has laid out in Fig. 5.1 a description of the types of global roles their employees could have, along with the capabilities required for each of these roles[1]:

In its model, all of IBM's employees are expected to have basic cross-cultural awareness and access to resources and knowledge, while global client-facing employees are expected to have the ability to "inspire across cultures."

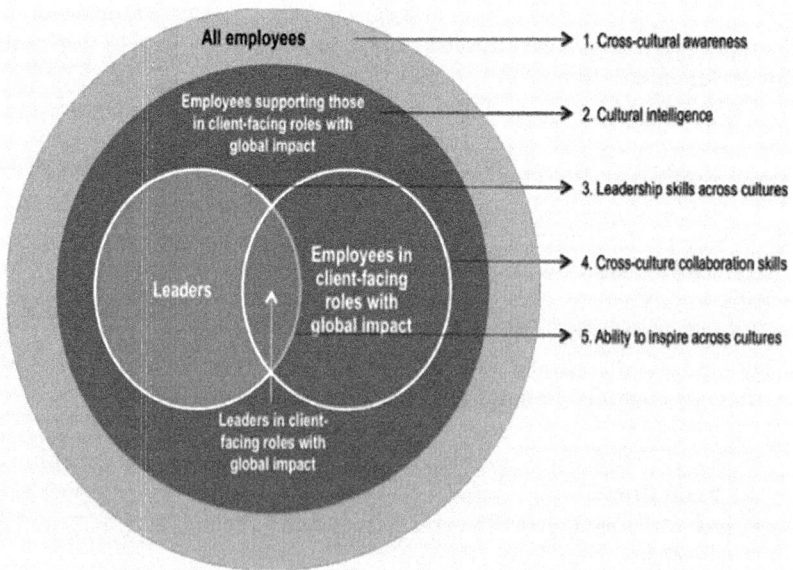

Fig. 5.1   Global roles and cultural requirements for IBM employees

Despite the growth of multinational companies and the rise of international trade, individuals and organizations continue to face several challenges with global leadership. First, differences in leadership expectations and management practices across cultures are not always apparent. Many large multinationals have developed sets of values and desired competencies that support their global strategy, and that they expect will be consistent and standardized across cultures. Facebook, Goldman Sachs, Nissan, PepsiCo, Samsung, Siemens, Shell Oil, and Unilever are among many companies that have rolled out globally statements of such values and competencies. Some of these organizations have translated their statements into several languages, and a few even have them on small cards or as screen savers on employees' computers. Of course, it is one thing for an organization to have a written set of statements and quite another to expect that employees will understand them or actually apply them to their day-to-day work.

How these values or competencies are applied across cultures can also vary tremendously. As House et al. (2004) have pointed out in their GLOBE study of over 17,000 managers in 58 countries, between 14 and 35 % of the cross-cultural variance on leadership styles can be explained by differing cultural values. More recent studies of the universality of leadership competencies have shown mixed results. For example, Gentry and Sparks (2012) used leadership competencies (e.g., change management, resourcefulness) from an instrument by the Center for Creative Leadership to determine to what extent they are "endorsed" by a sample of over 9000 practicing managers in 40 countries. They found convergence in endorsement for some but not all of these competencies. Other research has shown overlap among important leadership characteristics across cultures, but not complete convergence. In fact, there are some (Hollenbeck et al. 2006) who have argued against the value of leadership competencies, but others (as well as my own experience) suggest that individuals and organizations do find leadership competencies useful. Many global companies believe that their leadership competencies and (to a lesser degree) management practices transcend cultural differences (Denison et al. 2004; Schneider 1988). However, as mentioned previously, Sanchez-Runde et al. (2011), as well as the GLOBE study, have critiqued what they call this normative approach to leadership, which tends to be overly prescriptive and suggests that this will apply to all global managers regardless of where they are working.

Second, communicating, motivating, and managing are more difficult due to language, geography, and cultural barriers. Take Ken, who is the CEO of a small but successful R&D firm that develops formulas and conducts R&D for major brands. In expanding his operations, Ken decided to build a factory in China. In accordance with local laws, he leased the land and hired a Chinese construction company to build and manage the project based on the specifications designed by a US architect. To cut back on expenses, he decided not to hire a consultant to oversee the project nor did he send a manager on-site. When the project came in ahead of schedule, Ken and his team were pleasantly surprised. They decided to take a trip to China, and were very disappointed with what they found. They learned that the Chinese were working in 24-hour shifts, placing less emphasis on the quality of materials so as to be able to come in under budget.

The Chinese argued that they followed the design specifications as best they could, and suggested (very indirectly, of course) that the lack of direction and authority implied consent for the Chinese to complete the work according to local standards. Besides, their main contacts in the USA were middle managers who the Chinese did not perceive were important enough, and by implication, that the project itself was not a high priority for the company. On the other hand, the middle managers in the USA attributed some of the ambiguous responses they were getting from the Chinese as the result of their limited English language skills. A legal battle followed, and Ken's company had to abandon the project.

This was a painful lesson for Ken and in hindsight, he said that he should have done several things. One, he should have spent more time in China visiting the plant and building relationships with the local managers there. Second, he should have had a company representative on-site to oversee the project on the ground. Finally, he and his team should have undergone some type of cultural training to better understand how to do business with the Chinese.

Third, monitoring and tracking represent significant challenges due to distance. Multinationals expand overseas for compelling business reasons—to seek new markets for their products and services, to take advantage of countries' resources (what the economists call factor endowments, as well as human capital, such as an educated workforce or particular skill sets in that country), and/or to seek efficiencies (Dunning 2000). The challenge of physical distance can be even greater when it is combined with interaction frequency. Research has indicated that leader–follower interaction frequency is another type of distance, and can affect manager–employee relations and trust (Antonakis and Atwater 2002).

With respect to cultural distance (the differences in cultural dimensions between the home country and the host country), Colakoglu and Caligiuri (2008) found that this dimension not only predicted the number of expatriates in subsidiaries (that is, the greater the distance, the higher the ratio of expatriates in the subsidiary workforce) but also moderated the relationship between subsidiary staffing and performance; when cultural distance was high, a high ratio of expatriates tended to lower performance among subsidiaries. They and other researchers have used the Kogut and Singh (1988) measure of cultural distance, which is a composite measure of Hofstede's dimensions. As Stahl and Javidan (2009) have indicated, however, this index is problematic for several reasons, and results using this index should be interpreted with great caution.

Boeh and Beamish (2015), using a sample of Japanese–US dyads, found that the time required to travel between geographically separated locations affected subsidiary performance and survival. Ghemawat (2011) has shown that, on average, 60 % of firms' sales revenues in 2010 were outside of their home country—up from 57 % in 1990. What is interesting from his data is that, of all US companies that had foreign operations, most of them operated in just one another country (the median number being two), and 95 % in fewer than two dozen. Of the largest firms in the Fortune Global 500, 88 % derive more than one-half of their sales (an average of 80 %) from their home regions. He claims that despite the globalization of business, the majority of companies (at least in the USA) still limit their sales to nearby geographies. Rugman and Verbeke (2004) report similar data in their 2004 study of multinational companies that had at least 20 % of sales in each of the three regions of Asia, Europe, and North America and also had less than 50 % in any one region. They found that only nine multinationals met their criteria (IBM, Sony, Philips, Nokia, Intel, Canon, Coca-Cola, Flextronics, and LVMH).

Ghemawat and others may be limiting their analysis by considering only sales, and by including only large multinationals. As other researchers have pointed out, there are a number of "born global" companies (Knight and Cavusgil 2004) along with other small- and medium-sized enterprises that have plunged into the global business world seemingly overnight. Kimmit and Slaughter[2] state that in 2014, more than 60 % of all US imports consisted of intermediate input (parts and subassemblies), not final goods, sold to US consumers:

Decisions by multinational companies about where to invest have much less to do with domestic sales in the host country and much more to do with imports and exports of intermediate inputs.

Retailers and delivery companies are making it easier for shoppers to buy something from anywhere in the world.[3] UPS bought i-parcel LLC and FedEx bought Bongo International; these acquired companies specialize in allowing foreign shoppers to purchase goods on a retailer's site easily. They adjust the currencies and shipping methods depending on where the shopper is based and calculate shipping costs, taxes, and duties. According to the article, about a quarter of all e-commerce purchases are made with a foreign retailer. There is even a site, **www.sitejabber.com**, that allows consumers to review online businesses from all over the world.

However, especially for multinationals with subsidiaries in different countries, increased expenses of flying in and out of some markets have caused these companies to rely more on e-mails, teleconferences, and videoconferences to communicate and monitor progress. These work to some extent but are no substitute for face-to-face interactions in having a good understanding of the challenges and opportunities, as well as the progress that a subsidiary is making. Companies also use auditors to visit other countries. However, if the auditors do uncover problems, they tend to be after-the-fact and do not always pinpoint critical management or strategic issues within the country.

Sometimes even the distances within a country can be a challenge. When I was working for a company that was expanding within China, country management decided to place small branches across the country. These branches would be responsible for stocking products, where its sales representatives could pick them up and deliver them to their customers. This meant that the branches would need to report its inventory as well as sales on a regular basis. Given the lack of technology infrastructure in China at that time (and, in some regions, to this day), country management had to rely on the local branches' reporting of their results by telephone or by fax. This was far from reliable and led to inventory issues due to lack of accurate reporting.

Psychological distance (the extent that you feel that another person is similar to you or not) also seems to matter. Neuroscience has shown that the medial prefrontal cortex (MPFC) is a spot on each side of our brain that helps our memory and decision-making; different parts of it get activated when we are making judgments about ourselves versus others

(Denny et al. 2012). When others are those we consider to be different from us in some ways (e.g., culturally), those parts of our MPFC do not get activated as much, and so we don't think of others as compassionately as we might otherwise think of those who are like us.

It should be noted that scholars are continuing to investigate the definitions of distance and broadening its scope to more than physical, psychological, or cultural distance. For example, Berry et al. (2010) identified nine dimensions of distance—economic, financial, political, administrative, cultural, demographic, knowledge, connectedness, and geographic—and calculated various indices for each. While their interest was mainly on the impact of distance on the different types of foreign investment decisions that firms make, their approach should help other researchers and practitioners gain a better understanding of the impact of management practices and global leadership as a function of various dimensions of distance.

Table 5.1 shows a summary of many of the issues involved when global managers face challenges of cultural, physical, and psychological distance:

Fourth, cultural differences are sometimes used as a rationalization for performance issues or resistance to change. When managers are confronted with what seem to be performance problems, they try to get to the root causes so that the problems can be fixed. For example, let's say that a subordinate you are managing looks like she will not be able to deliver a project on time or on budget. Or you may have another subordinate who is unlikely to meet his sales or revenue targets. As a smart manager, you would presumably be communicating regularly with your subordinates so that there are no "surprises" at the end of the year. As a smart manager, you presumably also have a fairly good idea of your subordinates' motivation and skill set. If these subordinates have in the past shown great drive and persistence, as well as a high level of professional expertise, then you would explore other factors that may be contributing to these problems, such as lack of resources, unrealistic goals, or resistance from other departments. However, a global manager who is managing at a distance may not have all this information readily available. He may have only a superficial knowledge of the backgrounds of the overseas people with whom he is working. Could a performance problem be due to their lack of abilities or skills? Could it be because they have not clearly understood his expectations, either because of their difficulties with English and/or how they interpreted your expectations? Or could it be because they are not convinced that what you are asking them to do will work in their culture

Table 5.1   Issues in managing across distance

Issues likely to interact with culture
- It is easier to share knowledge than ever before
- Decision-making can become less hierarchical because knowledge is more easily shared
- A 24-hour work cycle is possible, providing a competitive edge in the information and service industries
- Time lags are reduced
- Geographically dispersed people behave differently:
  – They are less socially inhibited in their interactions (misattributions based on culture may lead to unfortunate and hasty electronic responses)
  – They are less hierarchical
  – People are less likely to change their minds or give up their position (which makes negotiation and problem solving even more difficult)
  – Explicit coordination becomes more critical
  – The development of trust may be inhibited (as with cultural difference)
  – Dispersed people communicate less frequently than do people who are co-located (when more communication is what they need)
- Communications are more task oriented
- Some people participate more than others
- Some people gain more influence than others
- Dispersed groups have a harder time dealing with conflict and achieving consensus (confounded by cultural differences and misattributions)
- Dispersed people may have inaccurate perceptions of one another (confounded by cultural differences and misattributions)
- The links between people may be weaker (as with culture)
- There are no social cues in an interaction (tone of voice, facial expression, body language)

Issues likely to interact with country
- People who need to work together may have unequal access to technology or unequal expertise in the use of technology
- There is less expense associated with travel, office space, and redundancy of resources (strong laws about termination and downsizing)

Issues with implications for development
- People can be recruited from anywhere in the world—wherever the talent is (But will they be given the opportunity to advance?)
- There is better access to experts (How to transfer knowledge?)
- There is the potential for greater job flexibility

Other
- Greater collaboration and interdependence is possible
- Dispersed groups take more time to accomplish goals if the work is interdependent
- Members of dispersed interdependent teams are not as satisfied with their team membership

Source: This is reprinted with permission from Dalton et al. (2002).

and rather than telling you directly, find ways to let you know, but very indirectly?

Fifth, complex organizational designs such as matrix and network structures can complicate reporting relationships and accountabilities. About 40 years ago, the matrix form of management became very popular, with companies such as Citibank, Dow-Corning, Nestle, Xerox, IBM, HP, and ABB in the forefront of its implementation.[4] The two-boss structure that was the essence of the matrix organization was seen as addressing the challenge of balancing business (or functional) units and geographies. Thus, for example, the head of Marketing for a country organization would report both to the country general manager as well as to a regional or global Marketing leader.

While it may have been a fad to some, organizations viewed the matrix as a way to resolve the classic structural issue of centralization or decentralization of resources to optimize productivity. However, the matrix organization required a different way of leading and managing, and many companies simply did not put in place the necessary groundwork to ensure the success of the matrix. Company after company started to abandon the matrix organization, with even management gurus like Tom Peters (Peters and Waterman 1982) decrying its complexity. Other more "advanced" and more complex forms of organizing started to emerge to the point where a leading expert, Jay Galbraith (1995), stated that the matrix was becoming rare: "The disappearance of the matrix is due, in part, to the trend toward more cross-border integration ... Also, newer forms are being adapted where the matrix would have been used in the past."

Yet, in discussions with many global managers and from an analysis of the organizational structures of global companies today, it seems like the matrix form is alive and well in today's organizations, albeit having evolved from its early days. The demands for speed, efficiency, coordination, collaboration, and customer responsiveness have led organizations once again to consider matrix structures, especially since these global companies are increasingly dependent on teams—virtual, project, cross-functional, and global. Even Galbraith (2009) has acknowledged that the two-dimensional matrix is now standard practice, and the three- and four-dimensional matrix is the current challenge especially for global organizations: "Complex businesses will need to be managed through complex organizations like the matrix." (p. 248)

The impetus for the kinds of teams that are so pervasive in organizations today is similar to what drove many to create the matrix form in the first place: the business need to be more nimble and to move quickly, to innovate, and to get people with different disciplines to work effectively together and make decisions based on the best possible information available. Many of the issues faced by those companies that started and abandoned the matrix form are still relevant and are continuing to be addressed by companies today.

A dramatic example of this is Cisco, which, a few years ago, announced a different kind of re-organization. Cisco's CEO, John Chambers, wanted to see the company move into more than two dozen new businesses, from consumer camcorders to giant TV screens for stadiums.

> In order to manage these initiatives, Chambers has replaced Cisco's top-down decision making with committees of executives from across the company. Some teams provide strategic advice and evaluate the progress of these projects. In total, Cisco now has 59 internal standing committees.[5]

Indeed, teams in organizations today are staffed by individuals from different functional areas, different geographies, and even with individuals outside the company (e.g., vendors). Leaders of such teams may come from a business or function but they report to an executive from a different business or, in some cases, to one of the company's top executives. In one organization, the executive committee charged a senior executive with assembling a team to address the efficiency and effectiveness of its staff functions globally. The leader of the team was a Senior Vice President who, in his role as team leader, reported directly to the CEO even though functionally he reported to the CIO.

An important foundational element in matrix organizations and teams today is that of trust. As Covey (2008) has pointed out, trust is central to many organizations today. With matrix organizations and teams especially, building that sense of trust is the oil that will make this form of organization run smoothly and be successful. A careful investment of time and effort early on to build this trust will pay significant dividends later.

In traditional organizations, roles and responsibilities are defined mainly through the organization chart and who reports to whom. In large global organizations, especially those in the technology and professional services industries, such structures are not as well defined. In these matrix and networked organizations, it is not always easy to figure out who to influence, and how to influence. Furthermore, despite the apparent re-emergence of the matrix, this form of structure does not always work well with organizations in countries with strong cultural values on uncertainty avoidance and power distance. As one interviewee, an executive from an Asian country, explained to me:

> Most of the managers in my team want to know who their boss is, and they want to take orders from their boss. Matrix gets very confusing to them. I realize that this is how our company is organized, but it will take time for people here to get used to this.

Sixth, influencing without authority is a competency that takes effort and skill. I met Walt in one of my consulting assignments. He had worked for the US government for over 20 years and ran a section of over 50, overseeing an important initiative in a cabinet-level department. Now he was a global team leader at a major technology company where his staff came from at least eight different countries. Walt, used to having the formal authority of people reporting directly to him, was frustrated at the lack of authority he had with his current staff who all reported "solid line" to different bosses.

"When I was in government, I could tell them what I wanted, and it would get done," Walt told me. "They knew I was the boss, and they had no choice. Now, I don't have any control over these people assigned to me. I am supposed to be leading this global team, and I report to the COO, so I'm supposed to have all this power, but it is so hard to get things done. And they are in so many different countries that just coordinating what they are supposed to be doing, with the time differences, is very frustrating."

This situation is typical of many global organizations today. Teams are formed where the team leader does not have formal authority over his or her team members, and team leaders need to use their influencing skills to get things done. Traditionally, leaders would rely on their position of authority, what French and Raven (1959) call legitimate power, to influence others. Figuring out alternative ways to influence others who do not report directly to them is a major challenge for global leaders.

Seventh, the opportunity costs are not always visible to corporate HQs, especially with subsidiaries that might not be strategically important. Many global companies today use highly robust tools for identifying opportunities in different markets (Gupta and Govindarajan 2001). There might be some "herd like" behavior where companies will go to countries like China because the competition is there, but for the most part, strategic processes are in place to identify these opportunities. In one company, for example, there were a number of executive discussions on whether the company should enter the South Korean market. After considerable market research, including some limited pilot testing of the company's products with consumers in that country, the decision was made to delay entry—wisely so. Tesco, the British-based retail grocer, decided to pull out of South Korea and is selling its 1075 outlets to a consortium led by an Asian private-equity firm. Tesco had pulled out of Japan and the USA in recent years. It has also seen its market share in the UK drop as German discounters Aldi and Lidl have been making inroads on Tesco's home turf.[6]

In general, however, unless a subsidiary is considered to be strategically important, it is easy for that subsidiary to get isolated and not be in HQ's radar screen. Birkinshaw et al. (2007) conducted research on how subsidiaries were getting HQs to pay more attention to them. They found that subsidiaries used a number of actions to take initiative (e.g., developing new products, penetrating new markets) and to build their profile (e.g., supporting corporate objectives, creating a center of expertise). Unfortunately, subsidiaries that are not considered strategically important may not get the level of attention, and therefore the resources, they need. The lost opportunities that might result include competition taking market share away from the subsidiary, business ventures that if nurtured might grow the subsidiary significantly, or attracting local talent to help build the human capital in the subsidiary. In fact, Ciabuschi et al. (2011) conducted research with 23 multinational companies and 85 innovation projects, and found that HQs involvement enhanced the impact of the innovations more so than the "internal embeddedness" of the subsidiary (defined as the close linkages between HQs and the subsidiary that drive adaption of such processes as product development, sales, and marketing).

These are some comments I have heard over the years from executives in HQs locations:

> We are a German (substitute any other nation here) corporation. Everyone should learn how to do things our way.
>
> They never tell you what they really think. You can't trust them.
>
> You ask them to do something, and they nod. But two weeks later, nothing has happened.
>
> They never look you in the eye. You can't have confidence in people like that.

We've sold our products the same way in many countries. Customers are mostly all alike anyway.

To take a different perspective, the following are representative comments from executives who are in regional or subsidiary roles on their perception of HQs:

They don't understand that our corporate strategies and programs will not always work in this country/region.

They are forcing a 'one-size fits all' policy for all markets. That will never work.

As long as my direct boss knows what I am up to, and I know what he expects, I should be all right.

In a recent study of over 1000 Asia-based executives in various industries, organizations, and functions, the Corporate Executive Board and Russell Reynolds found broad skepticism and a lack of trust among Asia-based leaders on their HQs,[7] as shown in Table 5.2:

These different points of view from HQs and regional executives suggest not only some gaps in understanding each other's points of view, but potential missed opportunities. For example, subsidiaries might not be

Table 5.2 Opinions of Asia-based leaders in local organizations and HQs

	Asia-based leaders in local organizations[a]	Asia-based leaders in HQs[a]
HQs understands the realities of doing business in Asia	12	20
HQs makes decisions aligned with the regional context	14	21
Cultural differences have no bearing on decision-making	14	28
HQs allows customization of solutions to the region	25	33
HQs consults local leaders before setting regional strategy	26	28
HQs listens to my opinion	29	38
I trust the leaders at my organization's corporate HQs	31	34

[a]Percentage indicating "agree" or "strongly agree"

taking advantage of resources and expertise from HQs or from other markets that might help them improve their subsidiary performance as well as fight competition in their markets. HQs might be missing opportunities to learn about local practices that might be fruitful to implement in other markets.

These challenges become very salient when managers engage in cross-cultural interactions that are at the heart of global leadership. Many years ago, while I was consulting with the customer service unit of a consumer products company, a colleague recommended a book called *Moments of Truth* by Jan Carlzon (1989), then president of Scandinavian Airlines System (SAS). This phrase, which has since entered the business vocabulary, described the contact between a customer and a company representative that can profoundly impact the customer's impression of the product and/or the company. Carlzon wrote:

> Last year, each of our 10 million customers came in contact with approximately five SAS employees, and this contact lasted an average of 15 seconds at a time. Thus, SAS is "created" 50 million times a year, 15 seconds at a time. These 15 million "moments of truth" are the moments that ultimately determine whether SAS will succeed or fail as a company. They are the moments when we must prove to our customers that SAS is their best alternative. (p. 3)

Managers working globally have many interactions with different stakeholders coming from different cultures. They include customers, vendors, subordinates, bosses, and colleagues in the various places where we do business. Some of these interactions could certainly be described as "moments of truth," where the outcomes of these interactions can lead to a more positive path and ultimately a productive and effective relationship—or its opposite. Molinsky (2013) has stated that "interactions are the micro building blocks of long-term adjustment to a foreign setting."

Identifying these critical cross-cultural interactions is important because they create the situational context that influences our thinking and our behavior. In fact, Nardon and Steers (2014) argue that in addition to the cultural and organizational context, global managers need to pay close attention to the situational context. These day-to-day cross-cultural encounters and interactions can become particularly challenging for global leaders, but they can also provide opportunities for building successful global leadership.

The following are nine such interactions or where one's global leadership will be put to the test. This set of interactions is not sequential, although clearly the first two can make or break a potential relationship you are trying to establish. Some of these interactions are one-on-one others are with a group. The specific practices used will also depend on the characteristics of the person or group with whom the manager is interacting, as well as prevailing cultural norms and practices. For example, greeting a male senior executive in Japan will take a different form than greeting a young female professional.

(1) Greeting someone
(2) Establishing rapport
(3) Leading a team
(4) Conducting a meeting/participating in a meeting
(5) Providing instructions or guidance; coaching and teaching
(6) Resolving disagreements and conflicts
(7) Negotiating
(8) Motivating others
(9) Giving and receiving feedback

Lucy Kellaway, the acerbic columnist of the *Financial Times*, wrote recently about the challenges of greeting people from different cultures.[8] She was giving a talk primarily to Asian women at a conference in Singapore and she was at a loss as to how to greet the various attendees at the conference:

> In the old days, the principle was when-in-Rome. So when actually in Rome you kissed on both cheeks anyone you knew reasonably well. In Holland, it was three cheeks. In Russia you might expect a crushing bear hug, in Japan a nod and in India hands clasped and a namaste. In the US and Germany you could look forward to a bone crusher of a handshake, in the Middle East something more like a limp fish.
>
> Global business has made matters more complicated. We no longer know whose culture trumps whose. Is it the host country's? Is it the majority in the room? As no one seems to know, what tends to happen is a general confusing, embarrassing free-for-all. We live in a permanent state of hello hell.

Rather tongue-in-cheek, she proposes a Global Greetings Protocol where the only permissible greeting in a business setting would be a handshake. If it were only that simple!

Given the research on our unconscious biases and first impressions (e.g., Olivola and Todorov 2010; Rabin and Schrag 1999), thinking through your approach to greeting people from other cultures is enormously important. Greeting someone, of course, is just one of the key interaction hot spots that can contribute to your success as a global leader.

The following is a simple approach to how global leaders can be effective in these cross-cultural encounters. First, understand what your "default mode" is in each of these situations. Most of us have a preferred way of approaching certain interpersonal situations based on our experiences and our own natural inclinations. Keep in mind that your preferred way may also be influenced by cultural assumptions and norms. For example, Dutch and Germans like to resolve conflicts by being very direct and raising issues in a straightforward way to "cut to the chase," as the expression goes. So what's your typical modus operandi when you're trying to resolve a conflict or disagreement? You might be thinking, it depends on who the person is. Yes, of course, and that is a reasonable response; nonetheless, you are likely to have a preferred approach, one that you use other things being equal.

Second, consider the cultural background and cultural norms of the person or group with whom you will interact. Most of us will recognize that we will need to adjust our approach depending on the specific characteristics of the person or group (e.g., their age, gender, position in the organization, educational level). Make sure to include these cultural norms (or more generally the cultural orientation) as another dimension to consider. For example, Hannah is a manager of a global IT consulting company who was recently appointed to lead a team of Indian consultants in Bangalore. Hannah has a reputation as a good leader who likes to empower and delegate, but she also needs to be aware of the expectations of her Bangalore staff.

Third, adjust your approach or style so that it is culturally appropriate for that person or group. What this means is that you will have to develop a repertoire of styles, and not always rely on your default mode, difficult as that may be at times. We tend to repeat those behaviors that either come naturally to us or that we have been using for a long time. The challenge for many global leaders is to go into "manual" mode and use those behaviors that are most appropriate for that culture. For example, this may mean that you don't always look a person directly in the eye in a culture where doing this with very senior executives may be considered inappropriate.

In Hannah's case, she has had to adjust her style to make sure that she is more directive and explicit about her communication, at least initially.

Feng was a Chinese student in my class who was not used to speaking up in the classroom. In China, students are not expected to raise hands, nor are class discussions encouraged. As a result, when she signed up for her MBA classes, she felt overwhelmed and intimidated. In advising her, we worked out a goal of being a more active participant in the class. She started out by writing down a question beforehand that she would ask the professor. Toward the end of a lecture, when the professor would ask if there were any questions, she would raise her hand and ask a question. Eventually, as she became more comfortable in asking questions, she then wrote down a couple of points she wanted to make about whatever was being discussed that day, and raised her hand to offer her opinion when her professor asked for comments. By the end of the semester, she was a more active participant although she still cannot just "jump in" to a discussion—at least not yet.

In addition to adapting their behaviors, Nardon and Steers (2014) suggest that global managers can influence the situational context through three types of activities: the attention that they give, the interpretation they make of the situation, and the behaviors that they select. Global leaders can have a great deal of influence in shaping both the objective context (e.g., the current organizational structure or reporting relationships) and subjective context (e.g., communicating the implications of a non-native manager getting promoted). They can become more effective by identifying opportunities in their cross-cultural interactions to manage the context of these types of activities. Applying the Nardon and Steers model, the following are some examples of how a global leader can manage the situational context (Table 5.3):

In summary, corporations that fail to address these challenges may revert to unwitting ethnocentric strategies. In fact, such ethnocentric organizations may have a tendency to define "what they are" in such broad terms that they limit their ability or willingness to adapt. Companies like Disney, Wal-Mart, and Marks & Spencer have all experienced failures in their expansion to overseas markets, while others like Yum Brands, Toyota, and Marriott have succeeded. Organizations might do well to re-examine their competencies, values, and their identity—those elements that define their core—and determine what they can and should adapt. Moore (2002), in discussing what gives companies sustainable competitive advantage, made a distinction between a company's core and its context. He argues that

Table 5.3   How a global leader can manage the context

Cognitive activity	Objective context	Perceived context
Attention	Remove titles from managers' names outside their door to de-emphasize status	Highlight the international backgrounds of employees who are promoted to key positions
Interpretation	Continuously remind employees of the opportunities the company has for job assignments involving global responsibilities	Encourage employees globally to make use of the company practice to e-mail senior executives of any issues or concerns they have, pointing out to them that this is an example of the importance the company places on two-way communication and transparency
Selection of behavioral options	Provide clarification on the career paths of employees desiring global assignments	Encourage or insist that global teams have adequate representation from various regions

[a]Adapted from Nardon and Steers (2014)

companies should differentiate as much as possible on what they consider their core activities, while executing their context tasks efficiently and in a standardized manner. For organizations that are globalizing, defining their core (e.g., their values, their competencies) and building their differentiation on what these core elements are, while recognizing the need to execute and adapt their contextual tasks, will help them become less ethnocentric.

NOTES

1. From IBM Global Business Services white paper "Developing Global Leadership" (2010).
2. "How to Make Sure Volvo Is Starting a Trend," in the Wall Street Journal, April 9, 2015.
3. Laura Stevens, "Borders Matter Less and Less in E-Commerce," The Wall Street Journal, June 24, 2015.
4. One of the first books on matrix management is *Matrix* by Stanley Davis and Paul Lawrence (1977).
5. Ben Worthen, "Cisco CEO John Chambers's Big Management Experiment," The Wall Street Journal, August 5, 2009.

6. Saabira Chaudhuri, "MBK Partners Clinches Deal for Tesco's Korean Operations," The Wall Street Journal, September 8, 2015.
7. From "Demystifying the Market for Executive Talent in Asia": http://www.russellreynolds.com/sites/default/files/demystifying_the_market_for_executive_talent_in_asia.pdf
8. "Do We Hug? Kiss? Shake Hands?" in the Financial Times, September 22, 2013.

REFERENCES

Antonakis, John, and Leann Atwater. 2002. Distance Leadership: A Review and Proposed Theory. *Leadership Quarterly* 13(6): 673–704.
Berry, Heather, Mauro Guillen, and Nan Zhou. 2010. An Institutional Approach to Cross-National Distance. *Journal of International Business Studies* 41: 1460–1480.
Birkinshaw, Julian, Cyril Bouquet, and Tina C. Ambos. 2007. Managing Executive Attention in the Global Company. *MIT Sloan Management Review* 48(4): 39–45.
Boeh, Kevin, and Paul Beamish. 2015. The Cost of Distance on Subsidiary Performance. *Asian Business & Management* 14(3): 171–193.
Carlzon, Jan. 1989. *Moments of Truth*. New York: HarperBusiness.
Ciabuschi, Francesco, Henrik Dellestrand, and Oscar Martín Martín. 2011. Internal Embeddedness, Headquarters Involvement, and Innovation Importance in Multinational Enterprises. *Journal of Management Studies* 48(7): 1612–1639.
Colakoglu, Saba, and Paula Caligiuri. 2008. Cultural Distance, Expatriate Staffing and Subsidiary Performance: The Case of US Subsidiaries of Multinational Corporations. *The International Journal of Human Resource Management* 19(2): 223–239.
Covey, Stephen. 2008. *The Speed of Trust: The One Thing That Changes Everything*. New York: Free Press.
Dalton, Maxine et al. 2002. *Success for the Global Manager: How to Work Across Distances*. San Francisco, CA: Jossey-Bass.
Davis, Stanley M., and Paul R. Lawrence. 1977. *Matrix*. Reading: Addison-Wesley Publishing Company.
Denison, Daniel R., Stephanie Haaland, and Paulo Goelzer. 2004. Corporate Culture and Organizational Effectiveness: Is Asia Different from the Rest of the World? *Organizational Dynamics* 33(1): 98–109.
Denny, Brian, H. Kober, Tor Wager, and Kevin Ochsner. 2012. A Meta-Analysis of Functional Neuroimaging Studies of Self- and Other Judgments Reveals a Spatial Gradient for Mentalizing in Medial Prefrontal Cortex. *Journal of Cognitive Neuroscience* 24(8): 1742–1752.

Dunning, John H. 2000. The Eclectic Paradigm as an Envelope for Economic and Business Theories of MNE Activity. *International Business Review* 9(2): 163–190.

French, John, and Bernard Raven. 1959. The Bases of Social Power. In *Studies in Social Power*, ed. Dorwin Cartwright. Ann Arbor, MI: Institute for Social Research.

Galbraith, Jay. 1995. *Designing Organizations*. San Francisco, CA: Jossey-Bass.

———. 2009. *Designing Matrix Organizations That Actually Work*. San Francisco, CA: Jossey-Bass.

Gentry, William, and Taylor Sparks. 2012. A Convergence/Divergence Perspective of Leadership Competencies Managers Believe Are Most Important for Success in Organizations: A Cross-Cultural Multilevel Analysis of 40 Countries. *Journal of Business Psychology* 27: 15–30.

Ghemawat, Pankaj. 2011. *The Globalization of Firms*. Unpublished manuscript from the Globalization Note series. IESE Business School. http://www.ghemawat.com/management/files/AcademicResources/GlobalizationofFirms.pdf

Gupta, Anil K., and Vijay Govindarajan. 2001. Converting Global Presence into Global Competitive Advantage. *The Academy of Management Executive* 15(2): 45–56.

Hollenbeck, George P., Morgan W. McCall Jr., and Robert F. Silzer. 2006. Leadership Competency Models. *The Leadership Quarterly,* 17 (4): 398–413.

House, Robert J., Paul J. Hanges, Mansour Javidan, Peter W. Dorfman, and Vipin Gupta. 2004. *Culture, Leadership, and Organizations: The GLOBE Study of 62 Societies*. Thousand Oaks, CA: SAGE Publications.

Knight, Gary A., and S. Tamar Cavusgil. 2004. Innovation, Organizational Capabilities, and the Born-Global Firm. *Journal of International Business Studies* 35(2): 124–141.

Kogut, Bruce, and Harbir Singh. 1988. The Effect of National Culture on the Choice of Entry Mode. *Journal of International Business Studies* 19(3): 411–432.

Molinsky, Andy. 2013. *Global Dexterity: How to Adapt Your Behavior Across Cultures Without Losing Yourself in the Process*. Boston: Harvard Business Review Press.

Moore, Geoffrey A. 2002. *Living on the Fault Line: Managing for Shareholder Value in Any Economy*. New York: Harper Business.

Nardon, Luciara, and Richard Steers. 2014. Managing Cross-Cultural Encounters: Putting Things in Context. *Organizational Dynamics* 43: 138–145.

Olivola, Christopher Y., and Alexander Todorov. 2010. Fooled by First Impressions? Reexamining the Diagnostic Value of Appearance-Based Inferences. *Journal of Experimental Social Psychology* 46(2): 315–324.

Peters, Thomas J., and Robert H. Waterman Jr. 1982. *In Search of Excellence: Lessons from America's Best-Run Companies.* New York: Harper Collins.

Rabin, Matthew, and Joel L. Schrag. 1999. First Impressions Matter: A Model of Confirmatory Bias. *Quarterly Journal of Economics* 114(1): 37–82.

Rugman, Alan, and Alain Verbeke. 2004. A Perspective on Regional and Global Strategies of Multinational Enterprises. *Journal of International Business Studies* 35(1): 3–18.

Sanchez-Runde, Carlos, Luciara Nardon, and Richard M. Steers. 2011. Looking Beyond Western Leadership Models: Implications for Global Managers. *Organizational Dynamics* 40(3): 207–213.

Schneider, Susan C. 1988. National Vs. Corporate Culture: Implications for Human Resource Management. *Human Resource Management* 27(2): 231–246.

Stahl, Günter, and Mansour Javidan. 2009. Cross-Cultural Perspectives on International Mergers and Acquisitions. In *Cambridge Handbook of Culture, Organizations, and Work*, eds. Rabi Bhagat and Richard Steers, 118–147. New York: Cambridge University Press.

Worthen, Ben. 2009. Cisco CEO John Chambers's big management experiment. *Wall Street Journal*, August 5.

CHAPTER 6

Addressing the Challenges
with Global Mindset

The following is a sample of comments from managers who were asked what global mindset meant to them:

> Global mindset means that you are aware of your environment, of others and the impact of ideas and events in your business, strategy or position.
>
> Taking a more macro look at things ... understanding that things won't work the same all over the world, and taking that into account.
>
> Having an understanding that countries have different cultures, and going into each country, one must always be aware and sensitive to that country's cultural ways.
>
> Someone who understands or has an open mind to understand different cultures and how these affect the outcomes of decisions.
>
> Putting yourself in the other culture's shoes.
>
> Listening and resisting reflexive judgments.
>
> Your way is not always the right way.
>
> Understanding that different countries/cultures have different ways of doing things. They value certain things differently. A global mindset has

---

My greatest challenge has been to change the mindset of people. Mindsets play strange tricks on us. We see things the way our minds have instructed our eyes to see. (Muhammad Yunus) (From Muhammad Yunus. BrainyQuote.com, Xplore Inc., 2015. http://www.brainyquote.com/quotes/quotes/m/muhammadyu462186.html, accessed August 23, 2015)

© The Editor(s) (if applicable) and The Author(s) 2016
R. Henson, *Successful Global Leadership*,
DOI 10.1057/978-1-137-58990-3_6

to take all of that into consideration and be open-minded and willing to compromise.

Not surprisingly, since many of these managers work in multinationals, their comments are in general consistent with what current research and practice have identified as among the descriptions of global mindset.

Global mindset is part of global leadership, and the following (Fig. 6.1) is a proposed model for understanding global leadership, based on a distillation of research and practice. The model proposes that global leadership has antecedents (the most important of which are cultural intelligence or CQ, certain personality and background characteristics, the quality and extent of cross-cultural contacts and experiences, and self-awareness) and three sets of components (foundational requirements—organizational and business savvy, results-orientation, and integrity and ethics; global mindset dispositions—flexibility, acceptance, curiosity, and empathy; and competencies—intercultural communication skills, cultural sensitivity, and learning agility). Successful outcomes for global leaders depend on a fit between these components and the context in which global leadership is exercised. Among the contextual factors are organizational (e.g., the opportunities the organization provides and the climate for encouraging employees to build their global mindset), developmental (the right set of experiences, whether these be job assignments, challenges, or types of training), and situational factors in the work or job environment.

This interaction then leads to potential outcomes. Four types of outcomes are proposed: personal (e.g., growth of the individual, success adjustment, personal satisfaction), relationship (establishing trust and effective collaboration with others), performance (successful achievement of job and role requirements), and organizational (having a positive impact on the productivity of a team or larger entity within the organization).

Antecedents

CQ and Personality

Several key antecedents are hypothesized to influence global leadership, with CQ being primary. Earley and Ang (2003) have linked CQ to global mindset. There is clearly an overlap between CQ and global mindset, although like others (e.g., Story et al. 2014), we suggest that CQ is conceptually separate from global mindset.

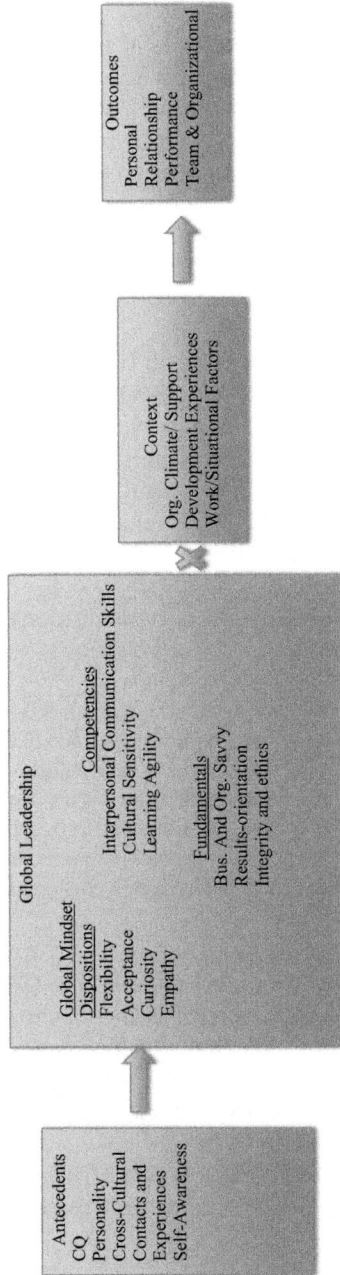

Fig. 6.1   A proposed model of global leadership

In Earley and Ang's conceptualization, CQ has three components: cognitive, motivational, and behavioral. That is, CQ is about knowing and understanding a new culture, being willing to learn, and having the skills to apply this knowledge and motivation. Ang et al. (2007) later added a fourth dimension, metacognitive CQ, which consists of those mental processes we use to gain knowledge of other cultures. Van Dyne et al. (2008) have reported on the development and validation of an instrument based on these four factors, which they labeled the Cultural Intelligence Scale or CQS. Most of the measures of CQ rely on self-reports; developing instruments that rely less on these self-reports, such as some kind of 360-degree observation, would be useful.

There has been considerable research by Early and others on CQ and its impact on various outcomes. For example, Huff (2013) found, in a study of over 100 expatriates living in Japan, that motivational CQ was the best predictor of adjustment (an aspect especially important for global managers with expatriate assignments) and, consistent with other research (e.g., Bhaskar-Shrinivas et al. 2005), language proficiency was not a strong predictor of work adjustment (although it was a predictor of general living adjustment).

Earley and Ang (2003) also looked at the relationship between CQ and adjustment to new cultures. According to them:

> this is not merely an issue of emotional intelligence, empathy, social intelligence, practical intelligence, tacit knowledge, and so forth. A new cultural encounter is unique in that the cues and information relied on from past experience are largely absent or misleading. Many times the actions and apparent intentions of others are so unexpected as to appear bizarre and random. A person with high CQ has a capability to encounter such a situation and comprehend, persevere, and act in such a challenging context. (p. 91)

The various studies on factors relating to expatriate assignment success also point to elements of global mindset and CQ as being important predictors of success, in addition to factors related to spouse and family acceptance and assimilation. For example, Yavas and Bodur (1999) found that being culturally sensitive, having empathy, and willingness to accept the challenge of intercultural experiences were important predictors of expatriate success.

Ramalu et al. (2012) surveyed over 300 expatriates working and living in Malaysia and found that the various dimensions of CQ had differential relationships with measures of cross-cultural adjustment. They used a measure of CQ developed by Ang et al. (2007) that included cognitive, motivational, and behavioral aspects. They also used Black and Stephens' (1989) measure of expatriate adjustment that included three scales: general adjustment (e.g., food, shopping), interaction adjustment, and work adjustment. Cognitive CQ was related to general and interaction adjustment, while motivational CQ was related to all three dimensions of adjustment.

Lisak and Erez (2015) found that three individual characteristics were predictive of those who emerged as leaders in multicultural teams: CQ, global identity, and openness to cultural diversity. The second of these measures is partly based on social identity theory (Brewer 1996), and they suggest that individuals who have a sense of belongingness to others with diverse cultural backgrounds will most likely have this global identity. Although not explicitly discussed by the researchers, it would seem that the quality (and perhaps diversity) of cross-cultural experiences and interactions might be a key factor to developing this identity.

Fernandez-Araoz (2014) analyzed data from his sample of 250 mostly Latin American managers and compared successful with less successful managers. He found that 70 % of successful managers and 85 % of less successful managers had relevant previous experience. However, 63 % of successful managers had a higher degree of emotional intelligence or EQ (which is related to CQ), while none of the less successful managers had a high degree of EQ. The failure rate of those with relevant experience and high EQ was only 3 %, while the failure rate of those with relevant experience and high IQ (but low EQ) was 25 %. Note that his sample consisted mainly of higher-level executives, but his research does point to the limitations of focusing on ability (i.e., IQ) and experience alone, clearly necessary but not sufficient conditions for success.

One of the most widely used measures of personality is the so-called Five-Factor model or Big Five, which consists of the following traits: Openness to Experience, Conscientiousness, Extroversion, Agreeableness, and Neuroticism or Emotional Stability (McCrae and Costa 2008). There has been some criticism of the use of the Big Five in research on cross-cultural management, and an alternative measure, the Multicultural Personality Questionnaire (MPQ) has been developed (Leone et al. 2005; van der Zee et al. 2013) with five dimensions: Cultural Empathy, Open-mindedness, Social Initiative, Emotional Stability, and Flexibility.

Still, research applying the Big Five has been considerable. Shaffer et al.'s (2006) analyses from several studies of expatriates showed that the Big Five dimensions were correlated with specific cross-cultural competencies but that none of them shared more than 20 % of their variance. Conscientiousness was found to be most highly correlated with expatriate adjustment. In fact, the research shows that this dimension seems to be the most predictive of performance across different jobs (Barrick and Mount 1991). In addition, Openness to Experience has been found to be positively related to CQ (Ang et al. 2006; Ward and Fischer 2008). Other researchers have found that CQ and these various personality measures are correlated, although they are also distinct from one another (Ang et al. 2006; Kim et al. 2008).

In a study of expatriates in Japan using the MPQ, Peltokorpi and Froese (2012) found that the MPQ dimensions all predicted cultural adjustment. Cultural Empathy and Emotional Stability contributed additional variance in predicting general adjustment. In another study, this time with Italian and Dutch student samples, Leone et al. (2005) found that the MPQ dimensions predicted "international orientation" better than did the Big Five traits. Like the previous study, their dependent measures focused primarily on adjustment and self-reported interest in an international career and not on successful performance in an international assignment.

Caligiuri (2000) used a different but widely used measure of personality, the Hogan Personality Inventory or HPI (Digman 1990; Hogan and Hogan 2001). She extracted the Big Five dimensions from the HPI and surveyed a sample of expatriates, who also had received ratings from their supervisors. Furthermore, she asked expatriates about their desire to terminate their assignment. Among her findings were the following: Extroversion, Agreeableness, and Emotional Stability were negatively related with desire to terminate the assignment, while Conscientiousness was positively related to ratings of performance. As a group, the Big Five predicted both dependent variables.

A related personality construct is that of psychological capital. Luthans (2002) defined this as follows:

> an individual's positive psychological state of development that is characterized by: (1) having confidence (efficacy) to take on and put in the necessary effort to succeed at challenging tasks; (2) making a positive attribution (optimism) about succeeding now and in the future; (3) persevering toward goals and, when necessary, redirecting paths to goals (hope) in order to

succeed; and (4) when beset by problems and adversity, sustaining and bouncing back and even beyond (resiliency) to attain success. (Luthans and Youssef 2007).

Note that although this is the same term used by Javidan and Teagarden (2011), Luthans defines this concept differently. Javidan and Tegarden identify the components of their concept as comprised of: passion for diversity, quest for adventure, and self-assurance.

Vogelgesang et al. (2014), using Luthans' definition, have studied the impact of psychological capital on the development of global mindset, although their initial results did not show confirmation of their hypothesis that psychological capital is an antecedent for global mindset as they defined it. However, because global managers tend to face complex and ambiguous cultural challenges, it seems reasonable to suggest that a sense of confidence and optimism would help. Choi and Lee (2013), in their study of 373 employees in South Korea, showed that psychological capital predicted perceived performance, turnover intention, and subjective well-being even after controlling for the Big Five personality traits. In summary, there is strong evidence that both CQ and certain personality characteristics (especially Openness to Experience and Conscientiousness) impact global mindset as well as certain global leadership outcomes, especially adjustment.

Youssef and Luthans (2012) point out that about 40 % of an individual's level of positivity is malleable, while 50 % is more or less hard wired. The remaining 10 % is determined by the situation. However, there is much debate as to whether personality characteristics other than positivity are as malleable. This has implications not only for individuals but also for organizations interested in developing global mindset in individuals. Caligiuri (2006), for example, suggests that organizations might be better off selecting these individuals prior to investing in international development activities and opportunities for them.

This emphasis on selection makes at least three somewhat unwarranted assumptions. First is that our measurement instruments are relatively precise in being able to identify those characteristics that we want to select. As Pfeffer and Sutton (2006) have mentioned, even IQ, the most powerful predictor of job performance across studies, only accounts for at best 16 % of the variance in performance. Second is that these antecedent personality characteristics are relatively fixed. There is evidence on the malleability of some of these characteristics (Dweck 2006) and the importance of practice. Third, having the right context, system, or environment can lead to successful outcomes in addition to, or perhaps in place of, having the right characteristics. For example, Groysberg et al. (2004) studied over a 1000 star analysts who worked for 78 US investment banks over an eight-year period. What they found was that the performance of these stars typically declined when they moved to another company. Not only did individual performance suffer, but the performance of the groups that these stars joined also slipped, and the company's valuation itself suffered. In their interpretation, companies tended to overestimate the individual factors that contribute to performance and underestimate other factors, such as the firm's reputation, systems and processes, leadership, internal networks, and training.

In a later study, Groysberg (2008) found however that women star analysts who switched firms performed just as well, on average, as those who stayed put. He learned from these female analysts that they had built skills that were more portable than their male counterparts; specifically, they went out of their way to build an external network, especially with clients and the companies they covered. Presumably, this helped them find firms where they had relationships with key individuals, as well as select firms where they believed they would have a good chance of succeeding. While personality traits may be important antecedents to the development of global leadership, paying attention to contextual factors is also important to consider; context does matter in performance.

Cross-Cultural Contacts and Experiences

The importance of having the appropriate skills and experience helps to establish an individual manager's credentials in many organizations. What kinds of cross-cultural contact and experiences matter the most as antecedents to global leadership? For example, there is evidence to suggest that international experience predicts adjustment to a new culture (e.g., Black 1988; Takeuchi et al. 2005). Tarique and Takeuchi (2008) found that international non-work experiences were positively related to CQ, although the length of experience was a significant moderator of the relationship between frequency and metacognitive CQ. Their study suggests that we need to consider multiple indicators of international experience.

Other researchers have examined the differences between conventional expatriates (CEs) and self-initiated expatriates (SEs) (Alshahrani and Morley 2015; Andresen et al. 2015). As defined by Crowley-Henry (2007), SEs are those seeking employment abroad on their own initiative and are hired as locals in the host country. In general, CEs tend to have, on average, a greater degree of international work-related mobility as well as non-work-related mobility, and a higher receptivity to international mobility developed during their childhood and early adult years (Tharenou 2003). Not all the research findings are consistent, perhaps due to the different samples of expatriates used by various researchers.

Clapp-Smith and Wernsing (2014) examined responses from a survey of 82 students who had gone to study abroad programs. They identified four categories of "transformational triggers" for these students: immersing with local customs and people, experiencing the novelty of "normality" (i.e., finding what other cultures consider as normal makes one question our own cultural assumptions about what is normal), finding time for self-reflection, and communicating in a new language (understanding the importance of language in communicating, both verbally and non-verbally). These four types of experiences seem to have "transformed" the cognitive frameworks of these students, although, as the authors themselves mentioned, organizations may need to help create the conditions for these experiences as well as help managers reflect on the implications of these experiences. The study is also not clear on the relative importance of these experiences, especially for managers who may already have some degree of cross-cultural experience. Nonetheless, for aspiring global leaders, experiencing these transformational triggers seem important antecedents to global leadership development.

Perhaps traveling and working in different countries will help, although there is at least one study with 356 Chinese professionals, where there was no significant relationship between the frequency of international experience and their scores on a measure of cross-cultural adaptability (Chang et al. 2011). Several studies suggest that the amount of travel, or the number of international business trips, may not be as important in contributing to global mindset (Story et al. 2014) as the quality of these experiences and the ability or willingness of the individual to reflect and learn from these experiences.

Some interesting research on biculturals (e.g., Hong 2010; Thomas et al. 2010), individuals whose identities are with more than two cultures (typically because they grew up in one culture and are now living in another), suggest that they have developed "cultural frame-shifting" (the ability to select and apply one of several cultural frames in reacting to cross-cultural situations) in response to situational cues (Cheng et al. 2006; Martinez et al. 2002). In fact, some studies suggest that this cognitive process takes place very quickly, even unconsciously. If you are not by definition bicultural, this concept of shifting your cultural frame of reference when interacting with colleagues from another culture is a useful one to consider, although you may have to work harder to develop this skill. Another supposed advantage of biculturals is that they can take on a boundary-spanning role, especially between HQs and the subsidiaries (Furusawa and Brewster 2015). It is certainly reasonable to suggest that boundary spanning and similar skills are not necessarily unique to biculturals. A third advantage that Lakshman (2013) proposes is that biculturals may have higher levels of attributional complexity (i.e., an ability to use differentiation and integration effectively in causal reasoning) than monoculturals and tend to be less susceptible to attributional biases.

Self-awareness

Self-awareness, the fourth antecedent, has also been shown to be an important predictor of global mindset (Bird et al. 2010; Levy et al. 2007). A component of self-awareness is cultural self-awareness, which is the recognition that part of one's behavior is a function of culture.

In summary, CQ, Openness to Experience, Conscientiousness, aspects of psychological capital, the quality (and diversity) of cross-cultural contacts and experiences, and self-awareness are hypothesized to be important antecedent characteristics of global leaders.

FOUNDATIONAL REQUIREMENTS

Business leaders today need three basic attributes that are important for international success: (1) business and organizational savvy, (2) a results orientation and/or a track record of good performance, and (3) integrity and ethics (Gregersen et al. 1998; Morrison 2001). Business savvy refers to your functional expertise and the application of this expertise to your work. It implies developing depth and breadth about your profession and your industry, and applying strategic thinking about your team and your company. For managers, in particular, this implies understanding the drivers of the business and the industry, for example, how do you make money in the business your company is in, and with its particular business model? Your education, technical background and relevant experience are important in many hiring and promotion decisions. The weight given to these considerations may vary by company, but having the right set of technical skills required for the position is almost always a primary criterion, at least for entry-level and mid-level managers. For global managers who are based in HQs and who are working cross-culturally, having these foundational requirements contributes to their role in training and transferring knowledge to their business colleagues in various subsidiaries.

Organizational savvy refers to your ability to understand how things get done efficiently and effectively in an organization, and having a good understanding of the culture and the politics of the organization. Understanding both the formal and informal networks is critically important to be an effective business leader. For global managers working cross-culturally, it is especially important to navigate the politics of the organization across borders, and to collaborate with business colleagues at a distance.

Business leaders are also expected to have a strong results orientation, that is, a relentless focus on improving results for which they are responsible. Bossidy and Charan (2011), among others, have written some practical guidelines for leaders who want to improve their results orientation (what they term "execution"). Especially for those with some experience, evidence of consistently high levels of performance is important to demonstrate. This commitment to results is important for global leaders working cross-culturally as they attempt to establish credibility both with their overseas business colleagues as well as with HQs executives.

In a world where information travels quickly and where your reputation is important, maintaining the highest level of integrity and ethics seems to be obvious. Yet the temptations and pressures become too strong for some; for others, the failure to maintain integrity may reflect a lack of clarity or reflection on one's values, inner strength, or beliefs about right and wrong. At the very least, a global leader will be expected to behave in a way that is consistent with the company's values and code of conduct. Your business colleagues overseas will observe your actions and make inferences about your integrity based on your behaviors. Since you are in a sense representing your organization, business colleagues will also make inferences about the company's commitment to a culture of integrity based on your actions.

Bill George, formerly CEO of Medtronic and now professor at Harvard Business School, states unequivocally (George 2008):

> Forty years of experience has strengthened my belief that the only way to build a great global company is with a single global standard of business practices, vigorously communicated and rigorously enforced. Applying

"situation ethics" in developing countries is the fastest way to destroy a global organization. To sustain their success, companies must follow the same standards of business conduct in Shanghai, Mumbai, Kiev, and Riyadh as in Chicago.

These foundational requirements are consistent with Bird et al.'s (2004) formulation. In their pyramid model, the foundational level consists of global business knowledge (e.g., knowledge about the business and its industry as well as the macro business environment), while the next level includes traits such as integrity, humility, and resilience (what they label as threshold personality traits).

GLOBAL MINDSET

In addition to these foundational requirements, our model proposes that global leaders need to have certain cognitive and affective dispositions that constitute global mindset. Welch and Welch (2015) argue that the single most important quality expatriates need to be effective is what they call "discernment," which they describe as "the combination of business savvy, cultural sensitivity, and good old wisdom."

Global mindset is an attitude and a predisposition that, *along with the foundational requirements and the necessary behaviors and skills (global leadership competencies)*, is one of the key components in this proposed model of global leadership.

The concept of global mindset has been discussed in the research and practice literature for at least 20 years, and although there has been much recent research on the topic, there is still disagreement on what constitutes global mindset and what its impact is. Gupta and Govindarajan (2002) define global mindset as "combin(ing) openness to and awareness of diversity across cultures and markets with a propensity and ability to synthesize across this diversity."

Levy et al. (2007) have provided an excellent summary of the research and approaches to global mindset, and they have summarized the different frameworks as consisting of three different perspectives: the cultural, the strategic, and the multidimensional. According to their analysis, the cultural perspective taps into the "cosmopolitan" concept of global mindset, specifically, openness and an "other" orientation; the strategic perspective taps into the cognitive complexity aspect of global mindset; while the multidimensional perspective incorporates individual perspectives and integrates them.

Javidan and Teagarden (2011) have defined global mindset as "an individual's ability to influence individuals, groups, organizations, and systems that are unlike him or her or his or her own." (p. 36). Javidan and his colleagues (Beechler and Javidan 2007; Javidan and Bowen 2013) have also done research on global mindset and have developed a conceptual model of global mindset that consists of three kinds of capital: intellectual capital (e.g., global business savvy, cosmopolitan outlook), psychological capital (e.g., passion for diversity, quest for adventure), and social capital (e.g., intercultural empathy, diplomacy). Story et al. (2014) have concluded that global mindset "involves mental fluidity to adapt to the global demands facing multinational organizational leaders and also a strategic business orientation they have that evaluates complex markets and maximizes global business opportunities." (p. 133).

Nummela et al. (2004) define global mindset as managers' perceptions of their firms' orientation toward proactiveness, commitment, and international vision. In their study of over 120 Finnish firms in the information and communications industry, they showed a positive relation between global mindset and objective measures of the international performance of the firms they studied. Similarly, Felício et al. (2012) showed that global mindset had a positive impact on the results of small firms that had internationalized.

The following approach to global mindset builds on the work of Caligiuri and Tarique (2012), Javidan and Teagarden (2011), Rhinesmith (1996), and the integrative frameworks proposed by Levy et al. (2007) and Bird et al. (2010). In our approach, global mindset consists of the following four elements (which can be easily remembered with the acronym FACE):

- Flexibility
- Acceptance (related to "cognitive complexity")
- Curiosity (related to "cosmopolitanism")
- Empathy/Emotional Connection

Like Bird et al.'s (2010) statement about their model, we do not claim that this model is definitive, but offer this in the spirit of building on others' research as well as seeking parsimony among all these different approaches. Table 6.1 shows how this model compares with other related research on aspects of global mindset:

Table 6.1 A comparison of global mindset models

FACE model	Javidan and Teagarden	Story et al.	Earley	Bird et al.	McCloskey et al.
Flexibility	Intellectual capital	CQ	Motivational CQ	Self-management, perception management (tolerance of ambiguity), relationship management (social flexibility)	Cognitive flexibility
Acceptance	Intellectual capital			Perception management (non-judgmentalness)	
Curiosity	Psychological capital	Global business orientation	Cognitive CQ	Perception management (inquisitiveness), relationship management (relationship Interest)	Cultural knowledge
Empathy	Social capital	CQ		Relationship management (emotional Sensitivity)	Cultural maturity Cultural acuity Interpersonal skills

Flexibility

Maria is a Brazilian manager for an accounting firm who was assigned to the US. Having visited the US several times as a tourist, she did not think that she needed to adapt her style to the American work culture. Because she tended to say everything that was on her mind (as do many Brazilians), she found that she had to "hold back" after she was advised by her mentor (a senior executive with the company) not to "spill everything" right away. She also learned to be more punctual when arriving at meetings and events.

Another interviewee, Jenna, is an R&D manager in the food division of a global consumer products company, and after assignments in Switzerland and Germany, this is what she had to say:

> I don't know Asian cultures but now I know to expect something different. I know what questions to ask and to be more sensitive to the signs. I think the cultural nuances become more obvious when you put yourself out there. You learn about your own culture, and where you're coming from

Bridget is a German national who was assigned by her company to work in the US subsidiary for a couple of years. Since she had vacationed in the USA with her family several times as a teenager, she did not expect to have to adjust too much to the workplace culture. Yet, during the first few months of her stay, she found herself disoriented in many ways. For one, she felt constantly rushed into finishing reports, making decisions, and submitting final deliverables quickly. She did not feel comfortable with the "trial-and-error" method used by her American colleagues. She was used to a more deliberate and cautious approach, where colleagues were more willing to talk through issues at length before a final decision was made. She felt that this upfront investment of time caused less re-work and improved efficiency. It was only through some coaching over time that she was able to adapt and recognize the benefits of a different approach.

Samira is an Arab from Bahrain who works for a German multinational and was assigned to Mexico. She described a meeting she had scheduled with a vendor to establish a business deal. The meeting was scheduled for 9:30 a.m., in a place about a two-hour drive from Mexico City. A local staffer was supposed to pick her up at 7:15 a.m. but he did not show up until 9:00. Then his car broke down on the way and he had to call a service operator to repair the car. They did not get to the client site until past noon since they ran into traffic along the way. When they arrived, the client did not seem fazed at all, and suggested they grab some lunch, where they talked about family, soccer, and the local economy before returning to the office to conduct the meeting. Throughout the day, Samira remained calm and clear-headed, recognizing the difference in Mexicans' attitude toward time. Coming from Bahrain, Samira could rely on her past experience to some extent, although this was countered by the norms of punctuality of her German company. She realized that she needed to be flexible.

The preceding are examples of global leaders demonstrating their flexibility. Some individuals like routine, and get very disturbed when their routine is disrupted. They like to have a great deal of structure in their lives, and prefer not to have to think too much in going about their routine activities. Working with people from another culture at the very least means having to do something differently, whether that's slowing down the way you speak, altering the way you make decisions, or how you engage other people to commit to a certain goal. In fact, you may not even be aware that you are on what I call "cultural cruise control." This disposition overlaps with the flexibility and emotional resilience dimensions of Kelley and Meyers' (1995) Cross-Cultural Adaptability Inventory. In their inventory, flexibility measures an individual's willingness to be open to new ideas and to relate to people different from oneself. Emotional resilience measures an individual's ability to handle the emotional pressures from visiting or living in a different culture.

Global leaders who are flexible will have some advantages over those who are not. First, they will be able to adapt more quickly to different and changing circumstances. Second, they will be able to manage their stress levels well, which should in turn help their overall productivity and effectiveness. Third, their flexibility will have a positive impact in their relationships with people from different cultures. There is evidence from research (e.g., Goldsmith and Morgan 2004), for example, that managers who respond to feedback from 360-degree reviews by adapting their style tend to be perceived positively, with their 360-degree results improving significantly a year later. Global leaders who demonstrate their flexibility will tend to improve their reputation among their global colleagues. There is also evidence to suggest that flexibility is a critical predictor of teamwork effectiveness (Driskell et al. 2006).

A recent study by Caligiuri and Tarique (2012) demonstrated the importance of flexibility and other elements to global leadership effectiveness. Over 400 participants from three large multinational conglomerates responded to their survey, which included measures of cultural flexibility, tolerance for ambiguity, and ethnocentrism, as well as supervisory ratings of global leadership effectiveness (sample items included ratings of the effectiveness of their employees on such areas as negotiating with people from other countries and supervising people who are from other countries). They found that cultural flexibility and tolerance of ambiguity were significantly related to global leadership success (but not ethnocentrism).

Some of the indicators of flexibility that you can rate yourself on, using a five-point scale (1 = Almost never; 2 = Sometimes; 3 = About half the time; 4 = Most of the time; 5 = Almost Always) include the following. When working or interacting with people from different cultures, how often:

- Do you adapt and vary your leadership style?
- Do you feel comfortable when faced with situations with much ambiguity?
- Are you able to distinguish between real agreement and polite responses?
- Do you adjust your work style or pace?
- Do you try to "bridge" HQs and subsidiary/regional perspectives in a way that enables both sides to better understand each other?

Acceptance

Imagine a Filipino manager who works for a global company who is about to have lunch with his new boss, Andreas, an expatriate from Finland who has accepted his first overseas assignment to head the subsidiary's marketing department based in Manila. Andreas has a grim look on his face, as he sits down in the company cafeteria. The manager asks Andreas how he is holding up with the weather, and he replies:

> Terrible, but that's the least of it. It's so hard to get anything done around here. No wonder this subsidiary is going downhill. You all just have to be more efficient. We have too many breaks and too many holidays. And when I ask for something, it takes so long for me to get something back. I don't know about you Filipinos. I don't see a lot of people taking initiative. You wait for me to tell you what to do, and then I find out that you don't do them anyway.

Acceptance is the opposite of the mindset that Andreas is displaying. Acceptance is about being open-minded, and not leaping too quickly to make judgments and evaluations. It suggests that a person, in Covey's (1989) words, seeks first to understand. It is related to Bird et al.'s (2010) sub-category of non-judgmentalness under Perception Management. The benefits to a global leader of having an acceptance disposition are significant. First, you are more likely to learn and incorporate new ideas and practices when you are open-minded and not prone to jumping to conclusions too quickly. Second, being accepting conveys to others your interest in learning about other cultures, which will help enhance your own effectiveness as a global leader.

Being open-minded does not necessarily mean agreeing with the practices or perspectives of other cultures. It means being able to learn and understand cultural differences without making quick value judgments about which culture is better or more superior. Lane et al. (2009) describe a process that they label D–I–E (for Describe, Interpret, and Evaluate), and they argue that we should "spend more time on description, treat interpretations as hypotheses, and defer evaluation until we have explored multiple possible interpretations." (p. 33).

Acceptance is related to reduced ethnocentrism (Caligiuri and Tarique 2012). Ethnocentrism implies a conscious negative attitude toward others' cultural values and behaviors, as well as a judgment that one's culture is superior to another's culture. However, for some managers, especially those who have never worked overseas or who have limited interactions with cultural diverse individuals, their lack of acceptance may not necessarily stem from a conscious ethnocentrism.

Acceptance seems to be closely related to cognitive complexity, which has been defined as "an ability to perceive multiple aspects of complex issues from multiple perspectives and to be able to see competing interpretations" (Lane et al. 2009). Research has shown that cognitively complex individuals have excellent information processing capabilities (Streufert 1970).

Fee et al. (2013) surveyed a group of 54 Australians and New Zealanders before and after their international assignments to 18 different countries in Asia and the Pacific. They measured individuals' cognitive complexity through Crockett's Role Category Questionnaire (Crockett 1965) before they left for their assignments and after they returned (typically, between 12 and 18 months later). They found significant increases in cognitive complexity scores for the group. However, prior knowledge of the cultures they were going to, and experience living in those cultures, did not contribute significantly to the increases in cognitive complexity. Rather, interaction with host country nationals both outside and at work accounted for 41 % of the variance in the scores. While there are some flaws in the study (e.g., no control group), there are two key take-away's here: that it is possible to improve one's cognitive complexity (this is not necessarily a fixed trait), and that certain kinds of experiences are more helpful than others—interacting with host country nationals being a key element, and which, presumably, prods us into stepping outside of our normal comfort zone. One of their conclusions for expatriates (and for anyone interacting with colleagues in other cultures) is as follows: "What you do during your assignment is more critical to cognitive change than less controllable antecedents like one's familiarity with the host culture."

One of the common mistakes that some global managers make, especially those who come from HQs and are either on their first overseas assignment or have taken on a global leader role, is to put on a unconscious cloak of superiority. This may stem from an assumption that, because they come from the main office, they know a lot more than the locals with whom they have to deal. That may be the case, but a condescending attitude will more than likely prevent them from learning from their business colleagues and establishing a certain level of trust.

Martin (2007) described one of the key characteristics of successful leaders as the ability to "hold two conflicting ideas in constructive, almost dialectic tension." He argues that most of us, when faced with two models, will avoid complexity and ambiguity by determining which of two models is "right" and which is "wrong." However, he continues: "We can use that tension to think our way toward new, superior ideas. Were we able to hold only one thought or idea in our heads at a time, we wouldn't have access to the insights that the opposable mind can produce." With acceptance comes a willingness to hold on to these opposing thoughts and recognizing the paradoxes and differences, rather than rejecting one or the other.

This characteristic applies to global leaders as well. For example, the opposing models may come from two different cultural assumptions about what motivates people in a work setting (empowering them versus giving them precise orders) or even at times, cultural paradoxes within a culture (Osland 2008). For example, the Japanese are known to be compliant and self-effacing, yet in past wars, their soldiers have had a reputation for barbaric cruelty. Holt and Seki (2012) have argued that this ability to manage paradoxes is an important aspect of global leadership. They have identified several sets of paradoxes for global leaders, one of which is cultural. Arguably, the other paradoxes (e.g., operating from a long-term perspective and at the same time ensuring that day-to-day operating details are planned and managed) are those that any leader needs to be able to address.

Some of the indicators of Acceptance that you can rate yourself on, using a five-point scale (1 = Almost never, 2 = Sometimes, 3 = About half the time, 4 = Most of the time, 5 = Almost always) include the following. When you are working with or interacting with people from different cultures, how often:

- Do you recognize and acknowledge the strengths of other cultures' business practices?
- Do you reflect on your actions and their possible impact?
- Do you find yourself being as open to ideas from these cultures as you are to ideas from your own culture?
- Do you feel confident in your ability to start conversations and establish rapport?

Curiosity

Leonor is a marketing manager for a non-governmental organization (NGO) who was sent to Ghana to help the Ghanaians create local marketing materials such as websites, brochures, and programs. She claimed that she did not want to "overthink" her preparation (both mentally and emotionally) so she arrived in Ghana with very little sense of the country but with a spirit of openness and optimism. As a Hispanic female from New York City, Leonor was not accustomed to standing out much and being followed by the curious locals. She was constantly being referred to as *obruni*, which is the Ghanaian term for an outsider (usually Caucasian). To overcome her initial discomfort, Leonor first shrugged this off as a cultural learning experience, and began to attend festivals and community events outside of work. The locals were impressed with her willingness to learn and to ask questions, and she even became somewhat fluent with the Twi language. Her interest also helped with her work, as she collaborated with local managers in adapting marketing materials that would be responsive to the Ghanaian population. Her Ghanaian colleagues even renamed her, using the Ghanaian term for Leonor.

In her free time, Leonor visited museums to learn more about Ghanaian history. She also noticed the strong similarities between Ghanaian cuisine and Latin American cuisine, which led to many conversations with her local colleagues and helped make her aware of the historic ties between Latin American and Ghana, many of whom were taken as slaves to the Americas (a sensitive subject to be sure, and one she broached very carefully).

How interested are you in learning about other cultures? Have you ever wondered why cultural practices differ so radically from country to country, and what might be some of the historical and cultural reasons for these differences? When you arrive at an unfamiliar location, do you look around and explore what is unfamiliar, or do you look to see what seems familiar to you (such as the nearest restaurant serving your country's cuisine) and gravitate toward those places? Curiosity is related to the sociological concept of cosmopolitanism. As described by Lane et al. (2009): "This is not just passive 'tolerance' but actively valuing and seeking out diversity which is seen as an asset. It is openness to different cultural experiences and a willingness to explore, learn and change." (p. 15).

This passion to learn, especially about other cultures, is an important antecedent of global leadership. In a recent interview, Carlos Ghosn (Stahl and Brannen 2013), the chairman of Reanult-Nissan who successfully turned around a Japanese car company in decline, commented:

> Working in a multicultural environment necessitates from the beginning a kind of thirst for learning. If you don't have a thirst for learning, if you think you know it all, and your system is the best, and you don't even try, this is not going to work. That's the most basic thing—that you want to learn more, develop your skills, broaden your horizon, and that you want to work in a multicultural environment because you are going to discover new things—about your business and also about yourself. (p. 497)

All too often unfortunately, expatriates and other global managers eager to prove themselves to their bosses in HQs take on their new assignment by trying to do too much too quickly, and without sufficiently understanding and learning about the local culture. Mussel (2013) has conducted some research to show that curiosity is a strong predictor of job performance. He created a Work-Related Curiosity Scale consisting of ten items (e.g., I carry on seeking information until I am able to understand complex issues). In one study of 320 incumbents of an industrial company, he found positive relationships between curiosity and various measures of job performance; this measure incrementally predicted performance above the Big Five personality measures. Kashdan et al. (2004) have developed a Curiosity and Exploration Inventory (CEI) designed to measure two scales: exploration (curiosity toward novel and challenging stimuli) and absorption (the ability to regulate one's attention and become immersed in novel and challenging situations). Ye et al. (2015) did not find this two-factor structure in their research of this inventory among Chinese university students in Hong Kong but did confirm the strong relationship between Curiosity and Openness to Experience.

There are three reasons for why curiosity is important for global leaders. First, as a global manager, it will help you better understand the different markets where your company might be selling its products and services so that your company's offerings will be better suited to those markets. Being curious, and asking questions about such business factors like different countries' consumer preferences, marketing approaches, distribution channels, major competitors, and recruiting strategies will help you devise relevant business strategies for these markets.

Second, asking questions, especially about various countries' management practices, will help you become a more effective manager of people. For example, learning about seniority systems in various countries (e.g., the Middle East) will give you insight into the challenges of implementing merit-based hiring and promotion systems in some countries.

Third, as Molinsky (2013) points out, showing genuine interest in the other culture will make it easier for your global colleagues to forgive you for cultural mistakes. Although this may be a bit more difficult to pull off, sometimes you can use your culture as an "excuse" in doing things a certain way. Phil, a Canadian, was sent by his cosmetics company to Brazil to head purchasing for the region. In meetings, Phil asked a lot of questions and got into so much detail that some of his Brazilian colleagues started to become a bit defensive. When he recognized the potential negative impact that his constant questioning was having on others, Phil explained to the local employees that as a Canadian, he had to prepare for long, hard winters and so he was brought up to pay a lot of attention to detail to make sure that his family and home were secure for the winter. This made a lot of sense to the Brazilians, and they became much more tolerant and open whenever he got into details in subsequent meetings.

In her company's London office, where Janice had been assigned from New York, she continued to use the same work style that got her recognized in America—being persistent, aggressive, and very demanding. When a co-worker failed to provide her with a deliverable on time, she approached him immediately to remind him of the deadline, and pushed hard for when she might expect the deliverable. She learned that this kind of behavior was considered highly aggressive in London, and she was stereotyped as the pushy American. Rather than be insulted, Janice said, "I began using this in my favor. I could use it to excuse my missteps and to find other ways to interact with my co-workers." However, she complemented her style by finding the time to build relationships with her co-workers, which she believed helped them to see her in a more positive manner.

There is a subtle but important distinction between using your culture as an excuse when you have made a cultural error and using it to justify not adapting at all. For example, your preferred management style as a leader might be to delegate and give your team a lot of autonomy. If your team were made up of very experienced people with deep knowledge of their functions, this would most likely be an effective style. However, if your team were made up of young professionals who are new in their jobs and who don't have a lot of confidence, this style would most likely not work for them. As an effective leader, you would have to adjust your style to make sure they are being properly led. To insist on sticking to your delegating style would not work. Similarly, letting your global team know that, for example, as a German executive, the German management style is what you will prefer to use would send a signal that you are not interested in learning and adapting your style.

Other interviewees (and my own experience) suggest that learning a few words in the local language can be helpful. Certain phrases in the local language are almost always helpful to learn: good morning, good afternoon, good evening, thank you, excuse me. Ideally, take some language lessons when you anticipate that you will be spending some time with people from a different culture, either through virtual meetings or when being sent on assignment. As Clapp-Smith and Wernsing (2014) have suggested, the process of learning to speak in a local language can be "transformational." It not only gives you more insights into another culture (e.g., the different terms used for different levels of management) but broadens your ability to communicate. One of our interviewees commented that his French language lessons helped him to begin to "think in the language."

Will is an Australian executive who was sent to Japan by his company, a global insurance firm. He made the effort to learn Japanese three months before his assignment by taking 90-minute weekly lessons from a tutor. Upon arriving in Japan, he was assigned a translator. In business meetings during his first month in Tokyo, his translator would begin translating about three to four seconds after the speaker finished. Will decided to take a risk after a month and during one business meeting, he responded to a question before the translator began. As Will recalled, everyone at the meeting was impressed and expressed appreciation to Will for making such an effort to learn the language. This little gesture on his part helped break the ice with his Japanese colleagues and started a fruitful, long-term relationship with them.

Schmidt and Rosenberg (2014), in their book *How Google Works*, gave this piece of advice for young graduates:

> Business, regardless of size or scope, is forever, permanently global, while humans are naturally provincial. So it doesn't matter where you are or where you came from, get out of there whenever you have the chance. Go live and work somewhere else. If you're at a big company, seek the international assignments. Your managers will love you for it and you'll be a much more valuable employee as a result. (p. 141)

Some of the indicators of curiosity that you can rate yourself on using a five-point scale (1 = Almost never, 2 = Sometimes, 3 = About half the time, 4 = Most of the time, 5 = Almost always) include the following. When you are working with or interacting with people from different cultures, how often:

- Do you try to get out of your comfort zone to experience new places, new people, or new ideas?
- Do you make an effort to learn some basic words of the language of their culture?
- Do you listen carefully to what others have to say?
- Do you show an active interest in their culture and way of life?
- Do you try to find out about current events and business news in these cultures?

Empathy

This is arguably the most important of the four dispositions. Wiseman (1996) suggests that empathy has four defining attributes: seeing the world as others see it (otherwise known as perspective-taking), being non-judgmental, understanding another's feelings, and communicating than understanding. Similarly, Krznaric (2014) defines empathy as "the art of stepping imaginatively into the shoes of another person, understanding their feelings and perspectives, and using that understanding to guide your actions."

The research on empathy indicates that there are two types: cognitive empathy and emotional empathy (Davis 1994; Smith 2006), and while the precise relationship between the two is not completely settled (Hoffman 1993; Staub 1990), most scholars seem to agree on this distinction. Questionnaires have been developed to measure each of these two types, the most common being the Interpersonal Reactivity Scale, or IRS (Davis 1994), and the Empathy Quotient (Lawrence et al. 2004). The IRS has 28 items measuring four different subscales: Empathic Concern, Perspective-Taking, Fantasy (people's tendencies to identify imaginatively with fictional characters in books or movies), and Personal Distress (measuring self-oriented feelings of distress during others' misfortunes). The following are sample items from the Perspective-Taking subscale:

- I sometimes find it difficult to see things from the "other guy's" point of view. (reverse-scored)
- I believe that there are two sides to every question and try to look at them both.
- Before criticizing somebody, I try to imagine how I would feel if I were in their place.

The following are sample items from the Empathic Concern subscale:

- Other people's misfortunes do not usually disturb me a great deal. (reverse-scored)
- I often have tender, concerned feelings for people less fortunate than me.
- Sometimes I don't feel very sorry for other people when they are having problems. (reverse-scored)

Baron-Cohen and Wheelwright's (2004) empathy quotient measure is similar to cognitive empathy, which they measure by individuals' level of agreement (or disagreement) with items such as the following:

- I can easily work out what another person might want to talk about.
- I can tell if someone is masking their true emotion.
- I find it easy to put myself in somebody else's shoes.

The evidence is strong that different parts of our brain are activated when we are using cognitive versus emotional empathy. Each appears to require different skill sets and tends to be used differently in different situations. According to Melloni et al. (2014), the amygdala, hypothalamus, and orbitofrontal cortex are involved with affective arousal; the medial prefrontal cortex, ventromedial prefrontal cortex, and temporo-parietal junction are involved with emotional understanding, and the corticocortical connections of the orbitofrontal cortex, medial prefrontal cortex, and dorsolateral prefrontal cortex are involved with emotion regulation.

Gilin et al. (2013) conducted some studies to determine the differential impact of cognitive versus emotional empathy. They defined cognitive empathy as perspective-taking, while emotional empathy is "the affective capacity to emotionally connect with others and experience sympathy and concern for others." Their hypothesis was that these two different types of empathy would work differently in different situations. When the goal is to understand an opponent's strategic intent, then cognitive empathy would be more effective than emotional empathy. With tasks that require collaboration with others, on the other hand, emotional empathy would be more effective than cognitive empathy or perspective-taking. Their findings support their hypothesis and they conclude:

> perspective-taking and empathy can each promote understanding that can lead to individual and joint competitive gains, but only when the underlying structure or content of the task requires that particular competency. (p. 11)

Roberge (2013) brings up an important distinction with the concept of emotional empathy. She suggests that emotional or affective empathy is about feeling for someone, as opposed to feeling as someone else does. "Affective empathy does not imply feeling similarity or emotional convergence, which refers to two (or more) people coming to feel more similarly … (it) is about 'feeling for' someone and not about 'feeling as' someone." The research on the impact of empathy on prosocial behavior (e.g., helping others) supports her point on the effectiveness of emotional versus cognitive empathy in these situations.

For global managers, both types are critical. When leaders are in a different culture, understanding how other people view things is important. Goleman (2005) has suggested that cognitive empathy is an outgrowth of self-awareness. For global managers, this also means being aware of how their culture impacts their own behavior. Managers who tend to be ethnocentric and who believe, for example, that their style of managing is superior to styles in other cultures will find it hard to develop cognitive empathy. Developing empathy will help global managers perceive more accurately a cross-cultural situation that they might be trying to understand. Perspective-taking is especially important for global managers in negotiation situations, for example, in working on joint venture agreements.

Galinsky and Moskowitz (2000) in fact have shown that perspective-taking might be a more effective strategy than stereotype suppression for decreasing stereotyping. In one of several experiments, participants (student undergraduates) were shown a photo of an elderly man and asked to write an essay describing a day in his life. One-third of the participants were given no explicit instructions, one-third were asked to suppress any stereotypes, and the remaining third were told to take the perspective of the individual in the photograph when writing their essay. The second group was told that "Previous research has demonstrated that thoughts and impressions are consistently influenced by stereotypic preconceptions, and therefore you should actively try to avoid thinking about the photographed target in such a manner." The third group was told to "imagine a day in the life of this individual as if you were that person, looking at the world through his eyes and walking through the world in his shoes."

They were then asked to write an essay about a second elderly man whose photo they were shown. Following this, the participants were shown a photo of a young African-American man and asked to write a third essay. The researchers wanted to find out whether the experimental instructions would generalize to a different social group. Raters who did not know which of the essays came from the different experimental conditions rated both the overall stereotypicality of the contents and its overall valence. The former is a standard measure used in research on stereotype suppression. Valence was measured to determine how positive the participants rated the evaluations of the target. What they found was that perspective-taking not only reduced the expression of stereotypical content but also increased the expression of positive content; stereotype suppression only affected the former and not the valence. For the second photo, both perspective-takers and suppressors wrote less-stereotypically based essays than did control participants, while perspective-takers expressed more positive evaluations of the target than did suppressors and control participants. No differences in stereotypical content were found for the third photo, perhaps because as researchers learned when debriefing the participants, they were sensitive to stereotyping by race (wishing to be politically correct, perhaps). However, perspective-takers expressed more positive evaluations toward the African-American target compared with the elderly targets.

The researchers conclude that "perspective-taking is a successful strategy for debiasing social thought. Perspective-taking tended to increase the expression of positive evaluations of the target, reduced the expression of stereotypic content, and prevented the hyperaccessibility of stereotype construct." (p. 720)

Apparently, based on several research studies, what happens in perspective-taking is that by considering another person's perspective, we see that we and the other person are not so different after all: "Perspective-taking results in the target becoming more 'self-like'; after perspective-taking, the cognitive structures for the self and the target share more common elements, resulting in a merger of self and other." (Galinsky and Ku 2004, p. 596).

Other recent experiments have shown that perspective-taking even helps to improve overall attitudes and evaluations of the target person's group. For example, in follow-up studies also using the photo of an elderly man, Galinsky and Ku (2004) found that those who were primed to take the elderly man's perspective also started to evaluate the elderly more positively than a control group. As the researchers pointed out, however, these findings may not generalize to collectivist cultures where individuals are "more likely to engage in outgroup derogation and intergroup bias ... and more likely to be (overly) generous when dealing with friends." (p. 602)

In another series of experiments conducted in Singapore and the UK, Wang et al. (2014) built on this research and found that perspective-taking increased willingness to engage in contact with negatively stereotyped targets, such as an "Ah Beng" (or local hooligan, in Singapore) and the homeless in the UK. In the second study, participants were shown a photograph of a homeless man; those in the perspective-taking condition were asked to "take the perspective of the individual in the photograph and imagine a day in the life of this individual as if you were that person." (p. 3) Participants in the control condition were simply asked to write a brief passage describing a typical day in the life of the individual in the photograph. After this task, they were then shown a photograph of a different individual.

In the same-target-group condition, participants were shown a photograph of another homeless man. In the different-target-group condition, they were shown a photograph of an African-American. Consistent with results from previous research, they found that those who were primed to the perspective-taking condition were more willing to engage in contact with the target group (although not necessarily with a different target group). Other research has shown that active perspective-taking is a predictor of successful global assignments (Hyung Park et al. 2014).

Another benefit of perspective-taking, especially critical for global leaders, is with improvements in the accuracy of what individuals believe the other person might be thinking or feeling. Ickes et al. (2000) have even developed a methodology to study what they call empathic accuracy. In one study, they first videotaped target participants while they talked about some event, topic, or problem. Then these participants watched their own videotape, stopping the tape when they remembered some thought or feeling while they were talking. They wrote these thoughts or feelings down and the time when these actually took place in the videotape. Perceivers then watched the video, which was stopped at the times when the target had recalled the thought or feeling. These perceivers then wrote down what they believed the target was thinking or feeling at these specific times. The researchers then compared the perceivers' responses to what the targets wrote down to obtain a measure of empathic accuracy.

They found that the perceiver's accuracy in understanding another person is not always a function of familiarity with the other person or his or her experiences but on the perceiver's motivation. This is somewhat reassuring for those working globally, for it suggests that our desire and interest in the other person, as well as our own self-concept, are strong predictors of how well we can accurately assess their thoughts and feelings.

Eisenberg and Lennon (1983) found a "female advantage" when people were asked to self-report their empathy; women tended to see themselves as more empathic. However, gender differences were not found with objective measures of empathy. It seems that "priming" women on their gender and role may make a difference: "If a woman is aware that the task she is completing is assessing her empathic capabilities, it may be important for her to perform well. She therefore may be more successful than a man completing the same objective measurement of empathy because of her increased level of motivation." (Klein and Hodges 2000, p. 721) One implication here is that global managers who believe that being empathic is important in their role, therefore, may be more motivated to be empathic and can in fact be quite accurate in their perceptions of others' thoughts and feelings—certainly a key advantage for succeeding as a global leader!

Are there limits to perspective-taking, especially when the person you are interacting with is very dissimilar to you in so many ways? For example, imagine a highly educated, young Dutch female executive on her first overseas assignment, getting ready to talk to an elderly Nigerian male working in an oil pipeline to determine problems in the flow of oil. How likely is it that she would be able to take the Nigerian's perspective to understand what the problem might be from his perspective? With some effort, this can still work, and in fact, some research supports this.

Lamm et al. (2009) used functional magnetic resonance imaging to examine how subjects would react to patients under different conditions. In their study, subjects were asked to empathize by imagining the pain (or non-pain) from two different groups of individuals. One group, who they described as neurological patients (and therefore dissimilar to the subjects), felt pain when touched by a soft object (such as a Q-tip), but did not feel pain when pricked by a needle. The other group was described as normal (and therefore similar to the subjects) and felt pain when pricked but no pain when touched by a Q-tip. Subjects observed sets of photographs of hands being touched by the Q-tip or pricked by a needle, with descriptions of the types of patients. They also completed the Empathy Quotient questionnaire to measure their dispositional empathy. They found that all subjects were able to empathize (i.e., infer the affective state of) even with those patients who were dissimilar to them, although it was more challenging to do so especially when the situation (i.e., the needle prick) was aversive to the subjects.

Other researchers are not as optimistic. Professor Paul Bloom suggests that there are limits to perspective-taking, especially when the stakes are high or when others' experiences are deeply significant, such as changing a religion or fighting a war.[1] Epley (2014), who has conducted considerable research on this topic, acknowledges the benefit of perspective-taking: "You maximize your use of what you already know about another person, information that you might otherwise mistakenly overlook." (p. 168) At the same time, he claims that in some of his experiments, perspective-taking can decrease accuracy by "overthinking one's emotional expression or inner intentions when there is little else to go on" (p. 168) This can be especially challenging, he states, when your belief about the other side's perspective is mistaken. Then perspective-taking can magnify the mistake's consequences. Epley (2014) states:

> We can all lecture other people about the danger of judging others until you've walked a mile in their shoes, but we easily overlook it when we're

doing the same thing ourselves. You don't overcome the lens problem by trying harder to imagine another person's perspective. You overcome it by actually being in that perspective, or hearing directly from some who has been in it. (p. 115)

Nonetheless, developing empathy is especially important cross-culturally because managers may be exposed to situations that are culturally very different and in fact may offend their sensibilities at first blush. When a colleague from Australia moved to Tokyo for a two-year assignment, she was shocked at the popularity of "love hotels" where she heard men could select the appropriate background sounds in the room and play them as they were calling their wives, explaining that they were going to be late coming home as they prepared for their trysts. The sounds ranged from the buzz of people and train announcements in Shinjuku station to pedestrians and cars honking their horns in Shibuya. While she (and many others like myself) could not accept this kind of behavior nor believed that we should show emotional empathy, she gradually gained a better understanding of the cultural reasons for this behavior by adopting a perspective-taking approach.

For global managers, learning about local cultural practices might give them insight into why these practices exist and the underlying cultural values. An executive working with Korean nationals, recognizing that he will be perceived as an authority figure by the Koreans, might put more effort in asking specific questions rather than asking them generally for their opinion. Ultimately, the benefit of developing empathy and of having a global mindset will help you become a more effective global leader.

Empathy helps builds trust, especially in relationship-based cultures. Developing trust is very important in business and personal relationships, and perhaps even more so when building relationships across cultures. Buchan (2009) has proposed a definition and model of trust based on work by Orbell et al. (1994). Her definition of trust is the expectation of another's behavior in a situation involving vulnerability where one may prefer the partner to do "a" but he/she has incentive or potential to do "b." This expectation is based on the trustor's evaluation of the trustee's competence and benevolence. However, culture influences trust in several different ways. For example, the evidence suggests that in individualistic cultures trust is built primarily on competence, while in collectivistic cultures trust is built through relationships. Western leaders who are working with colleagues and business partners from collectivistic cultures would do well to spend time building and nurturing relationships, and/or establishing connections with their colleagues' in-group.

Van Hoorn (2015) investigated the relationship between individualism–collectivism and a different aspect of trust, what he and others call the trust radius, that is, the width of the circle of people among whom a certain trust level exists. Using measures of in-group and out-group trust, and examining the data collected from the World Values Survey (1994), he found very strong relationships between individualism–collectivism and trust radius. That is, the more individualistic the culture of a society is, the broader the radius of trust within the society, with the reverse being the case for collectivistic cultures.

Some have argued that the market environment is also a strong driver of the basis of trust. In countries where there is weak rule of law, the argument goes, trust will be based more on relationships rather than competence. And as these countries develop their institutional systems, then the basis of trust shifts more toward competence and transactions (Johnson et al. 2002). They refer to "relational contracting" as the norm in countries like Russia, Poland, and Romania. Once relationships are built, then trust between supplier and customer (the cases they studied) gets strengthened. As they point out, "Continuing to deal with a particular supplier means being reluctant to deal with new suppliers." I learned about this first-hand in a discussion with an Asian country manager of a subsidiary about his company's interest in using a regional supplier versus the local supplier that the country manager had been using. Even though the regional supplier was offering a lower-priced deal, the country manager was reluctant to relinquish a relationship that he had built over the years with the local supplier.

Yet in countries like Japan, where the rule of law seems more advanced than in emerging markets, relationship-based trust still seems to be the norm. This suggests that cultural values may at times trump institutional mechanisms, at least with regard to trust. This is supported by the research that suggests that individuals from collectivistic cultures tend to have lower levels of trust in general than those from individualistic cultures (Huff and Kelley 2003), especially when it comes to those in the "out-group."

I have advised some of my clients of the three Cs in building trust: competence, commonality/connections, and commitment. The importance of each of these will most likely vary by culture. In task-oriented and assertive cultures, demonstrating your competence is important; you trust those who you believe can do the job. However, you will not trust even a competent person if you don't believe that person understands your perspective, which is what commonality implies. Showing your colleague that you will do what you say you will do, and that you can be relied on, are indicators of your commitment. Once you have established trust with your global colleague, you will be able to build a more fruitful working relationship and also influence him or her more effectively.

For Goleman (2005), managers who are effective in reading group dynamics and who are good mentors need to have high levels of emotional empathy. Goleman cites some research that individuals can develop emotional empathy by cultivating a certain detachment, learning how to step back and seeing their actions as if from above. This seems similar to what Heifetz and Linsky (2002) recommend for leaders—that they practice looking at their behavior and their interactions as if watching from the balcony. Global managers who are working with virtual teams and who need team members to collaborate with one another, as well as managers trying to resolve conflict situations, will need a healthy dose of emotional empathy. More recently, Goleman (2013) has proposed a third type of empathy, something he calls empathic concern—the ability to sense what another person needs from you.

John was an employee of an NGO working in Afghanistan. As part of his work, he and his team would meet with different tribal chiefs to discuss their needs and how his organization could help their tribes. In almost all cases, the team would be escorted to the tribal chief's tent, where they would be greeted by the chief and his entourage, and they would sit on the carpet and discuss their local issues. The first time that John went on such a visit, he noticed that every one of the local guards entering the tent took off their shoes and, following their example, John did the same. Several months later, when John and his same team returned to this tribe, his guards told the team that only John was welcome inside the tent because he was the only one who had shown respect by taking off his shoes.

It turns out that we have "mirror neurons" that help us to empathize. Rizzolatti et al. (2006) have conducted many experiments to demonstrate the importance of these mirror neurons to empathy. Somehow, observing another person experiencing emotion results in a direct mapping of that sensory information onto the motor structures that would produce the experience of that emotion in the observer. Another interesting finding from neuroscience is that the hormone oxytocin is related to empathy. Zak (2012) and others have discovered that when we see someone in moderate distress, oxytocin is released in the brain, which triggers an empathic response.

Empathy is important cross-culturally because it helps increase our understanding of another person's culture. When we empathize, we are trying your best to be non-judgmental. We are going outside your own mental map to try to understand a situation from that person's point of view. As Epley and Caruso (2008) have stated, "the ability to accurately adopt someone's perspective is better than chance but less than perfect."

However, can one empathize too much? The concern may be most relevant for emotional empathy, where managers might get "sucked in" and lose perspective and objectivity. Therefore, managers need to balance their emotional empathy within the context of their role and objectives. Epley and Caruso's position is that it is not easy to develop empathy, and they point to three barriers, which I will paraphrase here. The first barrier is "activating" or switching on in our minds a willingness to do this. As global leaders, this is sometimes difficult to do due in part to the variety of complex situations that they face. If they have not even made the effort to learn about other cultures, switching mentally to consider practices from another person's perspective will be difficult.

The second barrier is our natural tendency to react to things from our own perspective. In one experiment, Epley and Caruso (2008) asked participants to send either sincere or sarcastic messages to another participant, either over the telephone or via e-mail. They were asked to predict, for each of ten sincere and ten sarcastic messages, whether the recipient would interpret the message correctly or incorrectly. Recipients were not significantly better than chance at distinguishing between sarcasm and sincerity over e-mail, but not surprisingly, were significantly more accurate over the telephone. But the senders did not think there would be any difference in the recipients' accuracy when communicating over e-mail or the telephone. "The senders' intentions to communicate sarcasm or sincerity were so clear that it rendered them unable to appreciate ... that the perception of the person on the other end of the computer monitor would be very different from the person on the other end of the telephone."

I can recall many times when executives have told me that they don't understand why their messages are not being understood, or are being misinterpreted by employees. For example, if an executive working with Thai nationals has asked them for their opinions and they don't give him any, it must be because they prefer not being straightforward! The perspective that in some cultures, authority is so valued that voicing an opinion is tantamount to disrespecting the boss, is not something that would occur right away to this executive.

For example, when one interviewee, Sam, was sent to his company's Mexico plant to improve quality assurance operations, he did not think he would encounter any difficulties because the plant was a subsidiary of his company, a global multinational based in Switzerland. However, as he related later, he found the local employees reacting in one of two ways to his proposals. On the one hand, there was a great deal of resistance to change. He found some lab personnel unwilling to accept his proposals, claiming through their supervisors that such ideas would never work in the plant. On the other hand, he found others complying with his proposals simply because he was a person with authority who was telling them what to do. When he flew back to the USA, he learned that many of his suggestions were ignored. Sam was never able to figure out how to address the cultural challenges he faced, attributing his difficulties to "resistance to change" rather than trying to understand the underlying cultural dynamics.

Griffin and Ross (1991) described an experiment by Elizabeth Newton who assigned subjects to one of two roles: tappers and listeners. She paired participants into teams of two: one tapper and one listener. The tappers picked one of 25 well-known songs (such as "Happy Birthday" and "Auld Lang Syne") and were asked to tap out the rhythm on a table. Their partner, the designated listener, was asked to guess the song. Of the 120 songs tapped out on the table, the listeners only guessed 3 of them correctly, or 2.5 %. Before the listeners responded, the tappers were asked to predict how likely their partner was to be able to name the song. Tappers estimated that their partners would name the song an average of 50 % of the time, with these estimates ranging from 10 to 95 %. Newton asked another group of listeners, who were told in advance the name of the tune, for their estimates. Like the tappers, this group of listeners also predicted an average of 50 % accuracy. Griffin and Ross compared this situation to the work of the psychologist Jean Piaget who described children as too egocentric and unable to adapt others' perspective. Tappers were not aware that their subjective experiences differed from those of the listeners, nor did they make adequate allowance for this difference when they were asked to make their estimates.

Third, if we do recognize that we need to understand another person's perspective, our ability to do this may depend on whether we believe that person is similar to us or not. In either case, this may lead to problems. Let's say that you are a manager for a global company working with a group of Polish employees in your Warsaw subsidiary. You could make the assumption that because these employees belong to the same company as you they should react similarly to you. Or you could make the assumption that because these employees are Polish, your anticipation of how they will react will be based on your "stored knowledge" of what Poles are like—which may or may not be accurate. Each of these assumptions will not necessarily reflect the Polish employees' perspectives.

While in Singapore with a group of experienced expatriates and Asian executives, most of whom have regional roles working in global companies, I learned that one of their challenges was in managing within a matrix environment and convincing senior management that certain global policies and strategies might have to be adapted for different markets. In discussing their situation, we had a productive dialogue in looking at the situation from the senior managers' perspective—what could be going on in their minds, what might be driving their behavior? It had not occurred to them to consider another perspective until I raised the question.

Anil is a second-generation American Indian whose parents were from Kerala. As director of a global company specializing in enterprise resource planning, he was sent to Mumbai to help implement a project with one of India's leading cell phone service providers. The project was expected to be completed in half a year. About halfway through the project, an employee named Priya noted a script issue with one of the software products the group was working on. Apparently out of fear of being reprimanded by her male supervisor, Priya instead told her colleagues about the issue. Anil was unaware of this critical problem until he started to have a conversation with one of the employees over lunch, and who happened to mention this to him. Rather than being upset, Anil realized that the problem might stem from power distance compounded with the issue of women not feeling that their opinions would be listened to as much as those of the men's. Instead of confronting Priya directly, Anil approached her and reviewed the project specifications until she finally pointed out some of the problems with the deliverables. They were then able to collaborate and work together to resolve the issue.

Although empathy and perspective-taking may at times be difficult, developing this skill can be learned through practice and mindfulness. It is encouraging that in a recent experimental study by Lee et al. (2013), they were able to raise subjects' perspective-taking simply by giving them some reminders. In their study of negotiation, they used East Asian and North American students in a buyer–seller negotiation situation, and participants were made aware of the other party's culture and negotiation norms prior to the simulation. They found that negotiators who engaged in cultural perspective-taking claimed more value than negotiators who did not.

Some of the indicators of Empathy that you can rate yourself on, using a five-point scale (1 = Almost never, 2 = Sometimes, 3 = About half the time, 4 = Most of the time, 5 = Almost always) include the following. When you are working with or interacting with people from different cultures, how often:

- Do you change your verbal and non-verbal behavior when a cross-cultural interaction requires it?
- Do you try to put yourself in others' shoes to see things from their cultural perspective?
- Are you able to bring together divergent views and develop a consensus?
- Can you sense almost immediately whether something is going well or not?
- Are you able to show sincere interest, concern, and respect?

The four dispositions of Flexibility, Acceptance, Curiosity, and Empathy should help global leaders have a better understanding of the cross-cultural situation in which they work, and address the situational and cultural challenges they might face. The relative importance of these dispositions, and how they should be applied, will certainly vary by culture and by situation. For example, in some cultures, having strong empathy will be more important for leaders to develop than being curious. In summary, global mindset is about having dispositions of flexibility, openness, curiosity, and empathy about different cultures and the people from those cultures. While there is much that still needs to be learned about these dispositions and how leaders develop them, it is clear from the research and interviews, however, that these are important elements of successful global leadership.

GLOBAL LEADERSHIP COMPETENCIES

There have been numerous attempts to identify global leadership competencies. For example, Steers et al. (2012) proposed six multicultural competencies for global managers: a cosmopolitan outlook, intercultural communication skills, cultural sensitivity, rapid acculturation skills, flexible management style, and cultural synergy. After an extensive review of the literature, Bird et al. (2004) proposed three broad factors: perception management, relationship management, and self-management. Researchers have attempted to develop instruments to measure aspects of interpersonal competence (e.g., Koester and Olebe 1988; Chen and Starosta 2000) and interpersonal sensitivity (e.g., Hammer et al. 2003). Graf and Harland (2005) did not find much convergent validity when they assessed five related scales: the Behavioral Assessment Scale for Intercultural Communication Effectiveness, the Intercultural Sensitivity Scale, the Interpersonal Competence Questionnaire, the Social Problem-Solving Inventory, and the Self-Monitoring Scale.

McCall and Hollenbeck (2002), in their study of 100 global leaders from 16 companies in 36 countries, proposed the following global competencies needed for success in international business: flexibility in thought and tactics, cultural sensitivity, ability to deal with complexity, resilience and resourcefulness, honesty and integrity, personal stability, and sound technical skills.

McCloskey et al. (2010) developed a model of cross-cultural competence for soldiers and identified four levels of development (pre-competent, beginner, intermediate, and advanced). They created interview situations and assigned responses into each of these four categories. The following is an example of an interview situation in which the subjects were asked to respond:

> After being fired upon from inside the house, the US force conducts a search, finds the insurgent, and strikes a boy who had appeared to be pointing a weapon (which ended up being a stick) at the soldiers. The elder approaches the participant, furious that a child has been struck. The participant must determine how to deal with the elder and the village, both in the short term and over the next several weeks.

The five components of cross-cultural competence that they have proposed include the following: Cultural Maturity, Cognitive Flexibility, Cultural Knowledge, Cultural Acuity, and Interpersonal Skills.

Oxford Economics (2012) surveyed over 350 human resources professionals around the world, and found that three of the four areas where skills will be in greatest demand over the next decade include those critical for global leaders:

- Agile thinking skills (ability to consider and prepare for multiple scenarios, innovation, dealing with complexity and ambiguity, managing paradoxes, ability to see the "big picture")

- Interpersonal and communication skills (co-creativity and brain-storming, relationship building, teaming, collaboration, oral and written communication)
- Global operating skills (ability to manage diverse employees, understanding international markets, ability to work in multiple overseas locations, foreign language skills, cultural sensitivity).

Other leadership competencies have been suggested (e.g., Moran and Riesenberger 1994; Rosen et al. 2000). Many of these constructs overlap, and in integrating these approaches with my own experience and interviews with global executives, our model proposes the following set of global leadership competency essentials.

Intercultural Communication Skills

Accurate communication is challenging enough between two people with similar backgrounds and experiences; it can become extremely difficult for global managers without developing the required intercultural communication skills. As "senders" of communication messages, global managers need to understand that the content of their communication has to be clear, but that they also need to pay attention to the context of their communication (Arasaratnam 2014). This means paying attention not just to what they say but also how they say things—the non-verbals. As "receivers" of messages from their counterparts in other cultures, global managers need to build their listening skills.

Cultural Sensitivity

The skills to be able to build and maintain relationships with diverse individuals and groups from different countries are important to becoming an effective global leader. Bird et al. (2010)'s concept of emotional sensitivity, which refers to individuals' awareness of others' feelings, is also related to this competency. The dispositions of global mindset, especially acceptance and empathy, are important in developing this competency. As Shapiro et al. (2008) stated in their study of North American buyers with different levels of cross-cultural experience:

> Cultural sensitivity is an ability to environmentally scan and make sense of cross-cultural differences via... declarative, procedural, and situated

knowledge structures, and to use these understandings to enact culturally appropriate behavior such as mimicry, control, and role-playing. The highest levels of cultural sensitivity involve a form of reflexivity in which individuals forge transcultural understandings and critically apply these understandings to their own culture. (p. 82)

Learning Agility

On a recent trip to Boston, I met Brad, a young man who recently graduated with a major in Economics from an Ivy league university and who was working for a technology company, helping with lead generation of start-ups. As he was describing his job, which involved a lot of analytics and knowledge of mobile ads and internet applications, I asked him how much of what he was doing he had learned in college. He said almost none, since the field was so new and evolving very rapidly. However, the ability to learn quickly was a discipline and approach that he learned in school and that he believed continued to help him.

For recent graduates, there is no question that grades and subject matter expertise still matter. However, much of their knowledge acquired through coursework will more than likely either not be remembered or become obsolete in a few years' time. This is why Schmidt and Rosenberg (2014) have stated that one of the key selection criteria for recruiting candidates at their firms is their ability to learn. This desire and ability to learn from experience, and apply what is learned to different situations, is what researchers have identified as learning agility (Lombardo and Eichinger 2000). Based on the Lombardo and Eichinger research, Korn Ferry International, for example, has been assessing executives on their learning agility (De Meuse et al. 2008). Gary Burnison, chief executive of Korn/Ferry International stated[2]: "What we've seen through our research is that the No. 1 predictor of executive success is learning agility ... It comes down to people's willingness to grow, to learn, to have insatiable curiosity." DeRue et al. (2012) define learning agility as "the ability to come up to speed quickly in one's understanding of a situation and move across ideas flexibly in service of learning both within and across experiences." (p. 263).

There is evidence for the importance of learning agility as a factor among executives who derail, as well as in predicting future potential (DeRue et al. 2012; Eichinger and Lombardo 2004; Lombardo and Eichinger 2000). In identifying reasons for expatriate failure, research (e.g., Lee

2007; Tung 1987) shows that the ability to learn quickly and to adapt is an important factor influencing success or failure. Learning agility seems to be an important global leadership competency, given the complex and ambiguous situations that global leaders face.

A related construct is that of the ability to learn, although DeRue et al. (2012) have argued that learning agility is actually a component of this ability to learn. There is also research evidence on the importance of a general learning orientation in the workplace (e.g., Vandewalle 1997), with individuals having a high learning orientation tending to agree with statements such as the following:

- I am willing to select a challenging work assignment that I can learn a lot from.
- I seek out situations that might allow me to increase my knowledge or skills.

For expatriates and other types of global leaders, both learning agility and a learning orientation seem critical in adapting to different and ambiguous cross-cultural situations (Porter and Tansky 1999). Learning agility seems related to what Yunlu and Clapp-Smith (2014) refer to as metacognitive awareness—the ability to reflect upon, understand, and control one's learning. The conceptual difference seems to be that the latter emphasizes self-reflection, while the former emphasizes speed. Time for self-reflection is another of the transformational triggers for individuals living overseas (Clapp-Smith and Wernsing 2014). Learning agility is related to a flexibility disposition.

CONTEXT

Our model suggests that successful global leadership will to some extent depend on the fit between the individual and the environment. Individuals who have the foundational requirements, dispositions, and competencies could still fail if some of these contextual factors are not present or where the situational demands do not fit the individuals' strengths. This is consistent with Pfeffer and Sutton's (2006) view, who suggest that "a well-designed system filled with ordinary—but well-trained—people can consistently achieve stunning performance levels." (p. 96)

The specific factors in our model include the following:

- Organizational Climate/Support. To what extent does the organization provide an environment that encourages and supports the development of global mindset? An organization that is ethnocentric versus geocentric (Perlmutter 1969) will most likely not select or deliberately develop individuals who have global leadership capabilities. Similarly, McCall and Hollenbeck (2002) suggest that organizations providing timely support to global executives can help them not only through professional but also some personal challenges (e.g., family situation). In addition, the individual's direct manager can be an important factor in their success as a global leader. Providing these individuals with challenging opportunities, giving them timely feedback, and coaching them to improve their performance are some of the key behaviors that are critical.
- Development Experiences. McCall and Hollenbeck (2002) highlighted the importance of providing the right experiences to executives for their development as global leaders. Organizations can help provide some of these experiences through strategic global assignments and roles (e.g., starting a subsidiary in an overseas location, working with a joint venture partner in another country, leading a global project team). A global leader might not always have full control over these assignments, but seeking out these experiences and taking advantage of opportunities that are available, are important steps to take.
- Work/Situational Factors. Beyond these general organizational variables are factors more directly related to the individual. In Lane et al.'s (2009) formulation, they refer to these work/situational factors as "situational readiness." They include such factors as the willingness of the family and a concern with their elderly parents that global leaders, especially expatriates, might have. In an interview, Kim Taylor of J&J[3] describes arrangements that her company has made with some of her Asian regional leaders not to have to relocate in all cases, especially when these leaders have concerns with not disrupting their children's schooling or the care of their elderly parents. For global leaders with international assignments, these concerns could certainly impact their ability to adjust and be effective. In our model, situational factors also include work factors, such as job and role expectations. Assigning managers to take on jobs that require skill sets they cannot reasonably expect to acquire in the period of time while they are on assignment is a recipe for failure. In

one case, a manager who had strong project management expertise was assigned to lead a local team in a Middle Eastern country working on an important technology project. However, she did not have the necessary technical skills that the project required. In another case, a global manager with an introverted personality and who was very reflective found success working in Japan but when assigned to Australia, did not do as well. His Australian colleagues found it difficult to accept and trust someone who they perceived to be withdrawn and not expressing what was on his mind.

As Osland et al. (2009) have pointed out, there is a paucity of empirical literature in general on the subject of global leadership development. While this model proposes a set of contextual factors, the relative importance of each and their interaction with individuals' global leadership capabilities are topics for future researchers and practitioners. Note the study by Groysberg et al. (2004) mentioned earlier that strongly suggested the importance of certain contextual variables in the performance of "stars," especially around systems and processes.

In a related study, Groysberg et al. (2006) examined 20 high-level executives who were leaving one company (GE) to join another company at an even higher level of responsibility (e.g., Chairman, CEO). In their study, which covered the years 1989–2001, they found mixed results for what they called the portability of these executives; some were successful, others less so. For example, Robert Nardelli went to Home Depot and failed there; James McMerney went to 3M and thrived. Both were at some point considered to be potential successors to Jack Welch at GE.

Why GE? For many years, especially during Jack Welch's time, GE was well known as a breeding ground for leadership. (I know several executive recruiters who used to keep close tabs on up-and-coming GE managers because of the company's reputation for identifying and developing leadership talent.) What Groysberg and his colleagues found was that portability depended on a match between the executives' skills and the requirements of the new position in terms of four areas: strategy, industry, relationships, and culture/systems/processes. For example, companies' subsequent performance was better when those executives had strategic skills that were a good match with their new company's strategic requirements. If an executive's strengths were in cost-cutting but the new environment required skills in growing the business, the chances were that the executive would not perform as well. In other words, the portability of an executive (at least in the limited sample they studied) was a function of the match between the executives' strengths and the company's situation in these four areas: "The more closely the new environment matches the old, the greater the likelihood of success in the new position." Subsequent research by Fernandez-Araoz (2014) supports this idea that "origin and destination matter."

Will similar cautions apply to the portability of global managers who are assigned to different country subsidiaries? Or does having cultural sensitivity and a global mindset trump any potential mismatches in portability? A theme that Groysberg and others conducting research on portability have emphasized is the importance of context. A study of cardiac surgeons, for example (House and Pisano 2006) found that increases in the volume of their procedures at a specific hospital improved their performance but only at that hospital. The researchers concluded that an aspect of context, "the familiarity with the assets of a given organization," was in part responsible for their performance. For global managers working in different subsidiaries or with various global teams, such contextual factors might include the degree of cultural distance and familiarity with local networks.

As an example, several years ago, a multinational acquired a small business in an African country that was founded by a very successful entrepreneur. To help integrate this business with the company, it sent a British manager who I shall call Philip. He had been with the company for over 20 years, had been assigned to several overseas subsidiaries during that time, was highly experienced in operations, and was very familiar with the company's culture and processes. Unfortunately, Philip did not do well in his assignment. His constant clashes with the local founder and his attempts to run a command-and-control operation did not fit with the loose, free-wheeling culture of the local company. Using the Groysberg framework, there were mismatches in all of the four areas:

- Strategy. This was a situation that called for an executive with skills in blending together an entrepreneurial company with a massive global enterprise; Philip had never faced this kind of challenge before.
- Industry. As an emerging market, this country's regulatory environment was not sophisticated, consumers had little awareness of the brand that the global company represented, and the competition was mainly other local companies. These were unfamiliar challenges for Philip, and very different from what he had faced in the past.
- Relationships. Philip flew in "solo;" he had met the founder briefly but had no friends or allies in the company whom he could trust.

As a result, he had blinders on and was not able to get feedback or advice that could have helped him adjust his behavior and style.

• Company culture/systems/processes. Philip was used to working in a bureaucratic environment where processes were defined and well established. Nothing in his past experience prepared him for this situation.

While Groysberg's framework applies in this case, a certain level of cultural sensitivity and global mindset on Phil's part could have helped mitigate these risks. For example, being willing to learn about other cultures and building connections (two critical elements of global mindset) would have helped him understand the local company's industry and processes, as well as establish productive relationships. Assuming that companies have vetted their global managers on global mindset orientation, what if it is apparent that there will not be a good match? A company has three alternatives:

Find someone else in the company with a better match for the situation, while sending the manager to another country where there is a better match for him or her. This presupposes that the company has a pool of such managers and the capability to match them to the most appropriate situations. If not, at least find the closest matches.

Fix the manager by providing her with some counseling and coaching. A global manager who may not be familiar with the regulatory environment in the country she has been assigned to can prepare by learning from more experienced colleagues about what to watch out for, consulting with country experts, or doing a lot of homework.

Fix the situation to enhance a better match by sending the global manager to a subsidiary where she already has a network. For example, Emily was a global manager for a technology company who had led a global team whose members were primarily in India. When there was an opening for a manager to be assigned to the company's Indian subsidiary, she was the logical choice, and Emily was able to take advantage of the alliances that she had already built in the subsidiary to have a successful assignment there.

OUTCOMES

There are four types of outcomes that our model proposes are important in assessing the success of global leaders: personal, relationship, performance, and team/organizational. Much of the cross-cultural research on outcomes has focused on the adjustment of expatriates. These studies have suggested that between 10 and 70 % of expatriate assignments end in premature departure or underperformance (Clapp-Smith and Wernsing 2014). Hippler et al. (2014) analyzed data from a sample of 209 expatriates and have developed a measure of expatriate adjustment. Their scale includes factors such as the work environment, the job or task characteristics, work-life balance, and family life. They found positive relationships between their adjustment measure and self-rated performance. Peltokorpi and Froese (2012) propose a concept of cultural adjustment based on three dimensions: general, work and interaction.

These measures cover primarily the first two types of outcomes: personal and relationship. In other words, succeeding as a global leader means achieving personal outcomes such as personal and professional growth, and job satisfaction. It also means achieving good relationships with colleagues and people leaders are working with, especially those from different cultures. This is similar to the concept of interaction adjustment as proposed by Peltokorpi and Froese (2012).

Performance outcomes are also important for global leaders' success. These measures could be objective, for example, achieving certain performance goals, or more subjective, for example, manager ratings. Regardless, these outcomes are focused on specific job or role requirements. In addition, there are team outcomes that are important; they include areas such as whether the global leaders have been able to build an effective team, transferred knowledge to others, and have had a positive impact on the organization.

THE PERILS OF AUTHENTIC LEADERSHIP CROSS-CULTURALLY

Between our coaching calls, Naveen, an Indian vice president of a technology company based in Bangalore, diligently read the handful of articles I had assigned to him. In our next call, he seemed perplexed by the term "authentic leadership" that he had seen in a couple of the readings. What does it mean to be an authentic leader, he asked me. He had looked up the dictionary definition of authentic and its synonyms, which included genuine, real, not a fake. Nonetheless, he still seemed a bit confused. To be genuine and real with your team, how much do you have to "self-disclose" by letting them know about your strengths and weaknesses, your likes and dislikes? And does being genuine and real imply behaving and only using the leadership style that comes naturally to you?

Take an article by Goffee and Jones (2000). In that piece, they wrote that one of the qualities of inspirational leaders was that they revealed their weaknesses. "When leaders reveal their weaknesses, they show us who they are—warts and all. This may mean they're irritable on Monday mornings, that they are somewhat disorganized, or even rather shy. Such admissions work because people need to see leaders own up to some flaw before they participate willingly in an endeavor. Exposing a weakness establishes trust and thus helps get folks on board."

Part of Naveen's discomfort was a particular concern about the cultural appropriateness of such self-disclosure, especially in countries where the expectations of what an effective leader is may not include such complete transparency, at least initially. In fact, a couple of recent articles in *Harvard Business Review* suggest such caution in this regard. For example, Rosh and Offermann (2013) urge leaders to understand the organizational and cultural context before they self-disclose. Similarly, Ibarra (2015a) writes that many models of authentic leadership are particularly American, especially in the advice to tell a personal story about a hardship they have overcome. She points out that these are based on Western ideals of individualistic triumph over adversity.

In a recent study, Kokkoris and Kühnen (2014) examined how different cultures perceive "authenticity" in others based on their self-expression. The countries representing these cultures, Germany and China, are on different ends of the spectrum in terms of their individualistic and collectivistic orientation. An important facet of collectivism is contextualism, the extent to which the context is crucial in understanding other people. Easterners more than Westerners tend to consider the context when explaining behavior. On the other hand, in individualistic cultures such as Germany, dispositional information, such as the person's personal preferences, is more important. Therefore, according to these researchers, a person expressing both his likes and dislikes will be perceived to be more authentic by Westerners. They predicted that Germans learning about a person who expresses only his likes (culture-incongruent) would seek more dispositional information (culture-congruent), whereas Chinese learning about a person expressing both likes and likes (culture-incongruent) would seek more contextual information (culture-congruent) to better understand this person. Their sample consisted of 73 German students and 87 Chinese students in universities in Germany and China who were randomly assigned to two scenarios. In one scenario, they read about the likes and dislikes of a certain person named George (in Germany) or Yong (in China). In the other scenario, they read about his likes only.

The participants were then asked how much each of 12 statements described George (or Yong). These statements were based on a scale of authenticity developed by other researchers. A sample item was the following: George is true to himself in most situations. Finally, participants were asked how useful they would find each one of six additional pieces of information to get to know George better.

What did they find? In brief, the Germans found the person expressing both likes and dislikes to be more authentic than the person expressing only likes, whereas the opposite was true for the Chinese. Furthermore, Germans reading about a person expressing only his likes (culture-incongruent) would seek more dispositional information (culture-congruent), whereas Chinese reading about a person expressing both likes and likes (culture-incongruent) would seek more contextual information (culture-congruent) to better understand this person. The Chinese rated contextual information as more helpful to better understand a person expressing likes and dislikes than a person expressing only likes.

The choice for a leader is not necessarily whether or not to self-disclose but how much. Authentic leadership, as one of its pioneers Bill George (2008) has stated, is about practicing one's values and principles. In their surveys of over 75,000 leaders globally, Kouzes and Posner (2007) have pointed out that honesty is one of the four characteristics of admired leaders selected by their respondents in over 50 countries: "We simply don't trust people who can't or won't disclose a clear set of values, ethics and standards and live by them."

The following are some proposed principles for self-disclosure by global leaders. The first principle is to inform honestly. Whether you are talking about your accomplishments or your failures, embellishing them with exaggerations or half-truths will not work in the long term. We have all read about leaders who have padded their resumes or told stories about their past that, with a bit of fact-checking, turned out to be distorted. This does not mean that you cannot tell a good story about your past; indeed, good leaders will frame your experience in a way that helps them send a clear message to their team.

A second principle is to consider organizational and cultural norms in selecting what to disclose. Pay attention to these norms and make sure you do not violate them for they can quickly undermine your effectiveness as a leader. The research study cited above is simply one example of how different cultures react to what they perceive to be authentic behavior. As another example, some global organizations have cultivated very formal cultures, where employees dress very conservatively, managers and executives are addressed with their last names, and where meetings are run following strict guidelines. As a new leader from a different culture joining this organization, you may think that behaving this way is not being authentic, but behaving counter-culturally, at least initially, will not make you an effective leader in that organization.

A third principle is to consider your audience and, specifically, the relationship you have with your team and colleagues. Imagine calling a meeting with your new team, most of who have been with the company for a while, and confessing to them your skepticism at the extent to which people who have been in their jobs for a long time can adapt to change. An executive from outside the company who was brought in to head a business unit that had seen its profits and market share shrink, Martin made these comments in his first meeting with his direct reports. He had a hard time recovering from his misguided attempt at being authentic.

These principles should address Naveen's two questions above. Fundamentally, authentic leadership starts with having a deep understanding of yourself and how people perceive you. George (2008) and others (e.g., Goleman 2004) have written about the importance of self-awareness, and the challenges of arriving at this self-knowledge. Knowing your reputation and what others think about you, as well as the context or situation you find yourself in, are important. You may believe that you are being genuine, that you are acting as an authentic leader, but if others do not perceive you that way or where cultural norms go against your perceptions of authentic behavior, then there is a gap that you will need to address, and not simply dismiss it by saying, "I don't care what others think of me."

Developing a global mindset, and ultimately becoming an effective global leader, does not happen overnight. As Mendenhall (2006) has pointed out, "Developing global leadership competencies involves fundamental human transformation; it does not involve adding incrementally new techniques to one's managerial skill portfolio." (p. 425) Similarly, Osland et al. (2012) state: "It is likely that global leadership development is not a linear progression of adding competencies to an existing portfolio of leadership competencies, but rather a non-linear process whereby deep-seated change in competencies and world view takes place in the process of experiential overlays over time." (p. 242). It is important to point out, as

Tung (1987) has stated, that "a global mindset is not acquired or fostered overnight; rather, it takes time to nurture this orientation."

Some have suggested (McCall and Hollenbeck 2002) that the foundations of global mindset are actually laid during one's early years through cultural contacts and experiences. However, the research findings are mixed here, with some studies indicating that even managers who might not have had the extensive exposure to other cultures during childhood could become successful global leaders. Development of global mindset seems to be a virtuous cycle that consists of building self-awareness, practicing, and trying out new behaviors (and stepping out of one's comfort zone), getting feedback, and constantly being curious. These activities will tend to reinforce one another. The trigger for such development may very well be facing a situation that is very different than the past, and being unable to understand and/or figure out how to resolve it. A person who is "primed" to reflect and seek understanding will be in a better position to move forward more quickly in the journey to becoming a global leader.

NOTES

1. Paul Bloom, "Imagining the Lives of Others," The New York Times, June 7, 2015.
2. Lauren Weber, "What Boards Want in Executives," The Wall Street Journal, December 9, 2014.
3. Listen to the interview in ITunes: https://itunes.apple.com/us/podcast/leading-growth-in-asia/id635596651?mt=2

REFERENCES

Alshahrani, Saeed, and Michael Morley. 2015. Accounting for Variations in the Patterns of Mobility Among Conventional and Self-Initiated Expatriates. *The International Journal of Human Resource Management* 26(15): 1936–1954.

Andresen, Maike, Torsten Biemann, and Marshall Pattie. 2015. What Makes Them Move Abroad? Reviewing and Exploring Differences Between Self-Initiated and Assigned Expatriation. *The International Journal of Human Resource Management* 26(7): 932–947.

Ang, Soon, Linn Van Dyne, and Christine Koh. 2006. Personality Correlates of the Four-Factor Model of Cultural Intelligence. *Group & Organization Management* 31(1): 100–123.

Ang, Soon, Linn Van Dyne, Koh Christine, K. Yee Ng, Klaus Templer, Cheryl Tay, and Anand Chandrasekar. 2007. Cultural Intelligence: Its Measurement and

Effects on Cultural Judgment and Decision Making, Cultural Adaptation, and Task Performance. *Management and Organization Review* 3: 335–371.

Arasaratnam, Lily A. 2014. Ten Years of Research in Intercultural Communication Competence (2003–2013): A Retrospective. *Journal of Intercultural Communication* 35(7): 1–12.

Baron-Cohen, Simon, and Sally Wheelwright. 2004. The Empathy Quotient: An Investigation of Adults with Asperger Syndrome or High Functioning Autism, and Normal Sex Differences. *Journal of Autism and Developmental Disorders* 34(2): 163–175.

Barrick, Murray, and Michael Mount. 1991. The Big Five Personality Dimensions and Job Performance: A Meta-Analysis. *Personnel Psychology* 44: 1–26.

Beechler, Schon and Mansour Javidan. 2007. Leading with a Global Mindset. In *The Global Mindset: Advances in International Management*, vol 19, eds. M. Javidan, R. Steer, and M. Hitt, 131–170. Oxford: Elsevier.

Bhaskar-Shrinivas, Purnima, David A. Harrison, Margaret A. Shaffer, and Dora M. Luk. 2005. Input-Based and Time-Based Models of International Adjustment: Meta-Analytic Evidence and Theoretical Extensions. *Academy of Management Journal* 48(2): 257–281.

Bird, Allan, Joyce S. Osland, and Henry W. Lane. 2004. Global Competencies: An Introduction. In *The Blackwell Handbook of Global Management: A Guide to Managing Complexity*, eds. Henry Lane, Martha Maznevski, Mark Mendenhall, and Jeanne McNett, 57–80. Malden, MA: Blackwell Publishing.

Bird, Allan, Mark Mendenhall, Michael J. Stevens, and Gary Oddou. 2010. Defining the Content Domain of Intercultural Competence for Global Leaders. *Journal of Managerial Psychology* 25(8): 810–828.

Black, J. Stewart. 1988. Work Role Transitions: A Study of American Expatriate Managers in Japan. *Journal of International Business Studies* 19(2): 277–294.

Black, J. Stewart, and Gregory K. Stephens. 1989. The Influence of the Spouse on American Expatriate Adjustment and Intent to Stay in Pacific Rim Overseas Assignments. *Journal of Management* 15: 529–544.

Bossidy, Larry, and Ram Charan. 2011. *Execution: The Discipline of Getting Things Done*. New York: Crown Business.

Brewer, Marilynn B. 1996. When Contact is Not Enough: Social Identity and Intergroup Cooperation. *International Journal of Intercultural Relations* 20(3/4): 291–303.

Buchan, Nancy. 2009. The Complexity of Trust: Cultural Environments, Trust, and Trust Development. In *Cambridge Handbook of Culture, Organizations, and Work*, eds. Rabi Bhagat and Richard Steers, 373–417. New York: Cambridge University Press.

Caligiuri, Paula M. 2000. The Big Five Personality Characteristics as Predictors of Expatriate's Desire to Terminate the Assignment and Supervisor-Rated Performance. *Personnel Psychology* 53(1): 67–88.

Caligiuri, Paula M 2006. Developing Global Leaders. *Human Resource Management Review* 16(2): 219–228.

Caligiuri, Paula, and Ibraiz Tarique. 2012. Dynamic Cross-Cultural Competencies and Global Leadership Effectiveness. *Journal of World Business* 47(4): 612–622.

Chang, Wei Wen, Yu Hsi Yuang, and Ya Ting Chuang. 2011. The Relationship Between International Experience and Cross-Cultural Adaptability. *International Journal of Intercultural Relations* 37: 268–273.

Chen, Guo-Ming, and William Starosta. 2000. The Development and Validation of the Intercultural Sensitivity Scale. *Communication Communication* 3: 1–15.

Cheng, Chi-Ying, Fiona Lee, and Verónica Benet-Martínez. 2006. Assimilation and Contrast Effects in Cultural Frame Switching, Bicultural Identity Integration, and Valence of Cultural Cues. *Journal of Cross-Cultural Psychology* 37(6): 742–760.

Choi, Yongduk, and Dongseop Lee. 2013. Psychological Capital, Big Five Traits, and Employee Outcomes. *Journal of Managerial Psychology* 29(2): 122–140.

Clapp-Smith, Rachel, and Tara Wernsing. 2014. The Transformational Triggers of International Experiences. *Journal of Management Development* 33(7): 662–679.

Covey, Stephen. 1989. *The Seven Habits of Highly Effective People*. New York: Simon and Schuster.

Crockett, Walter H. 1965. Cognitive Complexity and Impression Formation. In *Progress in Experimental Personality Research*, vol 2, ed. B.A. Maher, 47–90. New York: Academic Press.

Crowley-Henry, Marian. 2007. The Protean Career: Exemplified by First World Foreign Residents in Western Europe? *International Studies of Management & Organization* 37(3): 44–64.

Davis, Mark H. 1994. *Empathy: A Social Psychological Approach*, vol X. Boulder, CO: Westview Press.

De Meuse, Kenneth, Guangrong Dai, George Hollenbeck, and King Yii Tang. 2008. *Global Talent Management: Using Learning Agility to Identify High Potentials Around the World*. Los Angeles, CA: Korn/Ferry International.

DeRue, D. Scott, Susan J. Ashford, and Christopher G. Myers. 2012. Learning Agility: In Search of Conceptual Clarity and Theoretical Grounding. *Industrial and Organizational Psychology* 5(3): 258–279.

Digman, John M. 1990. Personality Structure: Emergence of the Five-Factor Model. *Annual Review of Psychology* 41(1): 417–440.

Driskell, James E., Gerald F. Goodwin, Eduardo Salas, and Patrick G. O'Shea. 2006. What Makes a Good Team Player? Personality and Team Effectiveness. *Group Dynamics: Theory, Research, and Practice* 10: 249–271.

Dweck, Carol. 2006. *Mind Set: The New Psychology of Success*. New York: Random House.

Earley, Christopher, and Soon Ang. 2003. *Cultural Intelligence: Individual Interactions Across Cultures*. Palo Alto, CA: Stanford Business Books.

Eichinger, Robert W., and Michael M. Lombardo. 2004. Learning Agility as a Prime Indicator of Potential. *Human Resource Planning* 27(4): 12–16.

Eisenberg, Nancy, and Randy Lennon. 1983. Sex Differences in Empathy and Related Capacities. *Psychological Bulletin* 94: 100–131.

Epley, Nicholas. 2014. *Mindwise: How We Understand What Others Think, Believe, Feel, and Want*. New York: Knopf.

Epley, Nicholas, and Eugene Caruso. 2008. Perspective Taking: Misstepping into Others' Shoes. In *Handbook of Imagination and Mental Simulation*, eds. K.D. Markman et al. New York: Psychology Press.

Fee, Anthony, Sidney J. Gray, and Steven Lu. 2013. Developing Cognitive Complexity from the Expatriate Experience: Evidence from a Longitudinal Field Study. *International Journal of Cross Cultural Management* 13(3): 299–318.

Felício, J. Augusto, Vitor R. Caldeirinha, and Ricardo Rodrigues. 2012. Global Mindset and the Internationalization of Small Firms: The Importance of the Characteristics of Entrepreneurs. *International Entrepreneurship and Management Journal* 8(4): 467–485.

Fernandez-Araoz, Claudio. 2014. *It's Not the How or the What But the Who*. Boston: Harvard Business Review Press.

Furusawa, Masayuki, and Chris Brewster. 2015. The Bi-cultural Option for Global Talent Management: The Japanese/Brazilian Nikkeijin example. *Journal of World Business* 50(1): 133–143.

Galinsky, Adam D., and Gillian Ku. 2004. The Effects of Perspective-Taking on Prejudice: The Moderating Role of Self-Evaluation. *Personality and Social Psychology Bulletin* 30(5): 594–604.

Galinsky, Adam D., and Gordon B. Moskowitz. 2000. Perspective-Taking: Decreasing Stereotype Expression, Stereotype Accessibility, and in-Group Favoritism. *Journal of Personality and Social Psychology* 78(4): 708–724.

George, Bill. 2008. Ethics Must be Global, Not Local. *Bloomberg Business Week*, February 12. http://www.bloomberg.com/bw/stories/2008-02-12/ethics-must-be-global-not-localbusinessweek-business-news-stock-market-and-financial-advice

Gilin, Debra, William W. Maddux, Jordan Carpenter, and Adam D. Galinsky. 2013. When to Use Your Head and When to Use Your Heart the Differential Value of Perspective-Taking Versus Empathy in Competitive Interactions. *Personality and Social Psychology Bulletin* 39(1): 3–16.

Goffee, Robert, and Gareth Jones. 2000. Why Should Anyone Be Led by You? *Harvard Business Review*, September-October, 78(5): 72–79.

Goldsmith, Marshall, and Howard Morgan. 2004. Leadership Is a Contact Sport. *Strategy + Business* 36: 70–79.

Goleman, Daniel. 2004. What Makes a Leader? *Harvard Business Review* 82(1): 82–91.

———. 2005. *Emotional Intelligence.* New York: Bantam Books.

———. 2013. The Focused Leader. *Harvard Business Review* 91(12): 50–60.

Graf, Andrea, and Lynn K. Harland. 2005. Expatriate Selection: Evaluating the Discriminant, Convergent, and Predictive Validity of Five Measures of Interpersonal and Intercultural Competence. *Journal of Leadership & Organizational Studies* 11(2): 46–62.

Gregersen, Hal B., Allen J. Morrison, and J. Stewart Black. 1998. Developing Leaders for the Global Frontier. *MIT Sloan Management Review* 40(1): 21–32.

Griffin, Dale W., and Lee Ross. 1991. Subjective Construal, Social Inference, and Human Misunderstanding. In *Advances in Experimental Social Psychology*, vol 24, 319–359. San Diego, CA: Academic Press.

Groysberg, Boris. 2008. How Star Women Build Portable Skills. *Harvard Business Review* 86(2): 74–81.

Groysberg, Boris, Ashish Nanda, and Nitin Nohria. 2004. The Risky Business of Hiring Stars. *Harvard Business Review* 82(5): 92–100.

Groysberg, Boris, Andrew N. McLean, and Nitin Nohria. 2006. Are Leaders Portable? *Harvard Business Review* 84(5): 92–100.

Gupta, Anil K., and Vijay Govindarajan. 2002. Cultivating a Global Mindset. *The Academy of Management Executive* 16(1): 116–126.

Hammer, Mitchell R., Milton J. Bennett, and Richard Wiseman. 2003. Measuring Intercultural Sensitivity: The Intercultural Development Inventory. *International Journal of Intercultural Relations* 27(4): 421–443.

Heifetz, Ronald A., and Martin Linsky. 2002. *Leadership on the Line: Staying Alive Through the Dangers of Leading.* Boston: Harvard Business Press.

Hippler, Thomas, Paula M. Caligiuri, Johanna E. Johnson, and Nataliya Baytalskaya. 2014. The Development and Validation of a Theory-Based Expatriate Adjustment Scale. *The International Journal of Human Resource Management* 25(14): 1938–1959.

House, Robert S., and Gary P. Pisano. 2006. The Firm Specificity of Individual Performance: Evidence from Cardiac Surgery. *Management Science* 52(4): 473–488.

Hoffman, Martin L 1993. The Contribution of Empathy to Justice and Moral judgment. In *Readings in Philosophy and Cognitive Science*, ed. Alvin I. Goldman, 647–680. Cambridge, MA: MIT Press.

Hogan, Robert, and Joyce Hogan. 2001. Assessing Leadership: A View From the Dark Side. *International Journal of Selection and Assessment* 9(1–2): 40–51.

Holt, Katherine, and Kyoko Seki. 2012. Global Leadership: A Developmental Shift for Everyone. *Industrial and Organizational Psychology* 5(2): 196–215.

Hong, Hae-Jung. 2010. Bicultural Competence and Its Impact on Team Effectiveness. *International Journal of Cross Cultural Management* 10(1): 93–120.

Huff, Kyle. 2013. Language, Cultural Intelligence and Expatriate Success. *Management Research Review* 36(6): 596–612.

Huff, Lenard, and Lane Kelley. 2003. Levels of Organizational Trust in Individualist Versus Collectivist Societies. *Organization Science* 14(1): 81–90.

Hyung Park, Joon, Je'Anna Lea Abbott, and Steve Werner. 2014. A Perspective-taking Model for Global Assignments. *Journal of Global Mobility* 2(3): 280–297.

Ibarra, Herminia. 2015a. The Authenticity Paradox. *Harvard Business Review* 93(1/2): 53–59.

Ickes, William, Paul Gesn, and T. Tiffany Graham. 2000. Gender Differences in Empathic Accuracy: Differential Ability or Differential Motivation? *Personal Relationships* 7(1): 95–109.

Javidan, Mansour, and David Bowen. 2013. The 'Global Mindset' of Managers: What It Is, Why It Matters, and How to Develop It. *Organizational Dynamics* 42(2): 145–155.

Javidan, Mansour, and Mary Teagarden. 2011. Conceptualizing and Measuring Global Mindset. In *Advances in Global Leadership,* vol 6, eds. Mobley, William, Ming Li, and Ying Wang, 13–40. Bingley: Emerald Group.

Johnson, Simon, John McMillan, and Christopher Woodruff. 2002. Courts and Relational Contracts. *Journal of Law, Economics, and Organization* 18(1): 221–277.

Kashdan, Todd B., Paul Rose, and Frank D. Fincham. 2004. Curiosity and Exploration: Facilitating Positive Subjective Experiences and Personal Growth Opportunities. *Journal of Personality Assessment* 82(3): 291–305.

Kelley, Coleen, and Judith Meyers. 1995. *Cross-Cultural Adaptability Inventory.* Minneapolis, MN: National Computer Systems.

Kim, Kwanghyun, Bradley Kirkman, and Gilad Chen. 2008. Cultural Intelligence and International Assignment Effectives: A Conceptual Model and Preliminary Findings. In *Handbook of Cultural Intelligence: Theory, Measurement, and Applications,* eds. Soon Ang and Linn Van Dyne, 71–90. Armonk, NY: M.E. Sharpe.

Klein, Kristi, and Sara Hodges. 2000. Gender Differences, Motivation, and Empathic Accuracy: When it Pays to Understand. *Personality and Social Psychology Bulletin* 27(6): 720–730.

Koester, Jolene, and Margaret Olebe. 1988. The Behavioral Assessment Scale for Intercultural Communication Effectiveness. *International Journal of Intercultural Relations* 12(3): 233–246.

Kokkoris, Michail D., and Ulrich Kühnen. 2014. 'Express the Real You': Cultural Differences in the Perception of Self-Expression as Authenticity. *Journal of Cross-Cultural Psychology* 45(8): 1221–1228.

Kouzes, Jim, and Barry Posner. 2007. *The Leadership Challenge*, Fourth edn. New York: Wiley.

Krznaric, Roman. 2014. *Empathy: Why It Matters, and How to Get It*. New York: Perigree Books.

Lakshman, Chandrashekar. 2013. Biculturalism and Attributional Complexity: Cross-Cultural Leadership Effectiveness. *Journal of International Business Studies* 44(9): 922–940.

Lamm, Claus, Andrew N. Meltzoff, and Jean Decety. 2009. How Do We Empathize with Someone Who Is Not Like Us? A Functional Magnetic Resonance Imaging Study. *Journal of Cognitive Neuroscience* 22(2): 362–376.

Lane, Henry, Martha Maznevski, Joseph DiStefano, and Joerg Dietz. 2009. *International Management Behavior: Leading with a Global Mindset*, Sixth edn. Great Britain: Wiley.

Lawrence, Emma, P. Shaw, D. Baker, Simon Baron-Cohen, and A.S. David. 2004. Measuring Empathy: Reliability and Validity of the Empathy Quotient. *Psychological Medicine* 34: 911–924.

Lee, Hung-Wen. 2007. Factors that Influence Expatriate Failure: An Interview Study. *International Journal of Management* 24(3): 403–413.

Lee, Sujin, Wendi L. Adair, and Seong-Jee Seo. 2013. Cultural Perspective Taking in Cross-Cultural Negotiation. *Group Decision and Negotiation* 22(3): 389–405.

Leone, Luigi, Karen I. Van der Zee, Jan Pieter van Oudenhoven, Marco Perugini, and Anna Paola Ercolani. 2005. The Cross-Cultural Generalizability and Validity of the Multicultural Personality Questionnaire. *Personality and Individual Differences* 38(6): 1449–1462.

Levy, Orly, Schon Beechler, Sully Taylor, and Nakiye A. Boyacigiller. 2007. What We Talk About When We Talk about 'Global Mindset': Managerial Cognition in Multinational Corporations. *Journal of International Business Studies* 38(2): 231–258.

Lisak, Alon, and Miriam Erez. 2015. Leadership Emergence in Multicultural Teams: The Power of Global Characteristics. *Journal of World Business* 50(1): 3–14.

Lombardo, Michael M., and Robert W. Eichinger. 2000. High Potentials as High Learners. *Human Resource Management* 39(4): 321–329.

Luthans, Fred, and Carolyn M. Youssef. 2007. Emerging Positive Organizational Behavior. *Journal of Management* 33(3): 321–349.

Luthans, Fred. 2002. The Need for and Meaning of Positive Organizational Behavior. *Journal of Organizational Behavior* 23(6): 695–706.

Luthans, Fred, and Carolyn M. Youssef. 2007. Emerging Positive Organizational Behavior. *Journal of Management* 33(3): 321–349.

Luthans, Fred, Carolyn M. Youssef-Morgan, and Bruce J. Avolio. 2015. *Psychological Capital and Beyond*. New York: Oxford University Press.

Martin, Roger. 2007. How Successful Leaders Think. *Harvard Business Review*.

Martinez, Veronica, Janxin Leu, Fiona Lee, and Michael Morris. 2002. Negotiating Biculturalism: Cultural Frame Switching in Biculturals with Oppositional

Versus Compatible Cultural Identities. *Journal of Cross-Cultural Psychology* 33(5): 492–516.

McCall, Morgan, and George Hollenbeck. 2002. *Developing Global Executives: The Lessons of International Experience.* Boston, MA: Harvard Business School Press.

McCloskey, Michael, Kyle Behymer, and Elizabeth Papautsky. 2010. A Developmental Model of Cross-Cultural Competence at the Tactical Level. United States Army Research Institute: Technical Report 1278, November.

McCrae, Robert R., and Paul T. Costa Jr. 2008. The Five-Factor Theory of Personality. In *Handbook of Personality: Theory and Research*, Third, eds. Oliver Johns, Richard Robins, and Lawrence Pervin, 159–181. New York: The Guilford Press.

Melloni, Margherita, Vladimir Lopez, and Agustin Ibanez. 2014. Empathy and Contextual Social Cognition. *Cognitive, Affective and Behavioral Neuroscience* 14: 407–425.

Mendenhall, Mark E. 2006. The Elusive, Yet Critical Challenge of Developing Global Leaders. *European Management Journal* 24(6): 422–429.

Molinsky, Andy. 2013. *Global Dexterity: How to Adapt Your Behavior Across Cultures Without Losing Yourself in the Process.* Boston: Harvard Business Review Press.

Morrison, Allen. 2001. Integrity and Global Leadership. *Journal of Business Ethics* 31(1): 65–76.

Moran, Robert, and J. John Riesenberger. 1994. *The Global Challenge: Building the New Worldwide Enterprise.* New York: McGraw-Hill.

Mussel, Patrick. 2013. Introducing the Construct Curiosity for Predicting Job Performance. *Journal of Organizational Behavior* 34(4): 453–472.

Nina Nummela, Sami Saarenketo and Kaisu Puumalainen. 2004. A Global Mindset – A Prerequisite to Successful Internationalization? *Canadian Journal of Administrative Sciences* 21(1): 51–64.

Orbell, John, Robyn Dawes, and Peregrine Schwartz-Shea. 1994. Trust, Social Categories, and Individuals: The Case of Gender. *Motivation and Emotion* 18(2): 109–128.

Osland, Joyce S. 2008. An Overview of the Global Leadership Literature. In *Global Leadership: Research, Practice, and Development*, eds. Mark Mendendhall, Joyce Osland, Allan Bird, Gary Oddou, and Martha Maznevski, 34–63. New York: Routledge.

Osland, Joyce, Sully Taylor, and Mark Mendenhall. 2009. Global leadership progress and challenges. In *Cambridge Handbook of Culture, Organizations, and Work*, eds. Rabi Bhagat and Richard Steers, 245–271. New York: Cambridge University Press.

Osland, Joyce, Allan Bird, and Mark Mendenhall. 2012. Developing Global Mindset and Global Leadership Capabilities. In *Handbook of Research in International Human Resource Management*, Second edn, eds. Günter Stahl,

Ingmar Bjorkman, and Shad Morris, 220–252. Northampton, MA: Edward Elgar.

Oxford Economics. 2012. Global Talent 2021: How the New Geography of Talent Will Transform Human Resource Strategies. http://www.oxfordeconomics.com/Media/Default/Thought percent20Leadership/global-talent-2021.pdf

Peltokorpi, Vesa, and Fabian J. Froese. 2012. The Impact of Expatriate Personality traits on cross-cultural adjustment: A study with Expatriates in Japan. *International Business Review* 21(4): 734–746.

Perlmutter, Howard V. 1969. The Tortuous Evolution of the Multinational Corporation. *Columbia Journal of World Business* 4(1): 9–18.

Pfeffer, Jeffrey, and Robert I. Sutton. 2006. *Hard Facts, Dangerous Half-Truths, and Total Nonsense: Profiting from Evidence-Based Management.* Boston: Harvard Business Press.

Porter, Gayle, and Judith W. Tansky. 1999. Expatriate Success May Depend on a 'Learning Orientation': Considerations for Selection and Training. *Human Resource Management* 38(1): 47–60.

Ramalu, Subramaniam Sri, Raduan Che Rose, Naresh Kumar, and Jegak Uli. 2012. Cultural Intelligence and Expatriate Performance in Global Assignment: The Mediating Role of Adjustment. *International Journal of Business and Society* 13(1): 19–31.

Rhinesmith, Stephen. 1996. *A Manager's Guide to Globalization: Six Skills for Success in a Changing World*, Second edn. New York: McGraw-Hill.

Rizzolatti, Giacomo, Leonardo Fogassi, and Vittorio Gallese. 2006. Mirrors In The Mind. *Scientific American* 295(5): 54–61.

Roberge, Marie-Elene. 2013. A Multi-Level Conceptualization of Empathy to Explain How Diversity Increases Group Performance. *International Journal of Business and Management* 8(3): 122–133.

Rosen, Robert, Patricia Digh, Marshall Singer, and Carl Phillips. 2000. *Global Literacies: Lessons on Business Leadership and National Cultures.* New York: Simon & Schuster.

Rosh, Lisa, and Lynn Offermann. 2013. Be Yourself, but Carefully. *Harvard Business Review* 91: 135–139.

Schmidt, Eric, and Jonathan Rosenberg. 2014. *How Google Works.* New York: Grand Central Publishing.

Shaffer, Margaret A., David A. Harrison, Gregersen Hal, J. Stewart Black, and Lori A. Ferzandi. 2006. You Can Take It with You: Individual Differences and Expatriate Effectiveness. *Journal of Applied Psychology* 91(1): 109–125.

Shapiro, Jon M., Julie L. Ozanne, and Bige Saatcioglu. 2008. An Interpretive Examination of the Development of Cultural Sensitivity in International Business. *Journal of International Business Studies* 39(1): 71–87.

Smith, Adam. 2006. Cognitive Empathy and Emotional Empathy in Human Behavior and Evolution. *The Psychological Record* 56(1): 3–21.

Stahl, Günter K., and Mary Brannen. 2013. Building Cross-Cultural Leadership Competence: An Interview With Carlos Ghosn. *Academy of Management Learning & Education* 12(3): 494–502.

Staub, Ervin. 1990. Commentary on Part I. In *Empathy and Its Development*, eds. Nancy Eisenberg and Janet Strayer, 218–244. Cambridge, England: Cambridge University Press.

Steers, Richard M., Carlos Sanchez-Runde, and Luciara Nardon. 2012. Leadership in a Global Context: New Directions in Research and Theory Development. Journal of World Business 47(4): 479–482.

Story, Joana, John E. Barbuto, Fred Luthans, and James A. Bovaird. 2014. Meeting the Challenges of Effective International HRM: Analysis of the Antecedents of Global Mindset. *Human Resource Management* 53(1): 131–155.

Streufert, Siegfried. 1970. Complexity and Complex Decision Making: Convergences Between Differentiation and Integration Approaches to the Prediction of Task Performance. *Journal of Experimental Social Psychology* 6(4): 494–509.

Takeuchi, Riki, Paul E. Tesluk, Seokhwa Yun, and David P. Lepak. 2005. An Integrative View of International Experience. *Academy of Management Journal* 48(1): 85–100.

Tarique, Ibraiz, and Riki Takeuchi. 2008. Developing Cultural Intelligence: The Roles of International Nonwork Experiences. In *Handbook of Cultural Intelligence: Theory, Measurement, and Applications*, eds. Soon Ang and Linn Van Dyne, 56–70. Armonk, NY: M.E. Sharpe.

Tharenou, Phyllis. 2003. The Initial Development of Receptivity to Working Abroad: Self-Initiated International Work Opportunities in Young Graduate Employees. *Journal of Occupational and Organizational Psychology* 76(4): 489–515.

Thomas, David C., Mary Yoko Brannen, and Dominie Garcia. 2010. Bicultural Individuals and Intercultural Effectiveness. *European Journal of Cross-Cultural Competence and Management* 1(4): 315–333.

Tung, Rosalie L. 1987. Expatriate Assignments: Enhancing Success and Minimizing Failure. *Academy of Management Executive* 1(2): 117–125.

Van Dyne, Linn, Soon Ang, and Christine Koh. 2008. Development and Validation of the CS: The Cultural Inelligence Scale. In *Handbook of Cultural Intelligence: Theory, Measurement, and Applications*, eds. Soon Ang and Linn Van Dyne. Armonk, NY: M.E. Sharpe.

Van der Zee, Karen, Jan Pieter van Oudenhoven, Joseph G. Ponterotto, and Alexander W. Fietzer. 2013. Multicultural Personality Questionnaire:

Development of a Short Form. *Journal of Personality Assessment* 95(1): 118–124.

Vandewalle, Don. 1997. Development and Validation of a Work Domain Goal Orientation Instrument. *Educational and Psychological Measurement* 57(6): 995–1015.

Van Hoorn, André. 2015. Individualist–Collectivist Culture and Trust Radius: A Multilevel Approach. *Journal of Cross-Cultural Psychology* 46(2): 269–276.

Vogelgesang, Gretchen, Rachel Clapp-Smith, and Joyce Osland. 2014. The Relationship Between Positive Psychological Capital and Global Mindset in the Context of Global Leadership. *Journal of Leadership & Organizational Studies* 21(2): 165–178.

Wang, Cynthia, Kenneth Tai, Ku Gilliam, and Adam Galinsky. 2014. Perspective-Taking Increases Willingness to Engage in Intergroup Contact. *PLOS One* 9(1): 1–8.

Ward, Colleen, and Ronald Fischer. 2008. Personality, Cultural intelligence, and Cross-Cultural Adaptation. In *Handbook of Cultural Intelligence: Theory, Measurement, and Applications*, eds. Soon Ang and Linn Van Dyne, 159–176. Armonk, NY: M.E. Sharpe.

Welch, Jack ,and Suzy Welch. 2015. *The Real Life MBA: Your No-BS Guide to Winning the Game, Building a Team, and Growing Your Career*. New York: Harper Business.

Wiseman, Theresa. 1996. A Concept Analysis of Empathy. *Journal of Advanced Nursing* 23(6): 1162–1167.

World Values Study Group. 1994. *World Values Survey, 1981–1984 and 1990–1993*. Ann Arbor, MI: Inter-University Consortium for Political and Social Research.

Yavas, Ugur, and Muzaffer Bodur. 1999. Satisfaction among Expatriate Managers: Correlates and Consequences. *Career Development International* 4(5): 261–269.

Ye, Shengquan, Ting Kin Ng, Kin Hang Yim, and Jun Wang. 2015. Validation of the Curiosity and Exploration Inventory–II (CEI–II) Among Chinese University Students in Hong Kong. *Journal of Personality Assessment* 97(4): 403–410.

Youssef, Carolyn M., and Fred Luthans. 2012. Positive Global Leadership. *Journal of World Business* 47(4): 539–547.

Yunlu, Dilek Gulistan, and Rachel Clapp-Smith. 2014. Metacognition, Cultural Psychological Capital and Motivational Cultural Intelligence. *Cross Cultural Management: An International Journal* 21(4): 386–399.

Zak, Paul. 2012. *The Moral Molecule: The New Science of What Makes Us Good and Evil*. London: Bantam Press.

CHAPTER 7

Building Global Leadership for Individuals: Implications for Practice

The research studies covered, along with our interviews, suggest a number of implications for the practice of successful global leadership. In this chapter, we will consider nine such practices. The first two focus on self-awareness; the next five on different elements of global mindset; and the last two on building specific competencies or skill sets.

All of these practices involve a combination of active and passive learning, with an emphasis on the former. As Ibarra (2015b) has suggested, sometimes it is more effective to act and behave (practice and experience) than to think before acting. The focus of these practices is on the individual taking initiative; in the next chapter, I will cover the implications of the research and interviews on organizational practices.

1. Make a life-long commitment to develop yourself and learn from others.
2. Expand your cultural self-awareness.
3. Take steps to get out of your comfort zone.
4. Understand before judging.
5. Show boundless curiosity.
6. Develop empathy.
7. Maintain your ethical core.
8. Learn to integrate differences.
9. Build your global team player skill set.

© The Editor(s) (if applicable) and The Author(s) 2016
R. Henson, *Successful Global Leadership*,
DOI 10.1057/978-1-137-58990-3_7

PRACTICE #1: MAKE A LIFE-LONG COMMITMENT TO DEVELOP YOURSELF AND LEARN FROM OTHERS

Ernesto is a Mexican who comes from a very wealthy family and whose father is an executive in one of the country's largest corporations. He went to a US Ivy League school for his college education, and easily got a job working for a telecommunications company in Mexico City. On returning to Mexico after his college years, Ernesto joined the country club and the local alumni network to continue to associate with Mexicans and other expatriates who went to the same school as he did. As a research analyst in his company, Ernesto spends most of the day analyzing data, examining competitive trends, and attending meetings with his bosses. He sees himself as moving up in the company and eventually getting promoted to an executive position, if not in this company then in some other. Ernesto spends very little of his time interacting with the "lower classes" in Mexico and does not see much value in learning from them.

Vicente, another Mexican, also went to the USA for his college education, and now works for a consumer products company in Monterrey. His mindset is very different from Ernesto's. Vicente believes that he still has a lot to learn, and he believes that he can learn from many different people, especially those who have been with the company for a long time. He is not hesitant in approaching production people on the plant floor and asking them questions.

These two examples provide a study in contrast to the different approaches people take to development and learning, especially the opportunities for learning from different sources.

Developing yourself and learning from others imply that you not only have a desire to learn more about yourself but that you also have an awareness that there is a lot you don't know and that you need to learn from others. Furthermore, those who are effective in learning from others know how to ask questions, to listen, and to reach out and get information from multiple sources. This commitment to developing oneself implies a degree of self-awareness that is an important antecedent in developing one's global leadership.

Learning from others is especially challenging for managers as they move up the ranks. When many of them reach positions of power, especially executive positions in companies, these individuals not only tend to hear mostly positive news but are also surrounded by other managers who continually praise them for their knowledge and wisdom. Without being fully aware of this, executives become more isolated and are less likely to listen to those who may have contrary views. They start believing their own press, and become less interested in learning from others—especially their customers. When these executives work across borders, such as in overseas assignments, this mindset is likely to carry over, and their opportunity for learning from others cross-culturally diminishes.

Wiseman (2014) has suggested that with work cycles spinning faster, and with knowledge quickly becoming obsolete, we need to adopt more of a "rookie" mindset. She identifies four rookie mindset modes—the backpacker, the hunter-gatherer, the firewalker, and the pioneer—and her book provides details on each of these modes. Her overall message is that we all need to think and act like "perpetual" rookies. She is not suggesting that prior knowledge and experience are useless, but that we remain open and eager to learn. She provides suggestions for actions that each of the types can take. For example, for the hunter-gatherer mode, she suggests talking to strangers to expand your network and perspective. Of course, talking to strangers may not be a helpful strategy when you are traveling in some areas of an unfamiliar country.

However, the suggestion of recognizing that there are many sources of information that can be helpful, and that you need to be intrepid and open in seeking them out, is a good one. I am surprised at the information I pick up from taxi drivers when I get into a cab from the airport to my hotel in the course of my travels. When I was in Vietnam, for example, I learned that my taxi driver was actually a solider for the South Vietnamese army during the Vietnam War, and we had a fascinating conversation about his experiences and the views of the Vietnamese people about the war and about their economy. In Singapore, I spoke to a taxi driver who was nearing retirement age, and he spoke about his experiences with his country's independence, the current economic situation, and his dreams of retiring to mainland China in a couple of years.

Now these are not expert opinions, but occasionally starting conversations with strangers and even front-line workers provides you with an on-the-ground view of the feelings people have, especially about the economy and the political situation in their country. As Clapp-Smith and Wernsing (2014) have found, interacting with others from different cultural backgrounds is one of the transformational experiences of people living overseas.

A valuable source of learning within a company comes from what researchers refer to as "connectors" (Cross and Prusak 2002), individuals who may not necessarily have lofty job titles or are in senior management but who have an extensive network of people internally who they can connect with and who they can also connect with each other. Some of these connectors have been with the company for a while, and they know a great deal about the culture and the history of the company—important contextual knowledge that someone new to the company would find very helpful. They are also helpful in building your organizational savvy. Front-line workers are another great source; these could be production workers, sales representatives, or plant employees, some of whom have frequent contacts with customers or suppliers.

Learning from others includes getting feedback from them about your-self. According to Stone et al. (2010), those who seek critical feedback tend to get higher performance ratings. They point to at least two reasons for this. One, when you're getting feedback, you find out what you need to do better. You can ask questions that will help your understanding, and you can start to work on how to get better at something. Two, you send a message that you are not only interested in what others have to say but that you are also humble enough to listen to critical feedback. This can influence others' perceptions of you as someone who is open to change and willing to listen to others. Goldsmith and Morgan's (2004) research involving more than 11,000 leaders and 86,000 of their co-workers from eight major corporations concluded that leaders who ask, listen, learn, and consistently follow up are seen as more effective leaders.

Here are some strategies for implementing this practice:

- Periodically conduct an in-depth self-assessment. This is not always easy for we have a tendency to hold a cognitive bias called the "better-than-average-effect." There are many examples of this from research over the years (Alicke et al. 1995; Kruger 1999; Larrick et al. 2007). For example, over 90 % of drivers believe that they are in the top 50 % in driving ability. In his workshops, management consultant Marshall Goldsmith (Goldsmith 2007) sometimes asks people in the audience (most of whom are managers and executives) to raise their hands if they believe they are in the top 10 % of per-formers in their company. Typically, over 50 % of the audience raises their hands (of course, it is possible that Goldsmith's audience is not a random sample, and that it is likely that his audience may indeed be among the top performers in their organization). In a study of pris-oners, even this population rated themselves better than the average inmate and better than the non-prison community on a number of traits, such as being moral, trustworthy, honest, and compassionate (Sedikides et al. 2014).

We need to acknowledge therefore that we all have this tendency to view ourselves in a more favorable light than we should. This may be good for our self-confidence but may prevent us from doing what we need to do to improve ourselves if we start believing that we are better than average and therefore don't really need to change. As mentioned previously, this is a challenge especially for very successful executives.

In this self-assessment, it is important therefore to seek feedback from others. You want to be able to approach someone who has your best interests at heart, and who does not have a personal agenda. Start by making a short list of people in your life (both inside and outside of work) who you believe you can trust because they have integrity, can keep confidences, have good judgment, and seem to care for your interests. Perhaps this list will include a spouse or significant other, or a former boss. Schedule a time with them individually to get their feedback and advice. Make sure you probe and ask questions, and have them give you examples of what they mean if they make general statements (e.g., "Sometimes you come across as arrogant"). Above all, do not get defensive nor try to justify your past behavior should they bring it up. Listen, take notes, and thank them for their time and candor. Some managers use someone they trust from their human resources department, or an external coach, to provide them with honest feedback.

Look for broad themes in the feedback you have received over the years from different sources. Are there any common themes? What were the one or two strengths across these different settings that stood out? What about weaknesses; did you have the same weaknesses in school as you do today, or do you have some different ones?

Buckingham and Clifton (2001) point out that "you will excel only by maximizing your strengths, never by fixing your weaknesses." They do argue not to ignore your weaknesses but to find ways to manage around your weaknesses. The examples they give are of individuals who got others to help them complement their weak points. For managers, this might mean hiring people on their team who complement skills and attributes they lack that are important for the success of their group. For an analytical individual, this might mean working with someone who is intuitive and creative.

What if the weakness cannot be compensated for by others, and the characteristic in which that individual is weak is critical to executive success? As an analogy, Buckingham and Clifton cite Cole Porter, a very talented songwriter who, according to them, unfortunately wrote very weak plots for his musicals. Still, for these researchers, his words and melodies were so outstanding that it almost did not matter who was singing them or why. It is true that Porter wrote some flops, but he also wrote quite a number of hit musicals such as *Kiss Me Kate* and *Can-Can*.

I once coached a manager who I will call Steve. Steve had an MBA from a top-tier business school, and a background in Finance. He was very talented in his field, and was considered a high potential in the company where he was working. He had one major flaw: he was afraid of speaking in public, and was not at all a polished speaker. I advised Steve not to ignore this weakness if he wanted to eventually become the chief financial officer (CFO) of a major corporation. Regardless of how good his other strengths were, being a C-suite player today requires very good communication skills. You don't have to be a master orator, but you have to be good enough to communicate with your team, people within your company, with investors, and with the public. And you cannot rely on others or on your staff to complement this weakness; you have to overcome it yourself. Winston Churchill, Tiger Woods and Jack Welch[1] were stutterers, and yet somehow they overcame this deficiency to become more than decent public speakers.

Steve realized that he could not just compensate for his lack of public-speaking skills by become a world-class finance person. He had to work on this weakness so he could become at least adequate as a public speaker. The lesson here is to build on your strengths but at the same time, not ignore those weaknesses that may prevent you from reaching your career or professional goals. You don't have to be world class in overcoming those weaknesses, but be "good enough" so these do not undermine you.

Developing yourself also means making an effort to be good at your work or at your craft. This is what Ericsson et al. (1993) refer to as "deliberate practice, which they defines as 'activities designed, typically by a teacher, for the sole purpose of effectively improving specific aspects of an individual's performance."

Ericsson and his colleagues have studied the differences between those who are the best in their field (e.g., musicians, chess players) and those who are good but not outstanding. One variable that was not a differentiator was the number of hours spent practicing. Gladwell (2008) has suggested the 10,000-hour rule—that for someone to be an expert, one has to practice for about 10,000 hours. In his view, what seemed to matter was the amount of deliberate practice. Newport (2012) describes this well: (Deliberate practice) is "where you deliberately stretch your abilities beyond where you're comfortable and then receive ruthless feedback on your performance" (p. 101).

There has been quite a bit of debate about the 10,000-hour rule, the role of aptitude or natural ability, and what deliberate practice means. There is no question that to be good or expert at something, you have to practice and put in the time. The 10,000-hour rule is an average so there will be some variability depending on a number of factors, including the natural ability of the person and the nature of the endeavor. Someone who already has an aptitude for math will more than likely spend fewer than 10,000 hours reaching a certain level than someone who does not have the same aptitude.

I can practice the piano four hours a day for ten years and I could never be the next Vladimir Horowitz or Lang Lang. A manager who has an affinity for people and has a natural curiosity will find it easier to become an effective global leader than someone who struggles to connect with people.

In addition, as Rosenzweig (2014) points out, it may be that deliberate practice is more suited to some types of activities, like hitting a tennis ball with your forehand or playing a short musical piece on the piano. When the activity is of short duration, when feedback is immediate, when the order of the tasks in the activity is sequential (vs. concurrent), and when performance is absolute (vs. relative), then deliberate practice tends to be more useful than not. Rosenzweig gives the example of a cosmetics salesperson going door to door, where deliberate practice would help because these conditions are present.

Does learning how to become a global manager fall into the less useful category? On the surface, it would appear to be that way. After all, the duration is long, the feedback is slow, activities can be concurrent, and a global manager's performance might be compared to others'. However, by breaking a global manager's tasks and activities and focusing on specific sets of activities, global managers could benefit from deliberate practice. Take Youseff, a global manager I was coaching who wanted to improve his ability to lead global meetings (an important set of tasks for global leaders). We broke down his overall goal into specific sub-tasks, such as developing clear agendas and running meetings effectively. He identified the specific meetings where he wanted to practice his meeting skills, and solicited feedback from the team both during the meeting and after the meeting (in one-on-one discussions). He designed a short checklist of questions to ask members about their satisfaction with the meetings, and so was able to measure short-term performance. Over time, Youseff was able to pinpoint areas where he could improve, and through coaching and practice, was able to improve his meeting skills. While deliberate practice may have its limitations, setting aside the time to practice, along with getting feedback, will help you improve your global leadership.

There are two other factors that may be important in your willingness to develop yourself and engage in deliberate practice. The first is what Duckworth et al. (2007) refer to as grit—perseverance and passion for long-term goals. Duckworth has conducted several studies showing how gritty people can achieve high performance, above and beyond their intelligence and natural talent:

> Grit entails working strenuously toward challenges, maintaining effort and interest over years despite failure, adversity and plateaus in progress. The gritty individual approaches achievement as a marathon; his or her advantage is stamina. Whereas disappointment or boredom signals to others that it is time to change trajectory and cut losses, the gritty individual stays the course. (pp. 1087–1088)

In one of her studies, Duckworth collected data on the intelligence quotient (IQ) as well as Grit and Self-Control scores of finalists in the 2005 Scripps National Spelling Bee competition. She also collected data on how many hours per day they studied for the Spelling Bee finals. What she found was that Grit and Verbal IQ predicted advancement to higher rounds in competition, and gritty children put in more time studying—so grittiness and deliberate practice seem to go hand in hand.

The second is a growth mindset, especially with regard to individuals' response to failure. According to Dweck (2006), individuals with a fixed mindset tend to view failure as a reflection of their lack of ability and tend to get discouraged and disengage when they fail; individuals with a growth mindset see failure as a learning opportunity and are more likely to learn from their mistakes. Moser et al. (2011) conducted an experiment where subjects performed a task in which they received feedback. The researchers measured subjects' growth versus fixed mindset in addition to neural activities especially as the subjects were reacting to their mistakes.

Specifically, they measured error-related negativity (ERN) and error positivity (Pe), two widely studied event-related potentials (ERPs), which are electrical brain signals elicited during error processing that correspond to adaptive behavioral adjustments following mistakes. They found that individuals with a growth mindset attended to have an enhanced Pe amplitude, which they described as a brain signal reflecting conscious attention allocation to mistakes and improved subsequent performance. This is evidence from neural activity that growth versus fixed mindset individuals react to mistakes differently.

- Read and study. You can read randomly and surf the Internet to learn about other cultures and global issues, but it's better to be focused. Pick a country or two you are interested in (e.g., countries of the colleagues or customers you are interacting with), and invest the time by spending at least 15 minutes daily learning more about that country—its politics, its business environment, its history, its people, what consumers in that country are like—and what it's like to do business in that country. Remember, however, as Ibarra (2015b) has advocated, there are limits to such passive learning, and at best, this should be used to supplement (and not replace) learning from experience.
- Observe. When you are observing people from other cultures talk or interact, step back and pay attention especially to the non-verbals—their body language, their use of personal space, the tone and manner of speech. Tannen (2007) calls these "metamessages." People are communicating these metamessages, sometimes unconsciously, and we may in fact be receiving them unconsciously as well. In fact, most of us can sense when someone is listening to us and engaged in a conversation and when someone is not. Bazerman (2014) refers to "first-class noticers" as people who are attentive and notice things that others might miss.

Even in professional sports, teams are becoming more interested in reading "emotion metrics" of potential players to try to predict their impact on a team.[2] Some sports franchises are using Ekman's Facial Action Coding System (Ekman 1993) to try to analyze players' facial reactions and what that might mean for their ability to fit into a team. For example, the Milwaukee Bucks organization (a basketball franchise and a member of the National Basketball Association in the USA) was trying to decide between Dante Exum, a point guard from Australia, and Jabari Parker, a freshman player from North Carolina. Although both were excellent basketball players, the Bucks organization decided on Parker:

> Nothing against Exum, but emotional resiliency, stability and an immediate, assured presence were all key considerations in support of selecting Parker.

This conclusion was based on the results of their facial coding analysis, which presumes that individuals can infer a person's emotional and psychological state by analyzing facial expressions. This might be carrying things a bit too far, but the general point is that we do reveal our emotions and feelings, not only through the words we use but also through nonverbals, such as the tone of our voice, the expressions on our face, and the gestures we make.

Another opportunity is to observe the interactions during meetings with global teams or with people from different cultures. Find someone to help you debrief these meetings, especially around the group dynamics and interactions, to get a better understanding of how people communicate cross-culturally.

- Practice. For students who are entering a classroom for a new course, do you tend to look for a familiar face and then instantly sit down beside that person? Next time, look for a person you don't know, even someone who you think may be from another culture, and introduce yourself. After establishing rapport and gauging the person's comfort level, ask questions about his or her country in a general way. More often than not, that person will appreciate your interest and you will be able to make a connection and build a relationship.

Similarly, when joining other employees at town hall meetings, do you look for someone you know and try to sit beside him or her? Next time, try to look for someone you don't know and introduce yourself. You may or may not get a reciprocal welcome, but do not let that discourage you. You will eventually "click" with someone, and you will have expanded your own internal social network.

- Find and seek advice from a cultural mentor or a coach. Some organizations, such as Johnson & Johnson, the Australian bank ANZ, Deutsche Bank, and BASF assign such mentors to individuals going on international assignments. If you are fortunate enough to be with an organization with such a support system, then take full advantage of this.

Andrew was on an overseas assignment in South Africa and had been away from corporate HQs for over two years. During that time, there were two senior management changes. Even though he had weekly calls with his immediate manager in HQs, the conversations focused more on the status of his projects with questions on support he needed as well as project-related challenges. He found the discussions to be very much a one-way affair. He was not invited to staff meetings, and did not have a sense of the pulse of the office. When he returned, he had to figure out how he could once again be an asset to the company and felt like it was his sole responsibility to determine how he could contribute. His immediate manager had been replaced by someone from outside the company, who he met for the first time when he returned. Andrew did not feel that he was able to apply the knowledge and experience he had gained when he was abroad. Without anyone to support or advise him, Andrew soon left the company to join another firm that was looking for someone with South African experience in particular.

For global managers preparing for overseas or global assignments, identify someone who is knowledgeable about the national culture they are entering and about its business culture, and who can be trusted. Some of these individuals may be within their organization, while others might be professional colleagues from other organizations or social/networking groups. They are typically people who have traveled to the host country, or who may be from there.

- Be mindful. Being mindful means paying attention, ignoring distractions, staying focused on what is going on at the moment, and remaining engaged. Adopting a mindfulness attitude will not only enable you to be able to understand people from other cultures better but will also communicate to them your interest and ultimately your sincerity. This is especially important in cross-cultural interactions because there are times when a global manager may not be fully cognizant of the contextual cues, and he/she may have to respond quickly.

However, as Langer (1989) has explained, there are three barriers to being mindful. One, we become "trapped by categories." We tend to think in categories (such as with stereotypes) and although this may be useful, we become mindless when we rely almost exclusively on these categories. A second barrier is our own "automatic behavior," which has been referred to previously as relying on our default mode or being on cultural cruise control. Part of this is simply because of habit, but it is also driven by our mindlessness. The third barrier Langer offers is that of thinking or acting from a single perspective. Langer advocates "multiple perspective-taking"; the benefits of this approach have been discussed in an earlier section. When faced with head-scratching behavior, some may simply conclude, "I don't get it" or "How can anyone believe that?" A successful global leader will try to look at a situation or a behavior from that person's perspective, and consider alternate explanations.

Another approach recommended by other scholars emphasizes mindfulness meditation. Practicing this type of mindfulness can take many forms, from simple relaxation training, to focusing on specific muscle groups, to traditional meditation. Regardless of the mindfulness technique used, being mindful will help leaders increase their self-awareness and provide clarity on specific challenges they may be facing. Note that the concept of mindfulness I am using is closer to Langer's approach than it is to the other conceptualizations of mindfulness, which tend to emphasize present-focused consciousness, and paying close attention to both internal and external stimuli in an open and accepting way (Hyland et al. 2016).

Practice #2: Expand Your Cultural Self-awareness

Cultural self-awareness is first of all about understanding your own culture, and acknowledging that part of your behavior (as some anthropologists claim, as much as 25 %) may be due to cultural influences. This may be difficult to achieve, especially for those who have never traveled, or who have not been exposed to cultural diversity. Hall (2013) and Adler (2008) have used the analogy of a fish that cannot imagine what it is like outside the water because it has been swimming in that environment all its life.

The second aspect of cultural self-awareness is recognizing the differences between your culture and other cultures, especially when it comes to behavior in the work place. Carlos is a manager from Sao Paolo who works for a Brazilian bank. Because of his performance and his technical knowledge, he was sent to the bank's New York office on a three-month assignment to implement a new procedure and to learn about working overseas. Without much cultural preparation (since he was busy with work up to the last minute), Carlos showed up at the office in midtown on a Monday morning. As he described this to one of our interviewers, he felt like a fish out of water. The style that was so effective in Brazil just did not work in New York. He had assumed that this was the way things got done everywhere, and particularly in the bank, where he had been working for over ten years. With some coaching, Carlos eventually recognized the differences between interacting and managing in Brazil versus New York, but it took him a while to make the adjustments he needed to make.

Similarly, Gina, a manager for a global financial services company whose parents were Puerto Rican, recalled the excitement she felt when her company asked her to move to London for two years: "In my mind, London was just like New York. I had travelled internationally before and of course spoke English; I was set. I came to New York as a young child and growing up, thought it was the center of the world. I really subscribed to the cliché that if you can make it here, you can make it anywhere. I expected the world to conform to my beliefs."

She remembered some of her initial impressions of her British colleagues at the F/X desk where she worked. Most of them spoke more than three languages, and she met one colleague who spoke seven languages. When she mentioned to him that she wanted to learn another language, he commented, "You do not speak English, you speak American. We speak English." Rather than taking this remark as an insult, Gina reflected on her lack of cultural self-awareness, and her arrogance in thinking that coming to London would be easy because she already knew the language. Adler (2008) makes this insightful comment: "Although we may think that the biggest obstacle to conducting business around the world is understanding foreigners, the greater difficulty actually involves becoming aware of our own cultural conditioning" (p. 81).

A third aspect of cultural self-awareness includes understanding of different gestures and other non-verbals, which as mentioned previously, are important in building our intercultural competence. The ability to understand cultural rules and codes has also been shown to be a predictor of positive interpersonal outcomes. In an interesting series of studies, Molinsky and his colleagues (Molinsky et al. 2005) developed a measure which they called the Gesture Recognition Task (GRT). This was made up of a series of 15 real (e.g., a shoulder shrug) and 13 fake non-verbal gestures (e.g., twirling the right finger in front of the body from chest level to above the head). Several hundred US-born and non-native-born students participated in the study. In their first study, they also developed a measure of intercultural competence, and they found a positive relationship between performance on the GRT with self-ratings of intercultural competence. In a second study, performance on the GRT was also positively associated with ratings of observers who rated the students on their intercultural competence, reinforcing the importance of the ability to "read" cultural non-verbal behaviors.

Similarly, Morgan (2014) suggests that there are four areas of human communication where it is helpful for us to pay close attention to the signals from others: power, friendship, alignment, and lying. In different cultures, you need to be especially attuned to how these four areas play out. In his practice, Morgan has observed several common body language behaviors of powerful people. For example, they take up more space, and they talk differently. However, some of these behaviors may not apply equally across different cultures. For example, the body language behaviors of friend or foe may not be common across cultures. In Table 7.1, Gesteland (2012), for example, shows that a common expression like raised eyebrows has different meanings in different cultures (p. 81):

Even e-mail communication can be influenced by cultural differences. Holtbrugge and his colleagues (2013) did an interesting study of a sample of professionals in the information technology (IT) and services industry of large multinationals. The sample, which was obtained from professional social networking sites such as LinkedIn, consisted of 235 participants from 28 different nationalities, including India, Finland, Germany, USA, and China. According to the authors, 75–80 % of virtual team communication is done by e-mail. They constructed a 23-item questionnaire measuring such dimensions as directness, promptness, preciseness, and task-relatedness. The researchers found significant differences between respondents coming from high-context (e.g., Argentina, Brazil, China, Italy, Pakistan,

Table 7.1 Raised eyebrows

North American	Interest, surprise
British	Skepticism
Germans	"You are clever!"
Filipinos	"Hello!"
Arabs	"No!"
Chinese	Disagreement

Reproduced with permission

and Uruguay) and low-context (Austria, Denmark, Germany, Sweden, and the USA.) cultures in their e-mail communication styles, with high-context, polychronic cultures preferring more formal but more fluid e-mail communication, and low-context, monochronic cultures preferring more precise and prompt e-mail communication.

In the course of our interviews, some managers have actually questioned the need for cultural self-awareness. Their argument goes something like this. Learning about other cultures beforehand can be counterproductive. First, it might perpetuate stereotypes about people in that culture which might be difficult to counter once you are actually there. Second, more often than not, many cultural programs portray aspects of the culture and of doing business in that country that are not only dated but may also apply only to certain parts of the country. For example, one manager recounted a cultural training program that he attended prior to his being assigned to Germany. The impression he received from his training was that Germans were reserved and aloof, and that it was very difficult to make friends with them. That impression impacted the way he interacted with Germans initially. To his surprise, upon moving to a small town outside Munich, he found his neighbors to be very friendly and, well, neighborly.

These managers seem to have concluded that it is sufficient to have an open mind and not bother with any kind of cultural training whatsoever. Such a viewpoint is not particularly helpful for successful global leadership for the following reasons. First, it is highly unlikely that any global manager would not have at least some knowledge of the culture he or she would be entering. This is especially true for those who might be going for an international assignment in the USA. It is very likely that these managers would already have an impression of what Americans are like, and what it's like doing business in America. Cultural awareness or training would at least provide a different, or perhaps even a more balanced perspective than the impressions they may have already formed.

Second, by not preparing themselves for cultural differences, managers would most likely end up relying on those preferred behaviors and styles that have worked well for them in their home culture. For example, Bernice went to Nigeria for a six-month assignment as part of an NGO based in Italy. Almost up to the last minute, it seemed that Bernice was busy finishing up her current role and had no time to study cultural differences, other than to worry about housing, visa requirements, and immediate living accommodations. She also did not expect that there would be many differences between how Italians are managed versus how Nigerians are managed, especially since the staff she would have there were also working for an NGO. Unfortunately, this was not the case, and Bernice had to go through a rough period of adjustment.

Similarly, Chuck signed up to work as a new product manager for a Korean electronics company in the USA. In its American offices, there were a number of South Koreans as well as Indian consultants, so Chuck was vaguely aware of the cultural differences. However, he did not believe this was important enough for him to understand, given all his work priorities. Besides, he was not leaving the country anyway. However, he began to notice some workplace differences. For example, he noticed that the company cafeteria always had three sections for American, Korean, and Indian food. He also noticed that the lights would dim at 1 p.m. and 7 p.m. When he asked why, he was told that Koreans liked to take short naps at their desks before resuming work, since many of them came in at eight and did not leave until after midnight. Soon after he joined the firm, Chuck was sent to Seoul where he met with some of his virtual team members. At dinner, he made a casual joke about the North Koreans and their economy that he realized was not only misunderstood but also not appreciated. A senior executive later told him in private that he should avoid making comments about political situations.

Third, by ignoring cultural differences, especially when managing multicultural teams, managers sub-optimize the performance of teams. Worse, by suppressing these differences ("After all, we all work for the same company, so we have much more in common than what separates us," is the type of statement I sometimes hear from managers), team performance suffers—particularly if the outcomes include creativity, innovation, and solving complex tasks. Research by Lane et al. (2009) and others have demonstrated the impact of such "destroyer" or "equalizer" strategies when managing diverse teams. Ely and Thomas (2001) examined the impact of cultural diversity on work group performance. Although their research was with groups in a single country, they studied groups that were diverse on different dimensions, including race. Their conclusion, consistent with that of other researchers (e.g., Chatman et al. 1998), was that groups that adopt a "diversity perspective" tend to perform better than groups that do not: "A diversity perspective provides the cognitive frames within which group members interpret and act upon their experience of cultural identity differences in the group ... which influences members' sense of how much others in the group value and respect them" (p. 266).

The following are several strategies to enhance cultural self-awareness. One, find out what managers' impressions are about your own culture. Of course, some of their impressions may be based on simplistic and even outdated stereotypes. However, they can provide some insights into the cultural influences that impact workplace behavior in your culture. Two, learn about the successes and failures of managers from your country who have worked in other cultures. For example, a British manager might identify other British colleagues who have been sent overseas on expatriate assignments. He could find out who were successful, and what it was about them or their circumstances that made them effective. Learning about their experiences may give him valuable insights on his own cultural self-awareness. This practice will help global leaders develop the global mindset disposition of curiosity.

PRACTICE #3: TAKE STEPS TO GET OUT OF YOUR COMFORT ZONE

For global managers working with people with similar cultural backgrounds, it is likely that they do not often think about what might or might not be appropriate culturally. As a recent graduate with an MBA from a New York-area school, Vincent landed a job at a financial services company in Manhattan. He had never thought about an international career, but when the company merged with a global firm, he was asked to run a department in Hong Kong. The company did not provide him with any cultural training, and he arrived with an attitude of "this is how I am going to do it." Coming from the high-pressure environment of New York, where the workday typically started at 7:30 a.m. and did not end until about 7:30 p.m., Vincent was surprised to learn that in Hong Kong, the workday started at about 9 a.m. Initially, Vincent asked his staff to come in by 8 a.m. but despite their nods of agreement, they still came in at 9 a.m. In addition, they took one-and-a-half-hour lunch breaks, including naps at their desk.

Despite his discomfort, Vincent realized that something had to give, and it had to be him. He met another expatriate who had been in Hong Kong for a while, and gave Vincent some valuable advice: "Build relationships, and build your team first," he told Vincent. Vincent started to join his staff to socialize at least once a week, where he quizzed them on Hong Kong's history and workplace culture. He also made sure to give credit and praise to the entire team when major milestones were achieved.

Larry was an extroverted manager who liked to hug everyone he met as his way of establishing rapport with others. He was also an inveterate talker, and became anxious when there was silence during meetings that he felt he had to jump in and at least say something. When Larry took a short-term assignment in Thailand, he found himself very much out of his comfort zone. He had to curb his "instinct" to touch people and to talk through the silence in conversations, which he found very challenging. How did he do it?

First, Larry stepped back and reflected on the gaps between what the Thai culture accepted as appropriate and what his own preferences were. He made a list that included touching and incessant talk, plus several other behaviors. Larry came up with about a dozen of these behaviors. Second, he prioritized these behaviors and identified those that he felt were most important for him to change to step out of his comfort zone. He brought his list to the local Human Resources Director to get his feedback and advice. They both agreed that touching and his talkativeness were the top priorities. Larry knew this was going to be difficult since he had been operating in this manner for a long time. So he decided to start by taking some small steps. For example, he made it a point not to hug, or even shake hands, with his Thai colleagues unless they offered to shake his hands first. Of course, no one even thought about initiating a hug with Larry. He practiced bowing slightly to different employees in the organization. This was very difficult for Larry at first, but he eventually began to identify other ways to establish rapport other than that initial hug. During meetings, he recognized that some Thais were reluctant to speak, not only because their English was not very good but also because they were concerned about saying anything that might embarrass Larry or cause him to lose face. So during lulls in the meeting discussion, when Larry would ordinarily jump in, he counted to 20 silently before speaking. He also learned to ask more questions, rather than making assertions and giving his opinions.

To step out of your comfort zone, here are several other suggestions. First, consider the worst-case scenario: what is the worst that could happen if you tried this behavior? Chances are it might not be the unmitigated disaster that you might imagine when you are thinking about doing something different.

Sri was an introverted manager who found it painful to go to social gatherings with his department. He was a bit shy, and the prospect of making small talk with strangers terrified him. However, he knew that this was important to his career and he had to do it. Sri spoke with me about his concerns, and about strategies he might employ. When I asked him what was the worst thing that could happen, Sri said that he would just be ignored—which actually would not be so bad, because then he could just go on and introduce himself to someone else. Sri rehearsed with me some opening lines and introductory topics to at least get the conversation going. He learned how to introduce himself and give a firm handshake to those he was meeting for the first time. After a few such gatherings, Sri became more confident.

Second, take small behavioral steps outside your comfort zone. There are a lot of different ways you can do this. For example, when at a restaurant, order an entrée that you have never had before. Better still, go to places that offer a different type of cuisine than what you are used to. Once in a while, take a different route in your commute. Once a week, leave your mobile phone at home. The point of these small changes to your habits will be to help you expand the range of your comfort zone so you can become more adept at "going with the flow" in the future. People who are overweight and are determined to lose weight start with making small changes in their diet. People who want to quit smoking or drinking may go "cold turkey" but they also take some concrete steps to make sure they don't slip. If you are an extrovert and have a difficult time holding back on expressing your thoughts, try some small steps, such as counting to ten before speaking or making a conscious effort that in the next meeting you have, you will offer no more than three opinions during the meeting (instead of your usual dozen). This is not about converting you from an extrovert to an introvert (or vice versa), but about learning new behaviors that will ultimately make you more effective cross-culturally.

Third, reframe your approach; instead of thinking that you will have to change "who you are," imagine yourself as someone who wears different "hats" or roles for different situations but whose inner core remains the same. For example, Jared was a Ph.D. in engineering who always thought of himself as someone dedicated to his engineering profession. He graduated from a university with a top-notch engineering program, and his faculty advisors had convinced him that the pinnacle of the profession meant having an academic career. When Jared joined a technology company, he continued to read journal articles and tried to publish on the side. Over the years, he turned down opportunities for assignments that might have taken him out of his engineering role, even though these assignments would have meant a broader role for him in the company and certainly bigger rewards. During our coaching sessions, Jared and I discussed his career goals, and his deeply held image of himself as an engineering Ph.D. He began to realize that, working in his company, he could never reach the pinnacle of his profession as an academic, but that did not mean he was a failure, or that he was giving up his love of engineering. What it meant was that he could still see himself as an engineering "expert" but one dedicated to applying his expertise in his role with the company.

One year later, Jared accepted a position as manager of a product development group. He has been very successful and surprised even himself by realizing that he enjoyed being a manager, working with his team to develop group goals, and motivating them to work toward these goals. He also began to accept that he could no longer continue to think of himself as an academic Ph.D., but that his training and his background had helped him to establish himself in the company as a subject matter expert.

In summary, there are several steps you can take with varying degrees of effort to begin to step out of your comfort zone, and the payoff will be improving your global mindset disposition, especially with flexibility.

PRACTICE #4: UNDERSTAND BEFORE JUDGING

In earlier chapters, we reviewed research that suggests that we tend to evaluate and form judgments quickly. When we judge, we are prone to the fundamental attribution error, our tendency to overattribute others' behavior to internal rather than external causes (Jones and Nisbett 1987; Ross 1977; Winter et al. 1985). This very much applies in cross-cultural settings when as a manager we tend to minimize the impact of situational factors such as culture on an employee's behavior. Research by Moran et al. (2014) using functional magnetic resonance imaging (fMRI) suggests that there are different regions of the brain that are activated whether perceivers attribute dispositional or situational causes to other persons' ambiguous behavior.

The degree of difficulty we have withholding our judgment may depend on the nature of the cultural practice, and how deeply it might impinge on one's own underlying cultural values. For example, some may react negatively to the types of foods that people from certain cultures eat but with some reflection and explanations (as Anthony Bourdain does so well), they may get to understand why these foods might be desirable to others. However, there are other practices that might be more offensive because they will seem at odds with our own values. For example, certain cultures are more tolerant of discrimination and gender inequalities.

Understanding before judging does not mean acceptance of all kinds of practices. It does mean keeping an open mind and finding out more about the reasons for why such practices exist. In terms of judging others, Sutton (2007) has advised, "be slow to brand people" (p. 85). He goes on to state that "when a person rarely smiles, has a hard time looking others in the eye, or seems to have a permanent sneer, our natural reaction is to label him or her as a jerk ... it is best to withhold your judgment and watch what they actually do" (p. 86).

Gladwell popularized the term "thin slicing," and this is how he described it:

(Thin-slicing)... is a central part of what it means to be human. We thin-slice whenever we meet a new person or have to make sense of something quickly or reencounter a novel situation. We thin-slice because we have to, and we come to rely on that ability because there are ... lots of situations where careful attention to the details of a very thin slice, even for no more than a second or two, can tell us an awful lot.

Research on the interviewing process has indicated that interviewers in an employment setting generally make up their minds about a candidate during the first few minutes of an interview. Gomez-Mejia et al. (2012) have summarized the studies as follows:

Perhaps the most consistent research finding is that interviewers tend to jump to conclusions—make snap judgments—about candidates during the first few minutes of the interview (or even before the interview starts, based on test scores or resume data). One researcher estimates that in 85 percent of the cases, interviewers had made up their minds before the interview even began, based on first impressions the interviewers gleaned from candidates' applications and personal appearance.

A classic meta-analysis by Schmidt and Hunter (1998) showed that, among 19 different selection methods, unstructured interviews (where interviewers did not have any specific questions prepared in advance) were among the worst predictors of performance. The reason for this is simple enough: in the absence of standard questions, it is difficult to compare candidates across interviews, and interviewers' impressions therefore tend to be weighted more heavily.

As Nicholson (1998) has pointed out, perhaps it's a result of our hard-wired behavior from the Pleistocene era, where our ancestors had to judge very quickly whether a person from another tribe was a friend or foe. Over the past several years, I have worked with executives to help them identify and develop potential talent in their organizations, and I find that many executives not only make these judgments very quickly but also seem to make them very confidently (not surprising for them, of course). A manager who they may remember texting during a meeting, or another manager who made a less than stellar presentation are samples of behavior where executives generalize very quickly, and can sometimes derail otherwise fine talent. In addition, the research on interviewing shows that interviewers are more influenced by unfavorable than favorable information about candidates (Bolster and Springbett 1961). In my many years of working with executives on talent identification and succession planning, this conclusion applies equally to executives who are making judgments about potential candidates for succession.

Ambady and Rosenthal (1992) actually coined the term "thin slicing" many years before Gladwell popularized it. More recent studies have reinforced the power of thin slicing (e.g., Todorov et al. 2005). According to neuroscientists (e.g., Pinker 2014), the ability to pick up emotional cues evolved in the amygdala. The challenge for many managers working globally today is to be careful of these thin slices when interacting with people who are members of different cultures, since they not only look different but also talk and interact differently (even when conversing in English). Therefore the potential for creating unfavorable first impressions is significant.

Epley (2014) points to another human tendency with his concept of illusions of insight—that we think we know what other people are thinking, and that our confidence grows especially with people who we think we know well. Our inclination to develop quick first impressions, when combined with our confidence in believing that we have good insights into reading other people's minds, can be particularly challenging for global leaders.

One interviewee, Diya, is a second-generation Indian manager who has been assigned overseas several times by her company, a global financial services firm. This is what she had to say about her experience in working with others cross-culturally:

I feel that, in working with different cultures, there are some people who may lack the ability to speak English well. But even if they don't, they may be really strong in analysis or may have great quantitative skills. So I have learned to refrain from judging people based on my first impression, and I gave myself enough time to understand and evaluate a persons' strengths and weaknesses, and map these according to the skills required for a project or for the team.

In cross-cultural settings, there are at least two kinds of biases we may fall prey to. First is the "lack of similarity" bias that is created when we meet people who are not like us (e.g., Bates 2002; Moghaddam and Stringer 1998). The relevant dimensions of dissimilarity or difference may differ by situation. For example, in the workplace setting, gender is sometimes not as relevant as functional background. Marketing people tend to refer to those finance types concerned only with numbers, while salespeople tend to refer to those engineering types who overdesign their products with little regard for consumer needs. In cross-cultural situations, our unconscious bias favoring people who are like us, or not favoring those who are not like us, can kick into high gear very quickly. The dimensions of similarity or dissimilarity might include physical appearance, body language (e.g., the way someone shakes your hand or expresses himself or herself), thinking style, and certainly cultural background.

The second type of bias is when we fix on superficial, and sometimes irrelevant, characteristics that lead us to jump to hasty conclusions. One example (which Diya highlighted) is the bias executives hold with regard to the ability of non-native English speakers to speak English well. Many executives visiting other countries tend to place undue emphasis on locals who have a verbal fluency in English, especially those who understand the nuances and idioms of the English language. English verbal skills may have little to do with local managers' performance or their competence, but it inevitably impresses many executives who should know better. Neeley and Kaplan (2014) point to this as a blind spot for many executives.

Here are a few recommendations for avoiding these biases and withholding our first impressions (difficult as this may be). When you are about to engage with someone from another culture especially for the first time, step back for a moment and ask yourself what assumptions you might be making about that person or group. For example, suppose that you are getting ready to meet with a Russian manager in Moscow. From what you have read about Russian businesspeople and about the Russian culture, you will certainly have certain expectations about the person you are about to meet. You expect to meet someone who is most probably an ethnic Russian, who is rather formal (in terms of both attire and interaction), who does not use much body language or non-verbal communication, and who prefers to get down to business almost immediately. What information do you already have, or can you get, about this person to test these assumptions?

As you meet with and engage with the person, test those assumptions to see whether they are justified or not. As Langer (1989) has advised, beware of being trapped by categories. Some of your thinking and adjustments might be done "in the moment." For example, on meeting the Russian manager, you realize that he is younger than 30, and he informs you that he has only been in Russia for five years, having been raised in Ukraine. Furthermore, he got his MBA at IMD Business School in Switzerland. These are pieces of information that you learn about as you interact with your Russian business partner, and might change the approach you might take with him. For example, you might then decide to take a somewhat less formal approach and engage in some informal topics to break the ice and establish rapport. This is consistent with the suggestion (Little 2014) about carrying multiple categories mentally when forming an impression of others.

After the interaction, reflect on your behaviors. How did you adjust your approach, and did you feel that it was effective? What would you do differently next time around? If appropriate, ask for feedback (e.g., not necessarily about yourself, but you could ask about how the meeting went for him), although keep in mind that you might not get honest feedback, especially if you are in a position of higher authority than the person or group with whom you are interacting.

A longer-term approach would be to focus on two aspects. First, take the time to explore commonalities between the other person and yourself. In some cases, this may be around sports, cars, or certain movies, books, or games. In other cases, this might be around common experiences, for example, having children of about the same age, having parents who may not be well, and so on. Finding "common ground" is an effective way to reduce your unconscious bias and in many cases, helps to establish an effective relationship with your colleague cross-culturally. This facilitates a common social identity that, as research has shown, can lead to positive outcomes such as helping behaviors (e.g., Levine et al. 2005).

The second aspect differs from the first in the sense that you are looking forward, not backward, to what common goals you might share and the interdependence you need to have to achieve these goals. Psychologists refer to this as outcome dependency. There is research that suggests that focusing on outcome dependency facilitates perspective-taking and reduces stereotyping (Galinsky and Moskowitz 2000).

Brewer (1996) has developed a theory of optimal distinctiveness to account for the motivational basis of group identification in people. According to this theory, our collective social identities come from two social motives: the need to be included, and the need to differentiate ourselves from others. These are opposing drives. As we become immersed in social units, the need for differentiation increases and vice versa until there is an equilibrium point or balance between the two tensions. She has built on the work of Triandis (1995), who found that collectivists tend to make sharper distinctions between members of in-groups versus out-groups. Brewer's own research suggests that individualists are less concerned with in-group distinctiveness than collectivists.

When I worked for Citibank many years ago, a colleague of mine told me a story about Walter Wriston, who was then the chief executive officer (CEO) of the financial giant that in those days already had a huge global presence. He told me that before Mr. Wriston would get on a plane to travel to the bank's different overseas subsidiaries, he would have his assistant prepare a "cheat sheet" on index cards for each of the key managers that he would be meeting. This was before the digital era of laptops and smart phones. Each index card would have some personal information about the managers—their title, age, nickname, years with the company—and most important, the names and ages of their spouses and children, their favorite hobbies and interests. When Mr. Wriston arrived in the country he was visiting, he had memorized these little factoids about his hosts and would make sure to weave in what he knew about them in their conversations. He would ask his assistant to do the same thing for any other important people he was scheduled to meet, such as government officials and important customers. It was an effective way for him to show interest in the person and to build a relationship. You would not have known it from seeing Mr. Wriston, who gave the initial impression of being a bit aloof and distant.

This combination of doing your homework and being mindful when interacting with others is also part of what makes for successful networking.

Schumpeter, writing in the Economist[3] describes examples of those who work hard at networking:

> Mukesh Ambani, the boss of Reliance Industries, one of India's largest conglomerates, makes sure that he is briefed on people he is about to meet, and asks them about their interests. Mark Tucker, the boss of AIA, one of Asia's biggest insurers, follows up conversations with detailed e-mails, sent at all times of the day and night.

This practice directly impacts the global mindset disposition of acceptance.

PRACTICE #5: SHOW BOUNDLESS CURIOSITY

In an earlier chapter, we discussed the importance of curiosity as a dispositional element of global mindset. Curiosity in this context means having the desire and motivation to learn about other cultures, and especially about management practices in these cultures, and taking concrete steps to gain a better understanding of these cultures and practices. It also extends to finding out more about your colleagues' backgrounds. How well do you know your colleagues from other cultures? How much time have you invested trying to know something more about each of them? What do you know about their family, their education, and their work experience? Needless to say, global managers have to be careful about both the timing and the nature of some of these questions. For example, people from so-called coconut cultures are very private about their personal lives and it might take a while before you can get to know them better. It is safe however to ask questions about their culture; in general, business colleagues welcome such questions. For example, if you are a manager of a global team that is based in India and the holiday of *Diwali* is coming up, by all means use the opportunity to ask your Indian colleagues about this holiday and why it is important. If your colleagues are from a country whose soccer team is advancing in the World Cup, ask questions related to this event.

For some, there are few things more exciting than packing their suitcase and preparing to travel for work to an overseas location for a few weeks, months, or years. It's not only the challenge of working on a project or assignment that could add value to their organization but also about learning from others who are very different from them. Of course, not everyone shares this sense of excitement, adventure, and learning.

Phil was a commissioned officer in the US Marine Corps. He led the ground-level execution of the military's strategy on five separate assignments, or deployments. When he was assigned to Iraq in 2004, he was a bit nervous but excited to be able to "get some," the phrase the Marines used when they expected to engage with enemy troops. Although his troops dominated the battlefield and were able to demonstrate that the insurgents could not stand up to their firepower on the battlefield, Phil realized that what was also needed was winning the people's hearts and minds. Prior to leaving for Iraq, Phil and his troops received very basic cultural training, like not showing the soles of your feet or interacting with the local females.

Yet once in Iraq, much of their time was spent not on the battlefield but in interacting with the locals, many of who came from different tribes along the Euphrates River. Phil was intensely passionate in learning about the nuanced cultural differences between the Shiite, Sunni, and Christian people. He took the initiative to study the local language, and he led training sessions with his Marines to sensitize them to these cultural differences. Little things made a difference. He made sure his troops waved, shook hands, and smiled rather than pointing guns. He made them buy from local merchants and offered medical assistance to locals in need of medical attention.

What are the barriers to curiosity? For some, there may simply be a lack of interest, or perhaps even a superior attitude, toward other cultures. There are quite a few Western managers working in emerging markets who have little interest in learning about cultures because they believe that these cultures have nothing to offer them, nor can they learn much from them. Furthermore, they consider cultural learning as a low priority since their focus is on delivering quick results, and fulfilling the expectations of their bosses. For others, it may be that the willingness is there, but they hesitate because they don't know where to begin, or perhaps believe that they may embarrass themselves by asking the wrong questions.

Suresh is a second-generation Indian-American who works for a major US company but also is involved in his father's business, a privately run Indian investment group. He took a three-month leave of absence from his company to go to India to work on a project selling land in the Indian province of Gujarat to a major US company that was planning to open a store in India. Suresh had been to India only twice in his life, and he only spoke minimal Gujarati. However, he felt confident in his cultural adjustment since he was raised in a Gujarati household and was familiar with the native customs. Did he have a rude awakening when he arrived in Gujarat! He immediately stood out since he was very well groomed and well dressed, and spoke with an American accent. The locals referred to him as an NRI (non-resident Indian). Suresh made it a point to ask a lot of questions and to learn as much as he could about local customs. After a couple of months, his local contacts began to complement him on how well he was adjusting to India, even to the point where his non-local accent had subsided somewhat.

PRACTICE #6: DEVELOP EMPATHY

Jake Lambert turned the dials on his watch so that he had the correct time for Beijing. As an executive working for a global consumer products company based in the USA, Jake was on his first overseas trip. He had scheduled a meeting with several Chinese businessmen to discuss a potential partnership to manufacture some of his company's products locally. A friend of his from another company (not a competitor) who had used them several years ago recommended the local company to Jake.

On the plane, Jake opened his briefcase and reviewed the contract that was drafted by his company. The sooner he could come to an agreement with his Chinese partners the better—for the company and for him. Jake was not fond of going on airplanes, and flying these many hours made him a bit irritable. However, he was only going to be in China for two nights, with one day scheduled for visiting the manufacturing plant 40 miles outside Beijing.

In checking into the Marriott that afternoon, Jake found a message from Mr. Zhu, the head of the manufacturing company, inviting him to dinner that night. Jake was hoping that he could get a good night's sleep since he did not have much sleep on the flight, but he thought that perhaps he could speed things up by starting business discussions over dinner. He asked the hotel to make multiple copies of the contract that he intended to bring with him that night.

When he went down to the lobby at 7 p.m., he found Mr. Zhu and his five management team members waiting for him. Jake introduced himself, while each of the Chinese executives handed him their business card, somewhat formally, Jake thought to himself. He had forgotten his business cards in his hotel room. The dinner was in a private room at a fancy restaurant about a half hour from the hotel. Jake took the opportunity during the ride to begin asking questions about their company and their business. What experiences have they had with other US companies? What quality control procedures did they have in place?

Over dinner (which as Jake recalled, took over three hours with endless servings), Jake continued to steer the conversation toward the business side. He was frustrated that his hosts seemed reluctant to talk business and kept on asking questions about people in his company, and even about his family and his personal interests.

The next day, he visited the factory and was impressed by what he saw. Toward the end of the visit, he sat down with Mr. Zhu and showed him the contract that his company had prepared. Mr. Zhu barely glanced at it, and said that he would have to discuss this with his management team. Then he asked Jake when he would visit Beijing next so they could have another discussion.

Jake had no intention of flying back to Beijing. This was it for him. Either they agreed or not. His company had some contacts in Vietnam and this was a backup plan if the Chinese did not readily agree to these terms, which he thought were quite fair. Unfortunately, Mr. Zhu was non-committal and suggested they meet again for dinner that night. Jake politely turned down the invitation, saying that he was getting ready to fly back and had to catch up on his work that night. When Jake got back to the USA, he promptly e-mailed Mr. Zhu and requested a follow-up discussion. Mr. Zhu responded vaguely after a few days but Jack did not hear from him again, despite several e-mails and phone calls. Jake somehow felt that this was not going to work out, and he and his company decided to pursue another opportunity in Vietnam.

As an executive with limited global experience, Jake made a few critical mistakes that he may not even have been aware of. He should have recognized that doing business with the Chinese is different than doing business with other Western nationals. From paying close attention to rituals and protocols (e.g., greeting others and having business cards) to developing relationships through socializing and spending time together over meals to having a longer time horizon for completing deals, Jake and other Western executives needed first of all to place themselves in the other persons' shoes to see how others' perspectives might differ from theirs. Jake also did not realize the importance of formality in Chinese culture, and that greetings and protocols are among the interaction hot spots important in cross-cultural interactions.

Contrast this with the experience of the executives of a US-based global electronics company that was entering the Chinese market. Through local contacts, they arranged a meeting with the Ministry of Finance in Beijing. Thirty-five people attended the first meeting, all with headsets and translators. The meeting started with an hour-long presentation where the Chinese discussed their five-year plans, followed by a tea break for an exchange of business cards, and then by a presentation by the company executives on what they had to offer. Based on this request, the executives were then taken to various component-manufacturing firms in China. Through careful preparation and planning, and by considering the importance of these interactions from the Chinese perspective, the executives were able to establish good working relationships with their Chinese business partners; six months later, they had agreed on a joint venture with a local firm.

Recently, the *Boston Globe* reported on a University of Michigan study that found that college students in the USA today are 40 % less empathetic than they were in 1979 on both cognitive empathy and emotional empathy.[4] At the same time, Colvin (2014) reports that software and technology companies are increasingly looking to hire workers who show empathy because this will help them better understand the "customer's inner experience."

In one study, researchers (Konrath et al. 2010) found that American college students scored lower on Empathic Concern and Perspective Taking (two sub-measures of empathy) between 1979 and 2009. The authors suggest that narcissism, which has been increasing among American college students, is negatively correlated with empathy. In collectivistic and group-oriented cultures, it may be more difficult for narcissists to thrive since there are more social pressures to conform and to fit in than in societies like the USA. Individuals from cultures that are more group oriented, and which are high context, are likely to have learned more empathy as they were growing up, especially emotional empathy. It would be interesting to compare empathy scores across countries with different cultural orientations, and to study if this trend toward declining empathy scores applies to other countries as well.

Sutton (2010) mentions a perk that General Motors (GM) executives had where they were given a new car every six months; all they had to do was go to a room where they would spec out and order a car. There was a gas pump in the building where they could get gas at a huge discount. Sutton said he had argued with GM management that this perk should be abolished because he believed that executives should go through what other customers go through in buying a new car. I think he was implicitly suggesting that this would increase their empathy with the customer. He did not succeed in persuading GM executives to eliminate this perk.

As mentioned in a previous chapter, empathy is one of the dispositional elements of global mindset. Global leaders can prime themselves to show cognitive empathy by adopting a perspective-taking approach through these questions:

- Imagine looking at this situation through their eyes and being in their shoes—how would you view this situation?
- What might this situation look like from their point of view? How would they explain this?
- What might be going on in their minds that could explain why they are behaving this way?

Among negotiators, empathy—especially cognitive empathy—is what differentiates effective ones from those merely average (Drolet et al. 1998; Martinovski et al. 2006). The Federal Bureau of Investigation (FBI) has developed a behavioral change strategy model where empathy is one of the five critical steps to take in dealing with hostage negotiation situations (e.g., Vecchi et al. 2005). Among physicians, those with empathy skills seem to be sued less than those considered less empathetic. Many studies have shown that it is the quality of doctor–patient communication, more so than the quality of care or documentation, that is key to avoiding expensive malpractice lawsuits (Levinson et al. 1997; Neuwirth 1997).

The following are some strategies to begin to develop your cross-cultural empathy. One, when interacting with people and teams from different cultures, get to know the other person better. By doing this, you will minimize your tendency to stereotype, and to more fully consider each individual's unique personalities and motivations. The best way to do this is by spending time with others in both work and social settings. Let them get to know you as well. MacNab and Worthley (2013) conducted a study whereby over 350 subjects representing 31 different nationalities participated in experiential learning exercises focusing on dialectic logic (as a strategy to break down stereotype beliefs) and found greater awareness of negative stereotypes as well as a recognition of their inaccuracy as a result.

Two, reflect on what is going on in different situations and develop different alternative explanations. This is the metacognitive awareness that

Earley and Ang (2003) suggest is a component of cultural intelligence. Three, try to experience other cultures like a native. I remember one assignment I had in Mexico City, where I requested the local managers there to have me accompany a local sales manager as she made her rounds trying to recruit locals to sell products for the company I was working for at that time. I asked her not to take me to any fancy places but to go to where she would normally go in making her recruiting rounds. It was eye-opening for me; we went to some lower-income neighborhoods where some of the living quarters did not even have wooden floors. Yet in all cases, the women in the different households greeted me with kindness, even offering me coffee. That experience, which I still remember vividly, gave me many insights on the challenges that the sales managers had with their jobs and with a side of the culture I was not normally exposed to.

If you are going to America from your home country, for example, get some advice from your American colleagues on what might be places to visit in order to experience what is uniquely American in that locale. If you are in New York City, for example, get in the subway during rush hour and experience what a typical commute is like for New Yorkers. Your specific experiences in America will depend of course on where you end up living or working. Kansas City or Dallas would be very different, but the point is to try to replicate some of the experiences that people living in those cities have. A multinational company recently launched a program where its senior executives spend time having lunch in the homes of typical households in different cities. The households are paid for their troubles, of course, but the executives come away with a good understanding of the types of consumers who buy their products.

Three, listen for understanding. Research has shown that effective listening is difficult to master (Golen 1990). Michael Skapinker, a Financial Times executive who returned to writing after running several departments for the newspaper, wrote that one of the leadership lessons he learned was to "tell people what they have just told you." He reinforces the point that "there is no more powerful management tool than showing people that you have listened to them.[5]" Many times, however, we become concerned with what we are going to say that we stop paying attention to what the other person is saying. Sometimes we find our minds wandering in conversations, perhaps because we are getting ready to prepare a counterargument with the other person.

Bolton (1979) proposes three types of listening skills: attending, following, and reflecting. *Attending* is about your physical attention to another person; it is your non-verbal way of communicating that you are paying attention and are listening. Four positions seem to be very nearly universal: facing the person directly and at eye level as much as possible (avoid looking down on him or her), maintaining an open position with arms and legs uncrossed, maintaining an appropriate physical distance (this may vary across cultures), and occasionally nodding while the other person is speaking. While Bolton and others suggest facing the other person squarely and looking them in the eye as ways of attending, it is important to remember that these behaviors may not always be appropriate in certain cultures.

Following is about behaviors to keep the focus on what the speaker is communicating. One of these is what Bolton calls a "door opener," which is a non-coercive invitation to talk. This is especially helpful in cultures where the speaker may be hesitant to bring up some topics to you as a foreigner. Door openers include making statements such as "Please go on," "I'm interested in what you are saying," or "You look a little upset." A door opener avoids making judgments (e.g., "What did you do this time?") or even reassurance (e.g., "Things will get better") and advice (e.g., "Why don't you do something about it?").

Another type of listening is *reflective* listening. There has been a lot written about various ways to develop your reflective or active listening skills. The four that Bolton recommends are paraphrasing, reflecting feelings, reflecting meanings, and summative reflection. Reflective listening is an important skill for global leaders to develop, especially where there may be difficulties in language. Even when using translators, it is helpful to paraphrase or summarize to be sure you have heard correctly, and that the translator has correctly translated your statements.

Four, develop your question-asking skills and empathy vocabulary. Sometimes it can be awkward to ask questions, especially with people from another culture whom you don't know well and whom you may think would find your questions offensive or culturally inappropriate. Furthermore, there are questions that could put others on the defensive, especially when the questions seem to imply some kind of value judgment. As Earley and Mosakowski (2004) have commented, "inquiring about the meaning of some custom will often prove unavailing because natives may be reticent about explaining themselves to strangers, or they may have little practice looking at their own culture analytically."

With people you don't know well, start with innocuous questions, such as how the weather varies by the season, or what the educational system is like. You'd be surprised at how much you learn about the culture by asking even these types of questions. It also sends a message to your colleagues that you are in fact interested in them and in their culture. In some cultures where work is such an important part of a person's life, asking questions about a person's position and role can be a good way to start a conversation. Anticipate your conversations by thinking in advance of a few questions you will ask your colleagues to get a conversation started. Keep in mind that some questions that may be appropriate in some cultures may not be appropriate in others. For example, in group-oriented cultures like Japan, it is important for you to introduce yourself and mention your organizational affiliation almost immediately; expect your colleague to do the same. In France, where people value privacy, asking any kind of personal question to a person you just met would be considered rude.

When I was in Singapore on a business trip not too long ago, my questions about where the children of a local colleague went to school started a conversation about the Singaporean education philosophy and its advantages and disadvantages. As you build your trust, then you can ask more probing questions. The important lesson is to keep on asking questions in the spirit of curiosity and learning, and not to make value judgments about how your own culture is better than (or worse than) another culture.

There are certain words and phrases that are helpful and others that are not helpful in conveying emotional empathy. For example, saying "I know exactly how you feel" is not necessarily an empathetic response, since the person's reaction to this comment may be to think that you do not know how he feels since you are not that person, nor have you been in exactly that same situation as that person. Instead, use phrases such as "That must be difficult for you" or "That must have been challenging for you." The idea is to try to reflect back to the person what you heard and acknowledge the person's state without turning it to you or making a judgment about his or her situation.

Five, practice mirroring. There is a body of research on the effectiveness of mirroring, especially among successful salespersons and negotiators. In fact, as Pink (2013) points out, mirroring (or mimicry, as others describe it) is very human, "a natural act that serves as a social glue and a sign of trust." Mirroring can of course be seen as manipulative or deceitful, and if you simply ape another's mannerisms, this could elicit a negative reaction. However, if your intent is to build rapport and convey respect and acceptance of the other person, then mirroring can be very effective.

In a set of laboratory studies, Sanchez-Burks et al. (2009) trained confederate interviewers in mirroring; some interviewers mirrored interviewees while others did not. The researchers used both US Latino and US Anglo interviewers and interviewees. The interviewers asked questions about participants' current and prior job experiences, career goals, as well as personal strengths and weaknesses. All participants were from a Fortune 500 corporation located in the USA. To confirm the manipulations, two observers who were blind to the experiment coded the confederate-only videos to establish whether the confederates' behaviors varied across the mirroring conditions in ways that might provide alternative explanations for the results. There were no significant differences between the mirroring conditions. Professional recruiters served as coders to assess the "performance" of the interviewees on seven dimensions (e.g., impact, verbal communication skills, assertiveness, etc.). The researchers even measured response time (i.e., latency) to the interviewers' questions as a behavioral performance indicator.

What they found was that Latinos performed significantly better in the mirroring condition, while the absence of behavioral mirroring did not affect the performance of the US Anglo interviewees! This is one of the few experiments using mirroring that suggests that mirroring does have an impact, although the strength of the impact may vary by culture.

This applies cross-culturally as well. There are certain mannerisms or gestures that global leaders can incorporate into their own behavioral repertoire. For example, when working in Japan, I made it a point to bow slightly especially when greeting Japanese senior executives. There are subtle gestures in different cultures that you can observe and incorporate as your own.

PRACTICE #7: MAINTAIN YOUR ETHICAL CORE

Dan (not his real name) was a manager for a global company who was long considered to have the potential to become one of its executives. He had deep expertise in his functional area, and a wealth of experience in the industry; his business acumen and track record were outstanding. Unfortunately, while in charge of one of the company's divisions in an emerging market region several years later, he was asked to leave the company amid accusations of corruption and bribery when he was working overseas. Many of his colleagues were surprised to learn that a person like Dan could throw away his reputation and his career over this.

Global leaders will most likely face a handful of ethical decision points during their career; some of these may seem insignificant, but there will be perhaps as many as a dozen situations on average in the course of a global career where their integrity will be tested. As mentioned previously, research has demonstrated that situational forces have a powerful effect on our behavior (e.g., Krull et al. 1999; Miller and Ross 1975).

In general, managers working overseas are subject to three influences that might drive them to behave unethically. The first is the "out of sight, out of mind" syndrome. When global managers are thousands of miles away from HQs, and they have a great deal of autonomy, the temptations to stretch the truth, for example, by delaying the reporting of a failed business transaction in order to achieve this quarter's or this year's numbers, become very strong. Wal-Mart has been investigating a scandal in its Mexican operation,[6] and several executives have either resigned or been let go by the corporation. Siemens, Glaxo Smith Kline, and IKEA have also been in the news recently because of executives who have been accused of bribery in their overseas operations.

The second influencing factor is the local context in which global leaders may find themselves. Consider the data from Transparency International, an agency of the World Bank that ranks countries in terms of corruption.[7] Now imagine an expatriate in one of those countries where corruption is endemic and in which businesses are expected to pay bribes and engage in corrupt behavior. If his competitors are doing it, taking market share and sales away from the company's business, it would be very tempting to "do as the Romans do." An executive I spoke to, a Vietnamese national who has a regional role in supply chain with a major multinational company, described to me the blatant attempts by some country officials he has dealt with to ask for bribes, for example, when getting shipments out of port docks.

The third influencing factor is internal to the company: the extent to which the company itself values and recognizes ethical behavior. Most major corporations these days have codes of conduct and ethical guidelines. Yet the existence of these codes does not necessarily guarantee that its executives, and the majority of employees, will behave ethically. Even Enron, the failed Houston-based company, had an ethics booklet of some 60-plus pages given to all employees with a foreword by Kenneth Lay, the CEO at that time.[8] Employees watch the behavior of their senior executives to see if they are "walking the talk." They also observe those who are rewarded and promoted to try to figure out the basis for their rewards and promotions.

What is the evidence on the universality of perceptions of what constitutes ethical behavior? Resick et al. (2006) used the data from the GLOBE Research Program to study the endorsement of ethical leadership across cultures. Twenty-three of the 100 items in the GLOBE survey were selected as reflective of ethical leadership; they then factor analyzed the data, which yielded four factors: character/integrity, altruism, collective motivation, and encouragement. Interestingly, they found that participants from the 62 countries in the GLOBE survey generally supported these four factors, although there were clear differences in the degree of endorsement. For example, Nordic managers endorsed character/integrity highly, while Middle Eastern managers less so. The authors suggest that "the dimensions of ethical leadership ... represent a *variform universal*, which exists when a principle is viewed similarly around the world; however cultural subtleties lead to differences in the enactment of that principle across cultures" (p. 354).

In another study, Resick et al. (2011) asked managers from six countries (the USA, Ireland, Germany, China, Hong Kong, and Taiwan) to describe their perceptions of ethical and unethical leadership. Leader character was an element of ethical leadership that they found common in all six countries, while acting in self-interest and misusing power was a common fundamental component of unethical leadership across these six countries. However, they point out that the degree of emphasis on various elements of ethical leadership will likely vary by country. Dickson et al. (2012) have summarized the research on perceptions of ethical leadership behavior and concluded that three behaviors across cultures that indicate lack of ethical behavior are: the leader acting in his/her own self-interest/lacking accountability; dishonesty/deceptiveness/lack of integrity; and misuse of power/poor treatment of employee.

Parboteeah et al. (2005) conducted an interesting study on the extent to which national cultures affect individuals' willingness to justify ethically suspect behaviors, such as accepting bribes, avoiding fares on public transport, and cheating on taxes. Using data from the World Values Survey, they found that two of the six cultural values (performance orientation and assertiveness) they measured were positively related to willingness to justify ethically suspect behavior, while a third (collectivism) was negatively related. They suggest that "the emphasis on competition, achievement and individual outcomes creates a focus on the ends and less concern for the means to achieve such ends" (p. 134). While this seems reasonable, the impact of cultural values might be dissipated by the strength of more local organizational and social norms.

As others have pointed out (e.g., see Donaldson 1996), however, managers working in foreign settings believe that what they consider ethical in their home country may not necessarily be considered ethical elsewhere, and vice versa. Cultural relativists argue that there are no rights or wrongs that are universal. According to them, managers who are in countries where bribery and corruption are quite common and acceptable have little choice but to go along with the prevailing practice; otherwise, their firms would be at a competitive disadvantage. This position is not tenable, especially in today's business environment, where social media can easily expose multinational corporations, and where government agencies can pursue claims against these corporations, no matter where these unethical practices are conducted. For example, child labor laws may be ambiguous or may even be non-existent in some countries, but if a multinational corporation were to use child labor in these countries on the premise that it is acceptable (or at least not illegal) there, the media and the public could easily highlight this practice and damage the corporation's reputation, if not its profits, in the long run.

At the other extreme are the cultural universalists, who argue that there are certain ethical standards and values that should be followed regardless of the country where managers are doing business.[9] For example, some corporations have very strict rules regarding gift-giving, interpreting any exchange of presents as a potential bribe and therefore to be avoided. However, as many managers working overseas have learned, gift-giving is a common business practice in several parts of the world. Donaldson and Dunfee (1999) have proposed accepting local cultural values as long as they are compatible with certain "hypernorms." They also propose that organizations identify specific local norms that may reflect local history and culture. Some of the evidence that would support a principle having hypernorm status are the following: widespread consensus that the principle is universal; it is an element of well-known global industry standards; it is consistently referred to as a global ethical standard by international media; it is known to be consistent with precepts of major religions. Donaldson and Dunfee list 11 such indicators.

If the principle does have hypernorm status, the next step would be to determine whether the specific situation warrants overcoming the presumption of hypernorm status. These hypernorms do vary and change over time, but in general, they include not abusing basic human rights and the elimination of widespread corruption. An example of the evolution of these hypernorms is with gender discrimination in employment practices in the USA. At one point, this was accepted and widespread, and was not illegal. In a profile of Supreme Court Justice Ruth Ginsberg for the *New Yorker*, Jeffrey Toobin wrote about a case in the 1960s when the courts in the state of Idaho ruled against a woman who wanted to be made administrator of the estate for her late teenage son. The woman suspected her husband to have shot their son after taking out an insurance policy on the young man but the courts ruled that "males must be preferred to females." It was only through years of effort and the passage of such laws as the Equal Pay Act and the Equal Rights Amendment that such practices became illegal.[10]

As it turns out, a group of researchers (Paine et al. 2005) have identified standards that they claim are widespread, based on an extensive analysis of sets of conduct guidelines such as the Organization for Economic Cooperation and Development (OECD) Guidelines and the UN Global Compact, codes of conduct of a select group of multinational companies, and a review of the Sarbanes-Oxley Act. They have consolidated these and have come up with what they call the Global Business Standards Codes.

> Viewed together, the source codes contain provisions relating to the six traditional corporate stakeholders: customers, employees, investors, competitors, suppliers/partners, and the public. Although the stances toward these constituencies vary ... the codes uniformly recognize that companies have responsibilities to several groups.

These codes have eight general principles and a set of conduct standards for putting these principles into practice. According to the authors: "Employees from every level ... strongly support adherence to the 62 standards ... despite wide differences in cultural origins and business environments ... Even on items that we thought would be controversial—such as respecting dignity and human rights—we found strong support." They conclude: "These surveys bolster our earlier research, in which we hypothesized an emerging consensus on widely accepted standards of conduct for global companies, and they belie the assumption that relativism should guide cross-border business practices."

Donaldson and Dunfee do suggest that there is room for "moral free space," which they define as "the area bounded by hypernorms in which communities develop ethical norms representing a collective viewpoint concerning right behavior ... (it) implies that it is right and proper for communities to self-define significant aspects of their business morality" (p. 83).

Kiel (2015) has studied the work of anthropologist Donald Brown (1991), who identified close to 500 behaviors and characteristics that he believes all human societies recognize and display. From Brown's list, Kiel identified four universal moral principles:

- Integrity—telling the truth; acting consistently with principles, values, and beliefs; standing up for what is right; keeping promises;
- Responsibility—owning one's personal choices; admitting mistakes and failures; expressing a concern for the common good;
- Forgiveness—letting go of one's mistakes; letting go of others' mistakes; focusing on what's right versus what's wrong;
- Compassion—empathizing with others; empowering others' actively caring for others' committing to others' development.

Kiel and his research team conducted an extensive study where they surveyed random samples of employees as well as their CEOs on behaviors of these CEOs and their executive teams. They then calculated a Character score for each CEO and his or her team. They were able to identify ten CEOs whose ratings placed them near the top of the Character Curve. They called these individuals Virtuoso CEOs. At the bottom of this curve were ten CEOs who were described by their employees through the surveys as having weak character and who were out for themselves. They called these individuals Self-Focused CEOs. Specifically, these CEOs could not be trusted to keep promises, often passed off blame to others, frequently punished well-intentioned people for making mistakes, and were especially poor at caring for people. They calculated that "the Virtuoso CEOs at the top end of the curve created a return on assets nearly five times greater than did the Self-Focused CEOs at the bottom of the curve"—9.5 % versus 1.9 % over a two-year period. Since almost all of these companies were from the USA (two were from Canada), it would be interesting to extend this study to non-US companies. I suspect that they would get similar results. This research, along with the studies on hypernorms, suggests a closer agreement toward some universal principles than what is suggested by the relativists.

An important distinction to be made is between what is legal and what is ethical. Imagine a matrix, as suggested by Henderson (1982), with legal–illegal on one dimension, and ethical–unethical on another dimension. Keep in mind that the definitions of what is legal and what is ethical may vary by country and even within a country, and may change over time. Nonetheless, when managers are considering what is right and wrong, it seems reasonable that they take into account these two dimensions. Examples of *legal and ethical* practices include paying a just wage for workers, firing supervisors who physically abuse their subordinates, and fulfilling the terms of a contract with a local vendor. *Illegal and unethical* practices include promoting individuals in exchange for sexual favors, hiring outside parties to threaten and even murder competitors, and deliberately replacing ingredients in products with those that are unsafe and dangerous in order to save costs. *Unethical but possibly legal* practices include hiring practices that explicitly discriminate on the basis of ethnic group or gender, insider trading (where there are no such laws in some countries), and dumping toxic waste in a river used by local citizens where there are no laws prohibiting this. *Ethical but possibly illegal* practices include working overtime without pay in order to meet a critical deadline, allowing employees to use office computers to send money electronically to a family relative who desperately needs it to pay for an operation, and driving over the speed limit to deliver a product that a client needs urgently as a matter of life and death.

The US Foreign Corrupt Practices Act (FCPA) makes it illegal for an employee of an organization doing business in the USA or of a US corporation to engage in bribery, except for certain facilitation payments.[11] In some cases, in doing business overseas, some executives have commented that they have actually been greeted with relief by local officials after mentioning that the company they represented would refuse to make any such payments. Besides, as Chayes (2015) has suggested, "'facilitation payments' are not as innocuous as often suggested. Distinguishing between such 'petty' bribery and so-called 'grand' corruption ... is a flawed analysis" (p. 200). Although referring more generally to countries and governments rather than corporations, she mentions that many such corrupt schemes are vertically integrated, and that "a flat refusal to do so ... usually succeeds."

In summary, the research indicates that despite the relativity of certain ethical behaviors, there is increasing general agreement on what constitutes acceptable business behavior across borders. Furthermore, despite any short-term gains made by engaging in certain unethical behaviors, such practices are increasingly risky and can harm a firm's long-term reputation and profitability. For individual global managers, the foundational requirement of integrity and ethics continues to be an important element of global leadership.

The following are some strategies for maintaining your ethical core. First, learn what the laws of the countries are in the places where you are doing business, in addition to making sure that you know what the laws of your home country are. For example, do not assume that because bribery is commonly practiced in that country, it is therefore legal. Many countries in fact do have anti-bribery laws, although some of them may not enforce them uniformly or consistently. Nonetheless, as a visitor to that country, you are subject to their laws and you need to be careful not to do anything illegal. These laws may also include specific statutes sponsored by various agencies such as the UN and the OECD that have been signed by several countries. Over 8000 businesses in about 145 countries have declared their support for the UN Global Compact,[12] which has ten principles that cover human rights, labor standards, the environment, and anti-corruption. These principles are not legally binding, but they signal a growing agreement on some basic principles with regard to corporate right and wrong. It is your responsibility as a global leader to find out as much as you can about the legality and ethics of business practices in the host country.

Second, learn what your company's own code of conduct is. According to Donaldson, 90 % of companies have one, and, just like ignorance of the law is no excuse, ignorance of your firm's code of conduct will not absolve you of responsibility. Many global companies require employees to go through some training every year, and you should find out proactively what the requirements are for your particular employer. These companies expect their employees to adhere to their codes of conduct regardless of where they are doing business. Of course having a code of conduct does not guarantee that a corporation will always behave ethically. Even Johnson & Johnson, whose "Credo" describing its values is well recognized by many of its employees, has gotten entangled with some ethical issues recently, with recalls of its products such as 1-Day Acuvue, hip replacement devices, and over-the-counter medicines such as Motrin, Rolaids, and Zyrtec (Santoro 2013).

Third, and perhaps most important, is to consider your own ethical code. It is best to do this before you are actually faced with an ethical dilemma, and to anticipate as much as possible where you might want to draw a line in the sand with regard to ethical behavior. As human beings, we can be quite adept at rationalizing our behavior, so having a framework, or even a mental checklist, might help you not get swayed by the pressures of the situation. It is not always with the major decisions where your integrity is tested, but the minor day-to-day decisions that will chip away at your integrity and make you vulnerable to ethical lapses in the future. Cavusgil et al. (2012) have proposed a four-step framework for arriving at ethical decisions, and I have modified as follows:

- Determine whether or not you are facing a situation or decision that has ethical dimensions. Business decisions can be judged according to cost–benefit analyses, but these analyses may not always factor in ethical implications. In some cases, the ethical implications will be clear, such as the request for a bribe from a local supplier. In other cases, it may not be so clear. In parts of Asia where gift-giving is prevalent, a more tolerant approach may be more appropriate. Doing business in many parts of the world requires building relationships with partners, and often these are accomplished through exchanges of gifts and the sharing of meals. Nonetheless, make sure you are aware of your company's code of conduct regarding such matters.
- Do some investigating and fact-finding. Make sure you are aware of the context, and of prevailing cultural norms. Consider the issue from the viewpoint of different stakeholders, such as employees, the community, and senior management. Do not be so quick to condemn any approach that seems suspicious to you, nor should you immediately jump to the conclusion that there is no other alternative but to acquiesce to a request that seems unethical.
- Identify alternative actions and evaluate them based on ethical standards. Make sure to explore different alternatives, for example, by identifying "interests" versus "positions" (Fisher et al. 2011). This is where you will need some kind of an ethical framework or set of criteria to apply in determining your best course of action. Clearly, you will have some business-related criteria, for example, return on investment, increase in market share, capturing an important consumer segment, dominating a local market. Instead of paying off a local mayor, for example, your company may instead make a commitment to hire local people, thereby enhancing the mayor's standing and also improving the company's reputation in the community.

- Consult with others before making the decision. You might want to approach your manager, or someone in the company who has knowledge of the company's code of conduct and who could give you good advice. I know several global managers located overseas who have built relationships with fellow countrymen in a different industry in the overseas location. These individuals have been in their overseas location for several years and have valuable knowledge and experience that they are willing to share.

This presupposes that global managers will have the luxury of time to systematically analyze their choices and then make the right ethical choice. Yet in some circumstances, they will be faced with having to make a quick decision. That is why it is important for global leaders to internalize not only their company's code of conduct but also their own sense of right and wrong. The US Marine Corps (1995) has a good rule of thumb to follow:

"If you are prepared to talk about your actions, or lack thereof, in front of a national audience, made up of all your seniors, peers, subordinates and friends who share the same professional values, and whose opinions you value, then your behavior was, or is, probably ethical in nature" (p. 42).

For organizations, Buller et al. (2000) suggest that the following conditions are important in setting a climate that supports ethical behavior:

- Top managers value ethics as an integral part of the company's mission, strategy, and culture and demonstrate consistent commitment to the vision over time.
- The organization engages in a collaborative learning process with its international employees, suppliers, customers, and other partners to develop an understanding of and sensitivity to cross-cultural perspectives on ethics.
- The organization's human resource management practices (e.g., selection, performance appraisals, training and development) are designed to build and sustain an ethical climate.

PRACTICE #8: LEARN TO INTEGRATE DIFFERENCES

A colleague, whom I shall call Jeff, was meeting with the country manager of Taipei, who worked for the subsidiary of a global company. They had just completed a coaching session, where they reviewed the manager's 360-degree feedback and discussed how Asians might answer survey-type questions, when the manager, who I shall call Ron, told him that he wanted Jeff's advice on a sensitive issue. The subsidiary had been doing so well, he explained, that he got approval from his boss, an American regional Vice President based in Hong Kong, to find new offices for his expanding staff. His boss and he had agreed on a budget for the rental of new office space, and he and his executive team had settled on a couple of locations. As part of their decision process, they had hired a *feng shui* master to recommend which of the two office locations would be more suitable, and the *feng shui* master strongly recommended Office A over Office B. Unfortunately, Office A was also more expensive and the rental rates would be over the budget that his boss had approved. Together they problem solved several approaches. Ron and his team reviewed their sales projections and estimated that by raising their sales goals by a small percentage, they could more than make up for the increased cost of moving to Office B. When Ron called his regional Vice President and explained the situation, and his proposed solution, he was immediately given the green light to go ahead.

Integrating differences means creating win–win solutions, where differences (and conflicts) can be reconciled without disrespecting or denying the importance of different parties' viewpoints. In the same interview cited earlier in this book (Stahl and Brannen 2013), Carlos Ghosn also had an opinion on this topic of win–win solutions:

> The ability to find creative and mutually beneficial solutions is also important. For instance, we have a rule that we can never make a decision to pursue a project in which one side wins and the other side loses. Never—even if that means that ultimately the project is completed at a slightly slower pace than if we had imposed a top-down decision in which one team had to surrender. Some people don't understand this. In particular, some outside observers have said, "Come on, you are slowing down the Alliance. There are so many opportunities. You should decide today to make a decision where Renault wins and Nissan loses, and tomorrow you can make a decision where Nissan wins and Renault loses, and then everything's going to be okay because, at the end of the day, everybody wins." But this doesn't work. (p. 498)

Shell (2006) has identified the different bargaining styles people have when negotiating with others, and has developed an instrument called the Bargaining Styles Assessment Tool. According to Shell, there are five bargaining strategies people typically use: avoiding, compromising, accommodating, competing, and collaborating (or problem-solving). Global leaders who practice integrating differences come close to what Shell describes as the collaborative approach:

> High collaborators enjoy negotiations because they enjoy solving tough problems in engaged, interactive ways. They are instinctively good at using negotiations to probe beneath the surface of conflicts to discover basic interests, perceptions, and new solutions. They relish the continuous flow of the negotiation process an encourage everyone to be involved. They are assertively and honestly committed to finding the best solution for everyone. (p. 246)

Shell is well aware of cultural differences in negotiations, and in fact states that the most important difference in cross-cultural negotiations is the way the parties perceive the relationship factor (page 26):

> North Americans and northern Europeans tend to focus more quickly on the transactional aspects of the deal, whereas most Asian, Indian, Middle Eastern, African, and Latin American cultures focus more intently on social, relational aspects.

Perceptions of these differences will affect the choice of negotiation tactics (see Imai and Gelfand 2009, for a comprehensive review). It would seem that dimensions such as power distance, individualism, time orientation, and uncertainty avoidance would impact negotiators' preferences toward certain tactics. For example, Imai and Gelfand (2010) summarize that:

> U.S. negotiators, who tend to be more individualistic and low context, are more likely to share information *directly* and they tend to achieve high joint gains though this strategy. By contrast, Japanese, Russian, and Hong Kong negotiators, who tend to be more collectivistic and high context, are more likely to share information *indirectly* through their patterns of offers and achieve high joint gains through this strategy. (p. 341)

Given all this, why is this practice important, and how does one get better at integrating differences? A key element in this practice is taking into account different cultural and other factors without necessarily assuming that one is better or worse than another. Applying this practice helps a global leader to build the global mindset element of acceptance. Youssef and Luthans (2012) refer to this as being "ambicultural," where a global leader is looking for the best of both cultural worlds, rather than viewing the differences as a gap that has to be minimized or eliminated:

> consider the numerous occasions in which intra-cultural differences or diversity within an organization may be more pronounced than national intercultural differences across geographically dispersed operations on a particular phenomenon or cross-cultural dimension. Research and practices that attempt to systematically understand, affirm, and integrate the unique characteristics of diverse contexts would be in a better position to capitalize on these differences for a better understanding of the phenomenon or construct in question, rather than discounting inconsistencies as measurement error simply because they do not "fit" the preconceived differences or universalities. (p. 544)

There may be circumstances when such integration may be difficult if not impossible. However, the global leader's going-in position should be to integrate, and not to select between one or the other. Here are some strategies for integrating differences. One is to encourage input and discussion. In some cultures, this will not be a problem because your colleagues will be more than willing to contribute their ideas. In other cultures, however, you may have to draw out your colleagues. During meetings and in one-to-one conversations, make sure you make statements that reinforce your willingness and desire to listen to their ideas. For example, you might say, "I am interested in what you think about this idea" or "If you have any concerns, I would be really interested in learning about them." Ask your colleagues what they think, what might happen if a certain management practice were implemented in their country, or what some of the barriers might be in implementing such a practice, and what could be done to address these barriers.

A second suggestion is to allow for "soak time." Do not rush for a solution. Creative ideas may need time to percolate, and so making sure that you and your colleagues have had some time to think about, and discuss, ways to integrate different ideas is important. As an example, for many multinationals, introducing a Western-based performance management system to their Japanese subsidiaries has been a challenge. In one case, the subsidiary of a multinational was a very traditional Japanese firm, where employees were promoted based on tenure, and where supervisors and managers had no input on their employees' evaluations or on how they were to be rewarded. In fact, this was not a part of the managers' role.

This large multinational was following a practice long used by other major corporations and with which employees in many Western companies were very familiar. For an individual employee, goals are set at the beginning of the year, in discussions with the manager. The goals ideally would be aligned with group and department goals, and there would be metrics on what success looked like at different levels of the organization. Throughout the year, there would be ongoing feedback and adjustments to these goals and measures of success as needed. At the end of the year, there would be a formal review session, where the manager would review the employee's performance. The employee would be assigned an overall performance rating, which would be the basis for year-end bonuses and other financial rewards. The performance rating would also be one of the indicators of the individual's potential for promotions and career advancement in the company.

In the traditional Japanese performance management system, with its emphasis on collectivism and group cohesion, managers and employee do not discuss individual goals. In fact, employees have no individual goals—just group goals. Some multinationals have tried to resolve such differences between their corporate or global approach and the Japanese approach by simply dictating that from now on, this is the way things will get done by stating something like the following: "You (the subsidiary) are now part of our global corporation and because we need to do certain things consistently and in a standard way, this is the way you have to do it."

This global multinational, and the global managers assigned to the subsidiary, used a different implementation approach. First, a team was formed made up of local Japanese employees and managers from HQs. The team worked in Tokyo for several months, often up to late hours of the night (following Japanese business work practices), with breaks for dinner and the occasional Friday karaoke sessions. Second, they spent considerable time learning each other's systems, the context for these systems, and an assessment of the strengths and weaknesses of both systems. After weeks of discussion, they reached agreement on the overall objectives for the performance management system in the subsidiary, with some core principles that all believed were important in developing such a system, and an implementation plan. This was presented and approved by senior management of the subsidiary as well as the parent company.

These steps were far from linear. It was difficult for the Japanese to understand, much less accept, the assumptions behind the Western approach to performance management. At the same time, the global managers from HQs found it frustrating at times that the cultural gaps underlying the two systems were significant. It certainly helped that they got to know each other well through many face-to-face work meetings and social situations. Also, by reaching agreement on the overall objectives and core principles, the corporate and the Japanese teams were able to agree and align on most steps, thus gaining widespread acceptance by managers in the subsidiary. Most importantly, they recognized that the changes could not be made overnight, and so they developed a transition plan to implement this new system in stages. After a year, along with communication and training of managers at all levels, the system was successfully implemented in the subsidiary.

PRACTICE #9: BUILD YOUR GLOBAL TEAM PLAYER SKILL SET

When I ask students in my MBA classes how many of them belong to cross-functional teams, between half to three-quarters typically raise their hands. And when I ask them if they also belong to global teams (where members are from different cultures and are in different geographic locations), most of them keep their hands raised.

The reasons for the increasing frequency of these teams are not surprising. First of all, many organizations have recognized for some time that their talent pool is not restricted to their HQs location, and so using the best and the brightest, no matter where they are located, makes sense. Second, many organizational solutions require cross-functional as well as cross-border collaboration, and restricting team membership primarily to one function or to those coming from a single country (typically where its HQs office is located) is not a smart strategy.

Note that the extent of globalness of a team may also depend on the number of geographies as well as the number of cultures represented on the team. When a team is also virtual (communicating using electronic tools and not primarily meeting face to face), an added layer of complexity is added. Stanko and Gibson (2009) have suggested that virtuality is multidimensional, and have included dynamic structuralism as another dimension of cross-cultural or global teams (i.e., how frequently change occurs among members, their roles, and relationships to each other). While this dimension certainly is present in many global teams, it can also be present in domestic teams, and may not necessarily define the uniqueness of global teams. Hollenbeck et al. (2012) have suggested three dimensions for describing teams: skill differentiation, authority differentiation, and temporal stability. Foster et al. (2015) suggest adding the dimension of virtuality, which they define simply as the distance between team members at work and as a continuous variable.

What do we know about the effectiveness of these teams? From diversity research, the evidence on the relationship between diversity and team performance is mixed. Recently, Stahl et al. (2010) extended the research to international teams and found similar results—that cultural diversity leads to increased creativity and satisfaction, but not necessarily to improved performance. Social identity theory (Brewer 1996) suggests that in diverse groups, individuals are more likely to see themselves as belonging to different groups and therefore might be less likely, at least initially, to show empathy or to collaborate with others. Furthermore, according to Brewer, our social identity is based on two opposing needs—our need to assimilate and be included in a group, and our need to differentiate ourselves from others. When we categorize ourselves, our need for inclusiveness increases, but then our need for differentiation is activated. We can reach equilibrium when "the need for assimilation and belonging is met within the social group and the need for differentiation is met by intergroup distinctions (i.e., by the difference between the in-group and others)" (p. 296).

The more diverse a team, the more challenging it might be for members to identify with the team and be willing to cooperate and collaborate. As Earley (1993) has pointed out, "globally diverse teams (those with members from varying countries of origin and cultures) require a strong emphasis on commonality to be successful" and that "the key for a successful but highly heterogeneous team is the formation of a common social structure, emphasizing universally held goals, roles, and rules." With regard to global virtual teams, there is also evidence to suggest that national or cultural diversity may hinder innovation and team effectiveness (Gibson and Gibbs 2006; Swigger et al. 2004). Interestingly, Staples and Zhao (2006) showed that a culturally diverse virtual team actually outperformed a culturally diverse face-to-face team on a decision-making task, although in general the evidence on performance outcomes for virtuality is quite mixed.

Based on three of the classical works on teams - Lencioni's *The Five Dysfunctions of a Team* (Lencioni 2002), Hackman's *Leading Teams* (Hackman 2002), and Katzenbach and Smith's *The Wisdom of Teams*

(Katzenbach and Smith 2006), the following are four key success factors on what makes a team effective: the team has to have a compelling vision or goal, members need to trust one another, their skills (whether these are technical or social skills) need to be complementary, and attention needs to be paid to team processes.

This is consistent with research by Maznevski (2008), in which she defines four conditions necessary for the performance of any team: task definition (knowing what the task and objectives are), team composition (having the right combination of skills), roles (both task-related and process-related roles need to be present), and processes (especially communication, conflict resolution, and project management). She includes trust as one of the characteristics beyond these four basic conditions. For global teams, especially, trust is particularly important because of the greater cultural differences among team members.

These same key success factors can be applied to global virtual teams, although making these factors work effectively becomes more complex and more challenging. Some of the challenges are obvious: differences in geography, time, language, diversity, culture, size, and technology. For example, research by Mockaitis et al. (2012) showed that individuals in multicultural teams with collectivist orientations (as measured by a Collectivism scale as well as by the individuals' nationalities) tended to have higher levels of trust, interdependency, and commitment to information sharing than those with individualist orientations. Other challenges, such as gaining the participation and commitment of team members, are subtler. In addition, many global team leaders are managing teams whose members do not report directly to them. Therefore, these team leaders have to learn to exercise "influence without authority" (Cohen and Bradford 2007).

Other relevant cultural orientations that might impact the behavior of team members and ultimately team effectiveness may include authoritarianism, time orientation, expressiveness, and directness. There is research on how some of these orientations impact collaboration and team outcomes, but clearly more is needed. Since it appears that there may be different degrees or levels of global virtuality, the relative importance of these orientations based on the extent to which a team is globally virtual also needs to be studied further.

Surprisingly, many of the studies of global virtual teams do not consider explicitly the impact of the leader. An effective global team leader can help accelerate the establishment of these key success factors. In their study of 13 globally diverse virtual teams, Kayworth and Leidner (2002) found that effective virtual team leaders exhibited many of the characteristics of global leaders described here; for example, they asserted their authority in a flexible manner, and provided regular, detailed, and prompt communication.

According to research by Govindarajan and Gupta (2001), 82 % of the global teams they surveyed fell short of their intended goals. Govindarajan and Gupta identified five challenges of global virtual teams:

1. Cultivating trust
2. Overcoming communication barriers
3. Aligning goals of individual team members
4. Ensuring that the team possesses necessary knowledge and skills
5. Obtaining clarity regarding team objectives

How can the four success factors cited earlier help global team leaders address each of these challenges?

Cultivating Trust

In many parts of the world, building relationships takes precedence over immediately working on the task requirements. Like empathy, researchers (e.g., McAllister 1995) have identified two types of trust: affective- and cognitive-based trust. The former is about building the emotional bond between persons, while the latter is more concerned with gains and losses, and where competence and reliability are important qualifications for trust to occur. Similar to the earlier discussion on trust (Orbell et al. 1994), which focused on the trustor's evaluation of the trustee's competence and benevolence, McAllister suggests that the antecedents of affective-based trust include the trustee's citizenship behavior toward the trustor, and the frequency of interaction between the two. The antecedents of cognitive-based trust include the trustee's reliable role performance, their cultural or ethnic similarity, and the trustee's professional credentials.

In McAllister's formulation, cognitive-based trust is necessary before affective-based trust develops, at least in organizational settings. However, in many cultures, affective-based trust may have to be established before cognitive-based trust is built. For example, Kwan and Hong (2014) state: "In Chinese organizations, it is possible that affective-based trust serves as the foundation for cognitive-based trust development; that is, trusting someone's abilities follows when *Guanxi* (affective-based trust) has been developed" (p. 102).

Therefore, it is important for a team leader to make sure that at the very least, global team members know one another on a personal level. Structure interactions and meetings early on to make sure that members are comfortable working with each other and that they understand each other's background, experience, and what they can contribute. It is not enough to assume that because individuals all work for the same company, they have common interests or shared goals. Although it may be difficult to have face-to-face meetings due to time or resource constraints, doing so is a worthwhile investment. As Epley (2014) has pointed out, physical distance is an important aspect of our engagement with others. He cites evidence from war and battles that soldiers who are fighting are more reluctant to use their weapons when the enemy is close to them physically.

Pay attention to group and social processes; for example, make sure that you establish protocols on how the team will communicate, how they will interact with each other during meetings, and other "ground rules" on how the team will function (e.g., who is responsible for informing team members who may not be present for a meeting, how disagreements and conflicts will be resolved). Build opportunities for the team to spend time together socially. John Spencer, a major in the US Army, has raised concerns about what lack of bonding and cohesion can do with soldiers. When he was stationed in Iraq in 2003, he witnessed firsthand how soldiers bonded together; they ate together, spent time with each other, and had little contact with the outside world other than the occasional letters and packages. When he returned in 2008, the impact of cell phones and social media was evident. Soldiers would spend hours by themselves posting on Facebook and sending messages to their friends and families. As a result, Major Spencer observed: "I saw them arguing about what decisions to make … Groups seemed unable to learn from their daily challenges or direct any intergroup policing of individual actions." He is rightly concerned about the lack of conversation during non-combat time "when bonds of trust, friendships and group identity are built."[13] Spending time on social interactions is important not only for soldiers but also for teams, especially global teams.

Brian is a senior process engineer with over 20 years of experience working for a global pharmaceutical company. His company sent him to its Puerto Rico facility for 11 months to bring it up to standard for compliance with regulatory requirements as well as to establish lean and efficient manufacturing processes. Brian was responsible for managing about 30 employees. He had never been to Puerto Rico before but he assumed that, since it was a commonwealth and the subsidiary had been in place for over 30 years, the cultural challenges would be minimal. He did brush up on his Spanish before leaving, but was surprised to learn on his first week on the job that over half of the employees there did not speak English.

Since Brian was from corporate HQs, he felt that there was a trust gap between employees and him; employees seemed to react very defensively when questioned. Brian reached out to colleagues in HQs who had gone overseas for other assignments, and he asked for their advice. They suggested that he focus on developing team building with his staff. He solicited ideas from his staff on what social activities would interest them, and he eventually decided on getting together for lunch every Monday (paid for by the company), Happy Hour every Wednesday, and golf every Friday afternoon. Brian found that a number of good ideas were generated especially during the Monday lunches. As Brian said later on, "You have to empower the local people you are working with and demonstrate that you are not just there to be another boss; you must connect on a higher level." Brian also concentrated on accelerating his Spanish language skills over the next month, and soon, he was getting comfortable in interacting with his employees in Spanish.

Interestingly, there is some research that suggests that a level of distrust among team members might actually be helpful especially when dealing with non-routine decision tasks. Lowry et al. (2015) found that distrust in a group can actually be increased by using a less routine task and introducing an "environmental abnormality." This was operationalized through instructions given to some teams that a person in their group might be trying to undermine the decision results. They found that decision accuracy was higher in non-routine decision tasks with an additional distrust treatment than in non-routine decision tasks without this treatment.

Having a level of distrust will lead team members to be more suspicious, question more rigorously, and not take too many things for granted—all of which can help to improve decision outcomes. While this study is interesting, this research was based on virtual teams that were not diverse culturally (all were students from a US university), so one should use caution in generalizing from the results of this study. Furthermore, creating distrust may have unintended consequences, especially with regard to team cohesion and alignment of goals.

Overcoming Communication Barriers

While many global team members in multinational organizations may speak English, their level of confidence with speaking English will vary. To address this, leaders may need to use translators from time to time. Make sure that agenda items are communicated ahead of time, and minutes of meetings are circulated after the meeting. Allow some time toward the end of meetings to encourage members to make comments if some have not done so. Develop clear operating procedures for your team meetings (e.g., circulate agendas at least three days in advance, identify the purpose for bringing up a topic). Follow up individually with team members who do not seem to be participating as actively in team meetings, and probe carefully for possible reasons.

Aligning Goals of Individual Team Members

Do not assume that team members are all committed to the team goal. Consider the following strategies for building alignment. First, understand the work priorities and performance goals of each of your team members by initiating discussions with team members' bosses to make sure that they are aware of the commitments required by global team membership, and that they are fully supportive of their subordinates' participation. Second, watch for symptoms of non-alignment, for example, members not showing up for meetings, not volunteering for tasks, not delivering on their commitments. Third, engage and excite the team with a compelling vision. Identifying a business issue that members all agree is important for the organization to address will help the team to be purpose-driven (Pascarella and Frohman 1989). Fourth, make sure you link the business impact of your team's goals to the organization's success. Some researchers (e.g., Milton and Westphal 2005) refer to this as mutual empathy or collective empathy. Having a team goal will increase the level of collective empathy, which will in turn help to improve trust and collaboration within the team.

Ensuring that the Team Possesses the Necessary Knowledge and Skills

While team members may have the necessary technical skills, does the team have the right balance of cognitive and interpersonal styles? Successful global teams not only make sure skills are complementary but also that all members have opportunities to build their knowledge and skill base, not only in business and technical aspects but also in two important areas: understanding and dealing with cultural differences, and building collaboration skills. While Katzenbach and Smith's research suggests that complementary interpersonal skills may not be that critical as long as members can develop these while on the team, this balance may take on greater importance with global teams.

Obtaining Clarity Regarding Team Objectives

Is everyone on the team clear on what success looks like for the team? Are metrics well defined and does everyone agree with these metrics? If you sense a lack of clarity, or lack of agreement, address this by bringing in the team sponsor (the person or group that you as team leader are accountable to for the team's progress) to help clarify goals. Make sure that you define expectations and deliverables with the sponsor and communicate these to the team. The team sponsor can play a role in giving some recognition to the team as it makes progress. Is everyone clear on his or her roles and responsibilities (especially for those who may still have their regular "day job" in addition to being a team member)? Being aware of these challenges and some ways to address them should help the global team leader, and ultimately make participation more rewarding and fulfilling for everyone on the team (Thomas et al. 2012).

As an example of a global leader who has learned to manage his team effectively, let's take Andrezj, a project manager in the international division of a global financial services company. After a successful six-month assignment in Japan, his company sent Andrezj (who was born in Poland and then went to university in America) to South Korea for an extended assignment. Believing that he would not have to adjust in Seoul since both countries were Asian, he was in for a rude awakening. He found the Koreans to be very transparent and results oriented. At times he found them to be abrasive, where there were screaming matches that he learned to accept. On his first day, Andrezj was asked for his marital status, his salary, his religion, and even his political affiliation.

As with many Asian societies, relationship-building is important in Korean culture. For example, in Andrezj's first day in the office, he bought a sandwich from a vendor on a street corner and brought it back to his desk to eat. A colleague of his came over to ask him what he was doing sitting and eating lunch at his desk. Besides, all the lights were out because everyone went out for lunch, and several were sleeping with their pillow on their desk. His colleague took him out to lunch and later that afternoon, brought in a calendar and placed people's names from the company so he could have scheduled lunches with everyone for the next year.

He found out that Koreans work long hours, including Saturdays and most Sundays. Like Japanese, Koreans like to go out as a team after work. In the evenings, round one is the restaurant, round two is the bar, and round three is sometimes after midnight at *Noraebangs* (karaoke parlors). Andrej began to build trust, but he also realized that he had to make sure his team members understood how their work was contributing not only to the country's business but also to the broader corporate objectives. When the regional head visited Seoul, he made sure that his team had an opportunity to meet him and that they heard him speak about the importance of the work the team was doing.

Martin et al. (2014) suggest that managers and leaders of teams can improve cooperation and support among team members by paying attention to the things that teams share. However, they employ a slight twist to this—by recommending that the team focus on uncommon commonalities—those features members have in common with others that are rare to other external groups. According to them, this will fulfill people's desire both to fit in and also to stand out from other groups.

Along with this approach, it might be helpful to identify what the unique contributions of each member are. A team leader of global teams will need to be very skillful in drawing out similarities and differences of team members, especially when figuring out areas of competence. In some cultures, speaking about one's achievements may seem like boasting, and these team members may be hesitant to speak about some of their accomplishments in front of others.

There is intriguing research in the medical field on this aspect cited by Gawande (2011). For example, at the beginning of a case, if operating surgeons ask nurses for their names and what concerns they have, they are more likely to note problems and identify solutions. For Gawande, "Giving people a chance to say something at the start seemed to activate their sense of participation and responsibility and their willingness to speak up" (p. 108).

One of the most widely used models for team development is Tuckman's four-stage model of forming, storming, norming, and performing (Tuckman 1965). According to Tuckman, groups go through these predictable stages, although not always in a linear fashion. What does this mean for global team players? Let's say that you are a marketing manager in one of your company's subsidiaries and your direct boss, the country managing director, calls you into his office and lets you know that he has received an e-mail from the chief operating officer (COO) requesting your participation in a global task force that is charged with considering opportunities for globalizing marketing programs and reducing marketing costs by 20 %. For global teams, the forming stage actually starts sooner than the first face-to-face meeting among team members. Here are some questions it would be important to get answers to for you as a global team player or leader:

- Who is the "sponsor" of this team? In other words, who has commissioned the formation of this team, and to whom this team is ultimately accountable?
- What are the objectives of this team, and how will success be measured?
- Who is on the team, and why were they selected?
- How long will the team be operating?
- What is the time commitment expected? Depending on the answer, individuals may need to negotiate with their direct boss as to expectations for their regular job responsibilities while they are also participating in the team.
- Who is responsible for expenses of the team?

You may not be able to get all the answers immediately, but these are important questions to keep in mind. For a team leader, here are some suggestions based on research and practice for making sure that a global team goes through the forming stage successfully:

- To the extent that you have control over this, make sure that team members are selected based on their ability to collaborate and their global mindset as well as their technical or professional qualifications and expertise.
- Involve the team members' managers and make them aware of the importance of the team, the time commitments you are requiring from their subordinates, and how the team's objectives will have a positive impact on his or her organization or country.
- Use multiple methods of communication in your initial contacts with team members. For example, this may involve an e-mail from

a senior executive of the company inviting the employee to the team, followed by his or her manager having a conversation with the employee, and then followed by your e-mail as well as a telephone call from you.

- Learn as much as you can about each team member, and have everyone provide some basic information about themselves prior to the first meeting.
- Prepare carefully for your first team meeting, which should be ideally a face-to-face meeting. If this is not possible, make sure you select a time for your first conference call that will be convenient for a majority of the team members, even if this may not be convenient for you.
- Circulate an agenda prior to the first meeting, but do not overstructure it. Assuming that the meeting will be conducted in English, remember that some of your team members may not speak English fluently. Allow at least 25 % more time for discussions than you normally would in a meeting where everyone speaks English very well. If there are documents to be discussed at the first meeting, make sure you send these out at least one week before the meeting.
- During the first meeting, take time to explain the rationale for the team, the objectives, and the metrics to be used. If available, invite the team sponsor to the first meeting; this will signal to all team members senior management commitment and interest in the project.
  - Be sure to define roles and responsibilities, and the team's "operating ground rules." Invite comments and ask for feedback.
  - Allow at least ten minutes toward the end of the meeting and ask each member if they have anything more to add or comment.
- After the first meeting (and subsequent ones), send out the draft minutes and ask for comments. If you are meeting face-to-face, make sure you build some team-building and social activities after the meeting so members can get to know each other better and build relationships. Be careful not to put members in a position where they are uncomfortable sharing too much personal information in front of everyone. This is best done one-on-one initially.

As research has shown, the nature and characteristics of the task can be a strong predictor of how groups will perform (Hackman and Vidmar 1970). For example, teams do better on complex tasks than on simple tasks. Whereas many global teams will most probably work on complex tasks, it is important for a team leader to understand the task context and how this might influence performance outcomes.

In the storming stage, the major issue for global teams is resolving conflicts and building trust. As Govindarajan and Gupta (2001). have pointed out, there are many challenges to trust-building in global teams. Here are some strategies:

- Be sensitive to participation levels in your team, and follow up to determine root causes. For example, is the reason why Masato seems quiet is because of his English, because he may not be in agreement with some of the decisions, or because he is feeling pressure from his regular job and cannot devote the time to participate actively in the team? You need to make the time to establish a relationship with Masato (and possibly his manager) and figure out what the problem might be.
- Be aware of differences and conflicts, and proactively address these conflicts constructively. It is inevitable, especially in the storming stage, that you will find differences among team members. Some of these differences may be due to disagreements about the tasks or about the approaches being applied to address these tasks. Other differences might be related to interpersonal issues. Some team members may not get along with others, for a variety of reasons. As the team leader, you need to nip these issues in the bud before they become dysfunctional to the team. Interpersonal conflicts are more difficult to resolve; they will exist throughout the life of a team but are especially critical during the storming stage.
- Address performance issues and dysfunctional members sooner rather than later. Invariably, you will have one or more of these issues and/or members in your global team. Sometimes, it will take a while to figure out what the root causes are, but the patterns of non-performance will emerge: not showing up at meetings, not delivering on certain tasks they have committed to, having reports and documents that have many errors. There may be a team member who is a whiner and a pessimist, cynical about the group's work and about the impact the team might have on the project's outcomes. Sutton (2010) advises that good bosses (and, by extension, team leaders) "make subtraction a way of life." (p. 267) By this he means that good bosses get rid of the rotten apples and other barriers that get in the way of high performance. In addition, a good boss will first

diagnose the situation to determine whether coaching or feedback can help address the problem.

A senior executive in one of the organizations I used to work for had a reputation for being a mean-spirited and terrible boss, who not only consistently demeaned her staff but also did not collaborate well with her peers. Yet her division continued to perform and deliver results year after year, despite the rising turnover in her staff. Eventually a new CEO came on board and within two months, he offered the executive a retirement package. When the announcement was made that she had left the company, employees actually burst into applause, and several of the CEO's direct reports asked him what took him so long.

The norming stage, according to Tuckman, is when team members start to feel cohesive and an identity begins to form. For global virtual teams, it may take longer to reach this stage because of distance and lack of face time. Lane et al. (2009) have proposed that such global teams make sure that they "create a heartbeat." These heartbeat meetings and sessions are critical to keep the team engaged; with global teams that are co-located, it is admittedly easier to create these. Schedule regular activities and set milestones so that a team routine gets established.

In one assignment, I led a global team made up of managers from eight different nationalities (Mexico, Germany, Thailand, and England were among the countries represented). Fortunately, senior management provided us with the resources to meet face to face at a separate facility near our HQs location, and we worked daily for about a year until the project was completed. Every day, we had regularly scheduled meetings with specific agenda items and each member responsible for providing brief updates. Every other week, we would have a meeting with our executive sponsor. In addition, we had sub-teams that met every other day that were required to report on the outcomes of meetings and their progress during weekly team meetings. While these may seem like a lot of meetings and activities, it helped establish a "heartbeat" for the team as well as keep team members connected. With the aid of modern electronic technologies, global virtual teams can approximate some of these heartbeats. As a leader, it is important to create opportunities to establish these heartbeats for the team (Moore 2005).

In Tuckman's performing stage, the team is humming along, with a high level of trust among team members. As Tuckman states, "Roles become flexible and functional, and group energy is channeled into the task. Structural issues have been resolved, and structure can now become supportive of task performance" (p. 78). One barrier that global teams face perhaps more frequently than domestic teams is team stability. Hackman (2002) has pointed to the importance of keeping team members together over a period of time; his research indicates that team stability is an important predictor of group performance. Unfortunately, in global teams, team members are often replaced more than what might be optimal for team performance. In some cases, team members get promoted; in other cases, they leave the company or get re-assigned by their local general manager to some other high-priority project. While this is inevitable, the team leader has to make sure that there is some continuity, and create mechanisms whereby the departing team member debriefs his or her learnings to the incoming team member so there is sufficient knowledge transfer.

It is an unfortunate fact of modern organizational life that companies are separated by silos characterized by competition, hostility, and lack of communication across departments and functions—not to mention across geographies, in the case of global organizations. The CEO of a company got so frustrated by the finger-pointing between Sales and Marketing that he called both groups together and chewed them out for engaging in internecine warfare. He concluded by saying, "The enemy is not the other group—the enemy is the competition that is trying to take sales and market share away from us."

A global leader who can bridge this gap will add a lot of value. Sutton and Rao (2014) refer to certain people in organizations who fill these roles as knowledge brokers who become bridges for otherwise disconnected groups. Sarah is a marketing development manager working at the HQs of a global consumer products company. She is responsible for supporting marketing groups worldwide in their implementation of the marketing strategies for a particular product line. She spends over 50 % of her time on the road, traveling to different countries and working with local marketing managers to make sure she understands their specific issues, and that they understand the corporate perspective. When she discovers good ideas in a subsidiary, she encourages the local managers to share the information through quarterly meetings and monthly video conferences that she sets up and facilitates. According to Sutton and Rao, such knowledge brokers have five elements in common, and Sarah illustrates them well. I paraphrase their description (pp. 208–210):

- They are curious about strangers and their ideas. They are "relentlessly interested in and eager to meet people who know things that (they don't)—and to have detailed conversations with them." When Sarah is in a subsidiary, she tries to meet as many people as possible, and not just from Marketing. She even has conversations with the janitorial staff and the local subsidiary's chauffer.
- They live and breathe the mindset but are not obnoxious about it. Sarah makes sure to weave in the corporate perspective in her conversations with subsidiary managers, but she does not insist that they adhere to company policies, at least without listening to their perspective.
- They have strong opinions, weakly held. Sarah has a point of view based on her knowledge of the company's strategies, but recognizes that there may be some adaptations to marketing plans that will need to be made in various subsidiaries.
- They listen and learn. For Sutton and Rao, this means that they "ask more questions and make fewer statements ... (they give) advice only after hearing what you need."
- They convene, introduce, and connect. Sarah is constantly looking for opportunities to connect managers together who might have some common challenges or might have solutions that others might benefit from.

In a recent review of the literature on global team leadership, Zander et al. (2012) have identified boundary-spanning as another important capability of those leading global teams. More research on this topic is needed, especially around the different types of boundary-spanning activities that global leaders can play (Butler et al. 2012). In one particular organization that launched a major initiative, the global team leader was in charge of a team of 11 managers who represented different functions and geographies. None of these members reported directly to him, with all of them having matrix reporting relationships. The team leader not only had to concern himself with getting the right sponsorship he also had to reach out to each of the team members' managers and other functional leaders in the organization to get their buy-in on and support for the initiative.

It seems evident that a contingent or situational leadership style is important in dealing with globally diverse teams. There is research that suggests, for example, that for such diverse teams, a relationship style is more critical while for non-diverse teams, a task style was more important

(Milliken and Martins 1996). However, there is still much that we need to understand on the fit between leadership style and team diversity. How diverse does a team need to be? Are there other behaviors or demands that might compensate for the type of leadership style that might be appropriate, for example, if team members are all committed to the team goal?

As a former global leader myself with several global organizations, I have led global teams with members from different cultures; some of these teams have been face-to-face, and others have been virtual. In other occasions, I have been a team member in global teams. There are different challenges in managing each of these types of teams, apart from the cultural diversity of the members. However, the more culturally dissimilar the members are, the greater is the challenge for the team leader to create conditions that build trust, create open communication, and gain commitment toward team goals. This is clearly more difficult to do with virtual teams, but some of the strategies described here should help global leaders become more effective.

When Zoe was promoted to become the Asia-Pacific regional marketing head for her company, a major global consumer products firm, she was very excited. She had been head of marketing for Taiwan for the past five years, and had achieved outstanding results. Shortly after her promotion, Zoe flew to the USA to meet with her new boss and her counterparts from the other regions. She was determined to get an in-depth understanding of the company's global marketing strategy and its implications for her region. While in the USA, she also scheduled one-on-one meetings with some potential key stakeholders, such as the Head of R&D and the head of Human Resources. She spent time meeting with her new boss, hoping to understand exactly what his expectations were and what his perspective was on whether and how to adapt global strategies to fit local markets. She accompanied marketing researchers to retail stores where some of the company's key products were being sold to find out more about consumers and their preferences in the US market.

After returning to Taiwan, she then decided to visit each of the six countries that she was now responsible for and spend time meeting with the marketing teams to better understand their local customers. While in each country, she took time to explain the company's global marketing strategies and asked each team how they thought these strategies could be implemented in their market, and where they thought these strategies could be adapted to better fit local market conditions. She also described her marketing vision for the region, how excited she was to be working with them, and shared some of her expectations.

Rather than flying "in and out," as she observed previous executives had done, Zoe made sure to spend a week in each country. Working with the local marketing head, she developed an agenda for each country that involved meeting with the country head and his functional heads, meeting one-on-one and in groups with the marketing professionals, and visiting retail stores to learn about marketing and consumer practices in the country. Her evenings were not exactly free either. She scheduled dinners with several key executives (both from within the subsidiary as well as outsiders, such as key suppliers and government officials) and had at least one group dinner in each country.

At the end of each visit, Zoe shared with the local marketing head her observations, asked for feedback, and, with the team, identified follow-up actions for her team and herself. She asked the country manager for feedback, as well as for any additional support or resources that might be needed for the country's marketing team. In one country, there was quite a bit of concern and pushback about the pricing for one of the company's products that were about to be introduced. Both the country manager and the marketing head were not convinced that the proposed pricing from corporate would be competitive and would generate the expected revenue for the product. That week, Zoe and the country manager made calls to the Global Marketing head as well as the head of Asia-Pacific to express their concerns, and to present data based on market research on competitors' price points and consumer preferences. Based on these discussions, the pricing was modified.

It is too early to tell whether or not Zoe's approach will lead to outstanding results, but I believe, based on my experience and practices of successful global companies, that Zoe is on the right path to becoming an outstanding global leader. Let's examine more carefully what Zoe is doing. First, it is clear that Zoe is adopting a global mindset. She understands that while HQs may be driving global strategies, her role is not simply to push this strategy down to the countries but to make sure that she can synthesize and integrate, adapting where necessary to local market conditions.

Second, Zoe is making an effort to understand her company's overall strategy and priorities. At the same time, Zoe is aware that she needs to align her region to the company's goals, so a clear understanding of the company's priorities is important so that she can explain this perspective to her country teams.

Third, Zoe is also making an effort to understand local stakeholders' and customers' needs. As Bartlett and many others have pointed out (Bartlett and Beamish 2008), one of the key challenges of a global company is managing the tension between standardization and customization. By drilling down so that she is familiar with each market, Zoe will be in a better position to recognize and recommend solutions that meet both corporate needs as well as regional and local needs.

Fourth, Zoe is building relationships. She understands that in many Asian cultures, relationships come before task. People will need to trust you first before they will do business with you, and so Zoe is spending time building relationships. She is doing this through both formal and informal means, spending time in meetings as well as socializing after office hours.

While it is clear that global leaders use global mindset to improve their influence and effectiveness, there is much that we do not know about the process they use. Osland et al. (2009), for example, have suggested that global leaders use intercultural sense-making, which involves framing the situation, making attributions, and selecting scripts.

Perhaps global managers could do with some kind of a checklist. Gawande (2011) wrote about the Chairman of Surgery at the University of Toronto, who has been using a 21-item surgery checklist to catch potential errors in surgical care. What is interesting is that the checklist also includes a team briefing. "The team members were supposed to stop and take a moment simply to talk with one another before proceeding— about how long the surgeon expected the operation to take, how much blood loss everyone should be prepared for, whether the patient had any risks or concerns the team should know about" (pp. 100–101). In surgery, according to Gawande, you can have checklists for three of the four big killers: infection, bleeding, and unsafe anesthesia. The fourth killer in surgery is the unexpected. To prevent this, Gawande suggests having a checklist to facilitate a dialogue, where the staff has to stop and talk through the case together before surgery.

Unfortunately, according to Gawande, this kind of teamwork is not common in surgical teams. Some research he cites shows that team members who regularly used checklists showed great improvements in their ratings of their own teamwork. According to Gawande, "under conditions of complexity, not only are checklists a help, they are required for success.

There must always be room for judgment, but judgment aided—and even enhanced—by procedure" (p. 79).

What kinds of cross-cultural management situations might a checklist be used for? Actually, Useem (2011) has come up with his own checklist for leaders, consisting of 15 principles. Like Gawande, he argues that "when uncertainty becomes the norm and turbulence more commonplace ... a Leader's Checklist becomes more consequential" (p. 41).

Many of the 15 principles in Useem's leader checklist could apply to managers leading globally. They include articulating a vision, communicating persuasively, and building leadership in others. However, global leaders face different circumstances and need to take into consideration cultural variables. Useem himself suggests that his checklist must be customized for a leader's particular circumstances.

Similarly, Seibert et al. (2002) constructed a checklist to help with cultural awareness and sensitivity in medical settings. In the medical profession, according to the authors, culturally competent health care is a term that "requires that the health professional be sensitive to the differences between groups, to the differences in outward behavior, and also to the attitudes and meanings attached to emotional events" (p. 143). They suggest that a checklist could help health care providers be more aware of cultural issues, particularly in times of crisis and stress. Their checklist has ten areas of focus, and instructions for each of these ten areas. For example, under health care provider bias, the checklist item is to "Always remember, we all have biases and prejudices. Examine and recognize yours" (p. 145).

Based on a synthesis of the research covered in this book, along with the suggested practices, we propose a checklist for global managers in Table 7.2. The targets referred to in this checklist are those individuals, groups, or organizations from another culture with whom a global leader will be interacting. The checklist, along with the specific practices for implementing these principles, may vary depending on the situation. For example, an individual leading a global virtual team might have different practices and focus on different principles than an individual working on a long-term assignment within a subsidiary.

Table 7.2   A global leader's checklist

1. *Define your role.* Take steps to make sure you understand what you will be responsible for, and what the measures of success are
2. *Identify your default mode.* Examine your preferred leadership style or approach, especially when dealing with others from the same culture
3. *Learn the cultural code.* Find out as much as you can about the cultural norms, practices, and behaviors, and the dos and don'ts of the culture of the individual or group with whom you will be interacting
4. *Maintain your core.* You don't have to do as the Romans do; however, beware of assuming that you need not change at all
5. *Adapt your style.* While staying true to your values, adapt your behaviors to the host culture accordingly
6. *Ask questions and listen.* Especially during the early stages of cross-cultural interactions, do less talking and learn as much as you can
7. *Respect the culture.* Make an effort to understand the culture and appreciate cultural practices
8. *Build relationships.* You have a role to deliver results, but how you do this depends on your ability to build relationships with others
9. *Convey confidence and enthusiasm.* Demonstrate to your colleagues that you enjoy their culture and your role, and you believe that your colleagues' work can make a positive difference to the organization
10. *Recognize and celebrate.* Communicate your appreciation for the team's efforts and celebrate when milestones are reached
11. *Reflect on what you are learning.* Take the time to consider lessons learned; find a cultural mentor to give you feedback

NOTES

1. See   http://www.winstonchurchill.org/resources/myths/churchills-speech-impediment-was-stuttering,   http://www.stutteringhelp.org/tiger-woods-wins-golf-and-stuttering   and   http://stuttertalk.com/tag/jack-welch/
2. Kevin Randall, "Teams Turn to a Face Reader, Looking for That Winning Smile," the New York Times, December 25, 2014: http://www.nytimes.com/2014/12/26/sports/nba-bucks-looking-for-an-edge-hire-expert-in-face-time.html
3. See his January 17, 2015 column entitled "The Network Effect."
4. Keith O'Brien, "The Empathy Deficit," The Boston Globe, October 17, 2010 in http://archive.boston.com/bostonglobe/ideas/articles/2010/10/17/the_empathy_deficit/
5. Seven Lessons in Management I Learnt Over the Last Decade, from the Financial Times, January 8, 2015.
6. http://www.nytimes.com/2014/06/05/business/after-walmart-bribery-scandals-a-pattern-of-quiet-departures.html?_r=0

7. See their web site: https://www.transparency.org/
8. Seehttp://blogs.cfainstitute.org/insideinvesting/2013/10/14/the-enron-code-of-ethics-handbook-from-july-2000-is-a-fascinating-read/ and http://bobsutton.typepad.com/my_weblog/2009/03/the-enron-code-of-ethics-something-every-boss-should-read.html
9. McDonald (2010) offers the argument that differences in ethical actions could still be rooted in universal moral standards.
10. Jeffrey Toobin, "Heavyweight," The New Yorker, accessed August 19. http://www.newyorker.com/magazine/2013/03/11/heavyweight-ruth-bader-ginsburg.
11. http://www.justice.gov/criminal-fraud/foreign-corrupt-practices-act
12. See https://www.unglobalcompact.org/
13. See John Spencer's article in the New York Times, November 6, 2015, "A Band of Tweeters."

References

Adler, Nancy J. 2008. *International Dimensions of Organizational Behavior*, Fifth edn. Mason, OH: South-Western Publishing.

Alicke, Mark D., David L. Breitenbecher, Tricia J. Yurak, and Debbie S. Vredenburg. 1995. Personal Contact, Individuation, and the Better-Than-Average Effect. *Journal of Personality and Social Psychology* 68(5): 804–825.

Ambady, Nalini, and Robert Rosenthal. 1992. Thin Slices of Expressive Behavior as Predictors of Interpersonal Consequences: A Meta-Analysis. *Psychological Bulletin* 111(2): 256–274.

Bates, Reid. 2002. Liking and Similarity as Predictors of Multi-Source Ratings. *Personnel Review* 31(5): 540–552.

Bazerman, Max. 2014. *The Power of Noticing: What the Best Leaders See*. New York: Simon and Schuster.

Bolster, Bruce Irving, and B.M. Springbett. 1961. The Reaction of Interviewers to Favorable and Unfavorable Information. *Journal of Applied Psychology* 45(2): 97–103.

Bolton, Robert. 1979. *People Skills*. Englewood Cliffs, NJ: Prentice-Hall.

Brewer, Marilynn B. 1996. When Contact is Not Enough: Social Identity and Intergroup Cooperation. *International Journal of Intercultural Relations* 20(3/4): 291–303.

Brown, Donald. 1991. *Human Universals*, First edn. New York: McGraw-Hill.

Buckingham, Marcus, and Donald O. Clifton. 2001. *Now, Discover Your Strengths*. New York: Simon and Schuster.

Buller, Paul F., John J. Kohls, and Kenneth S. Anderson. 2000. When Ethics Collide: Managing Conflicts Across Cultures. *Organizational Dynamics* 28(4): 52–66.

Butler, Christina L., Lena Zander, Audra Mockaitis, and Ciara Sutton. 2012. The Global Leader as Boundary Spanner, Bridge Maker, and Blender. *Industrial and Organizational Psychology* 5(2): 240–243.

Cavusgil, S. Tamer, Gary Knight, and John Riesenberger. 2012. *International Business: The New Realities*. Englewood Cliffs, NJ: Prentice-Hall.

Chatman, Jennifer A., Jeffrey T. Polzer, Sigal G. Barsade, and Margaret A. Neale. 1998. Being Different Yet Feeling Similar: The Influence of Demographic Composition and Organizational Culture on Work Processes and Outcomes. *Administrative Science Quarterly* 43(4): 749–780.

Chayes, Sarah. 2015. *Thieves of State: Why Corruption Threaten Global Security*. New York: W. W. Norton.

Clapp-Smith, Rachel, and Tara Wernsing. 2014. The Transformational Triggers of International Experiences. *Journal of Management Development* 33(7): 662–679.

Cohen, Allan, and David Bradford. 2007. *Influence Without Authority*, Second edn. New York: Wiley.

Colvin, Geoff. 2014. Employers Are Looking for New Hires with Something Extra: Empathy. *Fortune* 170(4).

Cross, Rob, and Laurence Prusak. 2002. The People Who Make Organizations Go—Or Stop. *Harvard Business Review* 80(6): 104–112.

Dickson, Marcus W., Nathalie Castaño, Asiyat Magomaeva, and Deanne N. Den Hartog. 2012. Conceptualizing Leadership across Cultures. *Journal of World Business* 47(4): 483–492.

Donaldson, Thomas. 1996. Values in Tension: Ethics Away from Home. *Harvard Business Review* 74(5): 48–62.

Donaldson, Thomas, and Thomas Dunfee. 1999. *Ties That Bind: A Social Contracts Approach to Business Ethics*. Boston: Harvard Business Review Press.

Drolet, Amy, Richard Larrick, and Michael Morris. 1998. Thinking of Others: How Perspective Taking Changes Negotiators' Aspirations and Fairness Perceptions as a Function of Negotiator Relationships. *Basic and Applied Social Psychology* 20(1): 23–31.

Duckworth, Angela L., Christopher Peterson, Michael D. Matthews, and Dennis R. Kelly. 2007. Grit: Perseverance and Passion for Long-Term Goals. *Journal of Personality and Social Psychology* 92(6): 1087–1101.

Dweck, Carol. 2006. *Mind Set: The New Psychology of Success*. New York: Random House.

Earley, Christopher. 1993. East Meets West Meets Mideast: Further Explorations of Collectivistic and Individualistic Work Groups. *Academy of Management Journal* 36(2): 319–348.

Earley, Christopher, and Soon Ang. 2003. *Cultural Intelligence: Individual Interactions Across Cultures*. Palo Alto, CA: Stanford Business Books.

Earley, P. Christopher, and Elaine Mosakowski. 2004. Cultural Intelligence. *Harvard Business Review* 82(10): 139–146.

Ekman, Paul. 1993. Facial Expression and Emotion. *American Psychologist* 48(4): 384–392.

Ely, Robin J., and David A. Thomas. 2001. Cultural Diversity at Work: The Effects of Diversity Perspectives on Work Group Processes and Outcomes. *Administrative Science Quarterly* 46(2): 229–273.

Epley, Nicholas. 2014. *Mindwise: How We Understand What Others Think, Believe, Feel, and Want.* New York: Knopf.

Ericsson, K. Anders, Ralf T. Krampe, and Clemens Tesch-Römer. 1993. The Role of Deliberate Practice in the Acquisition of Expert Performance. *Psychological Review* 100(3): 363–406.

Fisher, Roger, William Ury, and Bruce Patton. 2011. *Getting to Yes*, Revised edn. New York: Penguin Books.

Foster, Mary, Augustus Abbey, Michael Callow, Zu Xingxing, and Anthony Wilbon. 2015. Rethinking Virtuality and Its Impact on Teams. *Small Group Research* 46(3): 267–299.

Galinsky, Adam D., and Gordon B. Moskowitz. 2000. Perspective-Taking: Decreasing Stereotype Expression, Stereotype Accessibility, and in-Group Favoritism. *Journal of Personality and Social Psychology* 78(4): 708–724.

Gawande, Atul. 2011. *The Checklist Manifesto.* New York: Picador.

Gesteland, Richard R. 2012. *Cross-Cultural Business Behavior: A Guide for Global Management.* Denmark: Copenhagen Business School Press.

Gibson, Cristina B., and Jennifer L. Gibbs. 2006. Unpacking the Concept of Virtuality: The Effects of Geographic Dispersion, Electronic Dependence, Dynamic Structure, and National Diversity on Team Innovation. *Administrative Science Quarterly* 51(3): 451–495.

Gladwell, Malcolm. 2008. *Outliers: The Story of Success.* New York: Hachette.

Goldsmith, Marshall. 2007. *What Got You Here Won't Get You There: How Successful People Become Even More Successful.* New York: Profile Books.

Goldsmith, Marshall, and Howard Morgan. 2004. Leadership Is a Contact Sport. *Strategy + Business* 36: 70–79.

Golen, Steven. 1990. A Factor Analysis of Barriers to Effective Listening. *Journal of Business Communication* 27(1): 25–36.

Gomez-Mejia, Luis, David Balkin, and Robert Cardy. 2012. *Managing Human Resources*, Seventh edn. Upper Saddle River, NJ: Prentice-Hall.

Govindarajan, Vijay, and Anil K. Gupta. 2001. Building an Effective Global Business Team. *MIT Sloan Management Review* 42(4): 63–71.

Hackman, J. Richard. 2002. *Leading Teams: Setting the Stage for Great Performance.* Boston: Harvard Business Press.

Hackman, J. Richard, and Neil Vidmar. 1970. Effects of Size and Task Type on Group Performance and Member Reactions. *Sociometry* 33(1): 37–54.

Hall, Edward. 2013. *The Silent Language.* Reissued. New York: Anchor Books.

Henderson, Verne. 1982. The Ethical Side of Enterprise. *Sloan Management Review* 23(3): 37–47.

Hollenbeck, John R., Bianca Beersma, and Maartje E. Schouten. 2012. Beyond Team Types and Taxonomies: A Dimensional Scaling Conceptualization for Team Description. *Academy of Management Review* 37(1): 82–106.

Holtbrügge, Dirk, Abigail Weldon, and Helen Rogers. 2013. Cultural Determinants of Email Communication Styles. *International Journal of Cross Cultural Management* 13(1): 89–110.

Hyland, Patrick, R. Andrew Lee, and Maura Mills. 2016. Mindfulness at Work: A New Approach to Improving Individual and Organizational Performance. Manuscript accepted. *Industrial-Organizational Psychology* 8(4): 576–602.

Ibarra, Herminia. 2015b. *Act Like a Leader, Think Like a Leader*. Boston: Harvard Business Review Press.

Imai, Lynn, and Michele Gelfand. 2009. Interdisciplinary Perspectives on Culture, Conflict, and Negotiation. In *Cambridge Handbook of Culture, Organizations, and Work*, eds. Rabi Bhagat and Richard Steers, 334–372. New York: Cambridge University Press.

Imai, Lynn, and Michele J. Gelfand. 2010. The Culturally Intelligent Negotiator: The Impact of Cultural Intelligence (CQ) on Negotiation Sequences and Outcomes. *Organizational Behavior and Human Decision Processes* 112(2): 83–98.

Jones, Edward, and Richard Nisbett. 1987. The Actor and the Observer: Divergent Perceptions of the Causes of Behavior. In Jones, Edward, David Kanouse, Harold Kelley, Richard Nisbett, Stuart Valins, and Bernard Weiner (Eds.). *Attribution: Perceiving the Causes of Behavior*, 79–94. Hillsdale NJ: Lawrence Erlbaum Associates.

Katzenbach, Jon, and Douglas Smith. 2006. *The Wisdom of Teams: Creating the High-Performance Organization*. New York: HarperBusiness.

Kayworth, Timothy R., and Dorothy E. Leidner. 2002. Leadership Effectiveness in Global Virtual Teams. *Journal of Management Information Systems* 18(3): 7–40.

Kiel, Fred. 2015. *Return on Character: The Real Reason Leaders and Their Companies Win*. Boston: Harvard Business Review Press.

Konrath, Sara H., Edward H. O'Brien, and Courtney Hsing. 2010. Changes in Dispositional Empathy in American College Students Over Time: A Meta-Analysis. *Personality and Social Psychology Review* 15(2): 180–198.

Kruger, Justin. 1999. Lake Wobegon Be Gone! The 'Below-Average Effect' and the Egocentric Nature of Comparative Ability Judgments. *Journal of Personality and Social Psychology* 77(2): 221–232.

Krull, Douglas S., Michelle Hui-Min Loy, Jennifer Lin, Ching-Fu Wang, Suhong Chen, and Xudong Zhao. 1999. The Fundamental Fundamental Attribution

Error: Correspondence Bias in Individualist and Collectivist Cultures. *Personality and Social Psychology Bulletin* 25(10): 1208–1219.

Kwan, Letty, and Ying-yi Hong. 2014. Culture, Group processes, and Trust. In *Culture and Group Processes*, eds. Masaki Yuki and Marilynn Brewer, 93–117. New York: Oxford University Press.

Lane, Henry, Martha Maznevski, Joseph DiStefano, and Joerg Dietz. 2009. *International Management Behavior: Leading with a Global Mindset*, Sixth edn. Great Britain: Wiley.

Langer, Ellen. 1989. *Mindfulness*. Cambridge, MA: DeCapo Press.

Larrick, Richard P., Katherine A. Burson, and Jack B. Soll. 2007. Social Comparison and Confidence: When Thinking You're Better than Average Predicts Overconfidence (and When It Does Not). *Organizational Behavior and Human Decision Processes* 102(1): 76–94.

Lencioni, Patrick. 2002. *The Five Dysfunctions of a Team*. San Francisco, CA: Jossey-Bass.

Levine, Mark, Amy Prosser, David Evans, and Stephen Reicher. 2005. Identity and Emergency Intervention: How Social Group Membership and Inclusiveness of Group Boundaries Shape Helping Behavior. *Personality and Social Psychology Bulletin* 31(4): 443–453.

Levinson, Wendy, Debra Roter, John Mullooly, Valerie Dull, and Richard Frankel. 1997. Physician-Patient Communication: The Relationship with Malpractice Claims among Primary Care Physicians and Surgeons. *Journal of the American Medical Association* 277(7): 553–559.

Little, Brian. 2014. *Me, Myself and Us: The Science of Personality and the Art of Well-Being*. New York: Public Affairs.

Lowry, Paul Benjamin, Ryan M. Schuetzler, Justin Scott Giboney, and Thomas A. Gregory. 2015. Is Trust Always Better than Distrust? The Potential Value of Distrust in Newer Virtual Teams Engaged in Short-Term Decision-Making. *Group Decision and Negotiation* 24(4): 723–752.

MacNab, Brent R., and Reginald Worthley. 2013. Stereotype Awareness Development and Effective Cross-Cultural Management: An Experiential Approach. *International Journal of Cross Cultural Management* 13(1): 65–87.

Martin, Steve, Noah Goldstein, and Robert Cialdini. 2014. *The Small Big: Small Changes That Spark Big Influence*. New York: Grand Central Publishing.

Martinovski, Bilyana, David Traum, and Stacy Marsella. 2006. Rejection of Empathy in Negotiation. *Group Decision and Negotiation* 16(1): 61–76.

Maznevski, Martha. 2008. Leading Global Teams. In *Global Leadership: Research, Practice and Development*, ed. Mark Mendenhall et al. 94–113.

McAllister, Daniel J. 1995. Affect- and Cognition-Based Trust as Foundations for Interpersonal Cooperation in Organizations. *Academy of Management Journal* 38(1): 24–59.

McDonald, Gael. 2010. Ethical Relativism vs Absolutism: Research Implications. *European Business Review* 22(4): 446–464.

Miller, Dale T., and Michael Ross. 1975. Self-Serving Biases in the Attribution of Causality: Fact or Fiction? *Psychological Bulletin* 82(2): 213–225.

Milliken, Frances J., and Luis L. Martins. 1996. Searching for Common Threads: Understanding the Multiple Effects of Diversity in Organizational Groups. *Academy of Management Review* 21(2): 402–433.

Milton, Laurie P., and James D. Westphal. 2005. Identity Confirmation Networks and Cooperation in Work Groups. *Academy of Management Journal* 48(2): 191–212.

Mockaitis, Audra I., Elizabeth L. Rose, and Peter Zettinig. 2012. The Power of Individual Cultural Values in Global Virtual Teams. *International Journal of Cross Cultural Management* 12(2): 193–210.

Moghaddam, Fathali M., and Peter Stringer. 1998. Out-Group Similarity and Intergroup Bias. *The Journal of Social Psychology* 128(1): 105–115.

Molinsky, Andrew L., Mary Anne Krabbenhoft, Nalini Ambady, and Y. Susan Choi. 2005. Cracking the Nonverbal Code Intercultural Competence and Gesture Recognition Across Cultures. *Journal of Cross-Cultural Psychology* 36(3): 380–395.

Moore, Fiona. 2005. *Transnational Business Cultures: Life and Work in a Multinational Corporation*. Burlington, VT: Ashgate Publishing.

Moran, Joseph, Eshin Jolly, and Jason Paul Mitchell. 2014. Spontaneous Mentalizing Predicts the Fundamental Attribution Error. *Journal of Cognitive Neuroscience* 26(3): 569–576.

Morgan, Nick. 2014. *Power Cues: The Subtle Science of Leading Groups, Persuading Others, and Maximizing Your Personal Impact*. Boston: Harvard Business Review Press.

Moser, Jason S., Hans S. Schroder, Carrie Heeter, Tim P. Moran, and Yu-Hao Lee. 2011. Mind Your Errors: Evidence for a Neural Mechanism Linking Growth Mind-Set to Adaptive Post-error Adjustments. *Psychological Science* 22(12): 1484–1489.

Neeley, Tsedal, and Robert Steven Kaplan. 2014. What's Your Language Strategy? *Harvard Business Review* 92(9): 70–76.

Neuwirth, Zeev E. 1997. Physician Empathy—Should We Care? *The Lancet* 350(9078): 606–606.

Newport, Cal. 2012. *So Good They Can't Ignore You*. New York: Hachette Book Group.

Nicholson, Nigel. 1998. How Hardwired Is Human Behavior? *Harvard Business Review* 76: 134–147.

Orbell, John, Robyn Dawes, and Peregrine Schwartz-Shea. 1994. Trust, Social Categories, and Individuals: The Case of Gender. *Motivation and Emotion* 18(2): 109–128.

Osland, Joyce, Sully Taylor, and Mark Mendenhall. 2009. Global leadership progress and challenges. In *Cambridge Handbook of Culture, Organizations, and Work*, eds. Rabi Bhagat and Richard Steers, 245–271. New York: Cambridge University Press.

Paine, Lynn, Rohit Deshpande, Joshua Margolis, and Kim Eric Bettcher. 2005. Up to Code: Does Your Company's Conduct Meet World-Class Standards? *Harvard Business Review* 83(12): 122–133.

Parboteeah, K. Praveen, James W. Bronson, and John B. Cullen. 2005. Does National Culture Affect Willingness to Justify Ethically Suspect Behaviors? A Focus on the GLOBE National Culture Scheme. *International Journal of Cross Cultural Management* 5(2): 123–138.

Pascarella, Perry, and Mark A. Frohman. 1989. *The Purpose-Driven Organization: Unleashing the Power of Direction and Commitment*. San Francisco, CA: Jossey-Bass.

Pink, Daniel H. 2013. *To Sell Is Human: The Surprising Truth About Moving Others*. New York: Penguin.

Pinker, Susan. 2014. *The Village Effect*. New York: Spiegel and Grau.

Resick, Christian, Paul Hanges, Marcus Dickson, and Jacqueline Mitchelson. 2006. A Cross-Cultural Examination of the Endorsement of Ethical Leadership. *Journal of Business Ethics* 63(4): 345–359.

Resick, Christian J., Gillian S. Martin, Mary A. Keating, Marcus W. Dickson, Ho Kwong Kwan, and Chunyan Peng. 2011. What Ethical Leadership Means to Me: Asian, American, and European Perspectives. *Journal of Business Ethics* 10(3): 435–457.

Rosenzweig, Phil. 2014. *Left Brain, Right Stuff: How Leaders Make Winning Decisions*. New York: PublicAffairs.

Ross, Lee. 1977. The Intuitive Psychologist and His Shortcomings: Distortions in the Attribution Process. In *Advances in Experimental Social Psychology*, ed. Leonard Berkowitz, 173–220. New York: Academic Press.

Sanchez-Burks, Jeffrey, Caroline A. Bartel, and Sally Blount. 2009. Performance in Intercultural Interactions at Work: Cross-Cultural Differences in Response to Behavioral Mirroring. *Journal of Applied Psychology* 94(1): 216–223.

Santoro, Michael. 2013. It's Time for J&J to Challenge the Credo ... Again. *Medical Marketing & Media*, October 13.

Schmidt, Frank, and John Hunter. 1998. The Validity and Utility of Selection Methods in Personnel Psychology: Practical and Theoretical Implications of 85 Years of Research Findings. *Psychological Bulletin* 124(2): 264–274.

Sedikides, Constantine, Rosie Meek, Mark D. Alicke, and Sarah Taylor. 2014. Behind Bars But Above the Bar: Prisoners Consider Themselves More Prosocial Than Non-Prisoners. *British Journal of Social Psychology* 53(2): 396–403.

Seibert, P., P. Strodh-Igo, and C. Zimmerman. 2002. A Checklist to Facilitate Cultural Awareness and Sensitivity. *Journal of Medical Ethics* 28(3): 143–146.

Shell, G. Richard. 2006. *Bargaining for Advantage: Negotiation Strategies for Reasonable People*. New York: Penguin.

Stahl, Günter K., and Mary Brannen. 2013. Building Cross-Cultural Leadership Competence: An Interview With Carlos Ghosn. *Academy of Management Learning & Education* 12(3): 494–502.

Stahl, Günter K., Martha L. Maznevski, Andreas Voigt, and Karsten Jonsen. 2010. Unraveling the Effects of Cultural Diversity in Teams: A Meta-Analysis of Research on Multicultural Work Groups. *Journal of International Business Studies* 41(4): 690–709.

Stanko, Taryn, and Cristina Gibson. 2009. The Role of Cultural Elements in Virtual Teams. In *Cambridge Handbook of Culture, Organizations, and Work*, eds. Rabi Bhagat and Richard Steers, 272–304. New York: Cambridge University Press.

Staples, D. Sandy, and Lina Zhao. 2006. The Effects of Cultural Diversity in Virtual Teams Versus Face-to-Face Teams. *Group Decision and Negotiation* 15(4): 389–406.

Stone, Douglas, Bruce Patton, and Sheila Heen. 2010. *Difficult Conversations: How to Discuss What Matters Most*. Penguin.

Sutton, Robert. 2007. *The No Asshole Rule*. New York: Business Plus Books.

Sutton, Robert. 2010. *Good Boss, Bad Boss: How to Be the Best … and Learn from the Worst*. New York: Business Plus.

Sutton, Robert, and Huggy Rao. 2014. *Scaling Up Excellence*. New York: Crown Business.

Swigger, Kathleen, Ferda Alpaslan, Robert Brazile, and Michael Monticino. 2004. Effects of Culture on Computer-Supported International Collaborations. *International Journal of Human-Computer Studies* 60(3): 365–380.

Tannen, Deborah. 2007. *You Just Don't Understand: Men and Women in Conversation*. New York: William R. Morrow.

Thomas, Robert J., Joshua Bellin, Claudy Jules, and Nandani Lynton. 2012. Global Leadership Teams: Diagnosing Three Essential Qualities. *Strategy & Leadership* 40(3): 25–29.

Todorov, Alexander, Anesu N. Mandisodza, Amir Goren, and Crystal C. Hall. 2005. Inferences of Competence from Faces Predict Election Outcomes. *Science* 308(5728): 1623–1626.

Triandis, Harry. 1995. *Individualism and Collectivism*. Boulder, CO: Westview Press.

Tuckman, Bruce. 1965. Developmental Sequence in Small Groups. *Psychological Bulletin* 63(6): 384–399.

Useem, Michael. 2011. *The Leader's Checklist*. Philadelphia: Wharton Digital Press.

U.S. Marine Corps. 1995. *Leading Marines*. Rockville, MD: Wildside Press.

Vecchi, Gregory M., Vincent B. Van Hasselt, and Stephen J. Romano. 2005. Crisis (Hostage) Negotiation: Current Strategies and Issues in High-Risk Conflict Resolution. *Aggression and Violent Behavior* 10(5): 533–551.

Winter, Laramie, James Uleman, and Cathryn Cunniff. 1985. How Automatic Are Social Judgments? *Journal of Personality and Social Psychology* 49: 904–917.

Wiseman, Liz. 2014. *Rookie Smarts: Why Learning Beats Knowing in the New Game of Work*. New York: HarperBusiness.

Youssef, Carolyn M., and Fred Luthans. 2012. Positive Global Leadership. *Journal of World Business* 47(4): 539–547.

Zander, Lena, Audra I. Mockaitis, and Christina L. Butler. 2012. Leading Global Teams. *Journal of World Business* 47(4): 592–603.

CHAPTER 8

Building an Organizational Global Mindset Culture: Implications for Practice

As a young professional in an emerging market, would you rather work for a global multinational or for a local company? Perhaps as recently as ten years ago, this question was a "no-brainer" for many bright talented men and women in emerging markets like Brazil, China, Thailand, and Chile. Working for a global company, especially one with a brand name and a strong reputation, was especially attractive for them. In many cases, the pay was greater but beyond that, the opportunities for developing professionally, as well as advancing (maybe even being sent abroad for an assignment), were far better than they were for local companies.

Executives of global companies paint a far different picture of the competition for talent today, especially in these emerging markets. First, a number of global multinationals' growth plans have stalled, or at least have slowed down. Second, in some cases, these multinationals have had to downsize and lay off local staff; in a few cases, companies have exited these markets entirely. Third, local companies, by contrast, have been growing and in some cases, have begun to expand outside their home country (Chattopadhyay et al. 2012). Fourth, as local companies have begun to build a strong managerial base and a more professional development process, the gap in the development of executives between global and local companies has narrowed. And fifth, the gap in compensation packages between global and local companies has also narrowed.

© The Editor(s) (if applicable) and The Author(s) 2016
R. Henson, *Successful Global Leadership*,
DOI 10.1057/978-1-137-58990-3_8

There are of course tremendous advantages that some global multinationals have. Many of these companies have been around for over 50 years, and they have a stable and deep history, which is still very appealing today to many young professionals in overseas markets. Furthermore, management practices such as managing by objectives, performance reviews, and coaching are well-established in these companies. Someone just out of school or coming from a state-owned company or family-owned business to join a multinational would have significant opportunities to learn about these modern management practices.

Nonetheless, the reality is that competing for talent in today's globalized world, especially for US- and European-based multinational companies, has become very challenging. Peter Drucker (1973) wrote presciently about multinational corporations many years ago when he said:

> It has to create unity within its own managerial organization and yet do justice to the diversity of peoples, nationalities and loyalties within it. And it has to create a unified business that can optimize factorial costs and factorial advantages within a common and yet live in peace … with a multitude of separate political sovereignties. (pp. 741–743)

Because of this complexity, Drucker did not believe that multinationals should diversify; in fact, he called the multinational conglomerate "an abomination." At the same time, he encouraged localization; he argued that local decisions had to be made at the scene of the action, although they had to be made within the framework of corporate strategy. He added that local management structures needed to fit the culture of the country in which they were based. The situation is somewhat different today, especially with many organizations recognizing that their corporate culture can be a competitive advantage. Furthermore, an element of this corporate culture that organizations like BMW, Colgate-Palmolive, IBM, Mondelez, and Unilever are trying to instill is a global mindset. Unfortunately, they are more the exception than the rule. Ghemawat (2012) cites a survey of senior executives by the Ashridge Business School that found that 76 % believe their organizations needed to develop global leadership capabilities, but only 7 % think they were currently doing so very effectively.

If global mindset is an important attribute for individuals, might it also be a cultural attribute that an organization could develop? Earlier, we mentioned Dweck's (2006) concept of growth mindset. Recently, Dweck has been exploring the idea whether organizations can have growth mindsets.[1] So far, her research seems promising. In her work, she describes various CEOs and their management approaches, implying that the CEO creates the mindset for the organization. For example, she points to Lee Iacocca, former executive of Ford and head of Chrysler, as someone who believed in his own inherent superiority and was constantly finding ways to enhance his own greatness. He was constantly worried about his subordinates getting credit, and so he was always finding ways to get rid of them. There are other contemporary examples of strong leaders who have influenced the mindset of the organizations they led for the better (e.g., Yvon Chouinard of Patagonia, Howard Schultz of Starbucks, Tony Hsieh of Zappos) of for the worse (e.g., Sepp Blatter formerly of FIFA, Tony Hayward formerly of BP, Robert Nardelli formerly of Home Depot).

Dweck discusses the fixed mindset that was pervasive at Enron, where people competed with each other in a cutthroat manner and the former CEO encouraged a winner-take-all attitude. She and her team have developed a survey that has been implemented among employees at seven Fortune 1000 companies. Employees rated the extent to which they agreed with a series of statements, such as "When it comes to being successful, this company seems to believe that people have a certain amount of talent, and they really can't do much to change it."

Dweck concludes that there is a great deal of consensus about what the prevailing mindset is in these employees' organizations with regard to growth. Her research shows that employees in growth mindset companies are:

- 47 % likelier to say that their colleagues are trustworthy
- 34 % likelier to feel a strong sense of ownership and commitment to the company
- 65 % likelier to say that the company supports risk-taking
- 49 % likelier to say that the company fosters innovation.

There has been much written about the various practices organizations implement to try to instill a common corporate culture. For example, many Japanese companies with overseas subsidiaries used to require employees to wear uniforms and participate in morning calisthenics. Wal-Mart had employees in many overseas locations gather around every morning for the Wal-Mart cheer. These corporate artifacts and behaviors are at the tip of the iceberg that is above the water. Corporate culture, like national culture, has visible and invisible aspects. Schein (2010) refers to three levels of culture: artifacts, values, and basic assumptions. At the tip of the iceberg are rituals and organizational practices, while underneath the water are those less visible attitudes, values, and assumptions.

Most organizations, especially those that have a presence in many countries, are constantly looking to create the "glue" that will bind employees' hearts and minds together. Talk to managers in some of these multinational companies, and you will hear them refer to the Ford Way, or the Unilever Way, or the Toyota Way. Do these work? Every corporation, like every individual, is to some extent a product of its national culture. It makes assumptions especially around management practices that are in part based on values and beliefs of the national culture of its founders and executives.

Could a global corporation today create a culture that somehow transcends or trumps national culture and even global culture, and, more specifically, develop a culture that reflects a global mindset? For example, Erez and Gati (2004) suggested that the core values of a global culture had six elements: freedom of choice; free markets; individualism; innovation and tolerance of change; tolerance of diversity; and interdependence/connectedness. One of the most intriguing pieces of work in this area is by Denison et al. (2004). Through their research, they have identified four organizational cultural values, or traits (as they put it), that are strongly related to organizational performance. These are:

- Involvement—empowering employees, building teams, and developing human capability at all levels to build a sense of commitment and belief that their work is connected to the goals of the organization.
- Consistency—having leaders who "walk the talk" by role modeling core values, and a set of processes that are aligned with these values.
- Adaptability—an organization that listens to its customers, takes risks, learns from its mistakes, and is constantly improving.
- Mission—having a clear sense of purpose and direction, along with a vision of how the organization will look in the future.

Using data from this organizational cultural model that they have collected from 230 organizations in Europe, North America, and Asia, along with other data from 218 organizations from seven countries (including Canada, Australia, Brazil, USA., Japan, Jamaica, and South Africa), Denison et al. found generally high correlations between overall performance and these cultural indices: "The link between company cultures and effectiveness appears to be both strong and consistent. In addition, the scores for the culture measures are essentially the same for the samples of organizations in each of these ... regions" (p. 106).

What about practices, those behaviors that are on the surface of the iceberg, to use an analogy? What is the relationship between these practices and cultural values? In an interesting study, Fischer et al. (2005) surveyed 1239 employees from various organizations in six countries (Argentina, Brazil, Malaysia, New Zealand, Turkey, and the USA) to analyze the impact of cultural dimensions on perceptions of organizational practices. They focused on 71 practices, factor analyzed the data, and identified three factors: employee orientation, formalization, and innovation. Sample items for employee orientation included:

- Managers give employees freedom to express their ideas
- Employees have a say in matters that directly involve them
- Managers encourage employees to speak up when they disagree with a decision.

Sample items from the formalization factor include:

- Everything in the organization is done according to a previously defined procedure
- What employees have to do is strongly determined by formal procedures
- Control and centralization are important.

Finally, sample items for innovation include:

- People are always searching for new ways of approaching problems
- There is a lot of investment in new products in this organization
- This organization frequently searches for new markets for existing products.

What they found were significant effects of cultural differences (e.g., individualism) on the degree of implementation of these organizational practices. In general, cultural effects for their sample were significantly and consistently larger than any industry effects. The take-aways from this research are consistent with the Covey distinction between principles and practices. First, organizational cultural values at the abstract or "principle" level can generalize across cultures. Specifically, taking Denison's model into account, organizations that are attempting to create a culture of involvement, consistency of word and deed among their leaders and with their processes, continuous improvement and risk-taking, and clarity of vision will find that these principles can resonate with their employees in different countries. Not only that, but perhaps even more importantly, having these values in place seems to help companies gain competitive advantage.

Second, organizations should be careful not to assume that these principles will translate into the same behaviors and practices in different countries. To build a universal corporate culture, organizations need to focus on corporate values such as the ones identified by Denison rather than specific practices that may need to be adapted from culture to culture.

To apply one of these principles, "involvement" for companies based in North America might mean giving employees more freedom to make decisions. For companies based in Asia, it might mean giving employees information about the company's plans which will make them feel more included and part of the company—an important consideration especially in collectivist cultures. "Adaptability" for companies based in North America might mean allowing individual employees to make mistakes and encouraging them to take risks. For companies based in Asia, this might mean asking groups to find ways to continuously improve their processes.

Denison et al. suggest that " … a concept like empowerment is important around the world, but we would not argue that this means the same behaviors would necessarily constitute empowerment in a different national context … (this cultural) model probably says much more about the presence of a desirable set of traits than it does about how those traits are expressed."

It seems reasonable to propose therefore that organizations can build a global mindset culture above and beyond having employees with global mindset (although a critical mass of the latter might facilitate the former). What would such a global mindset culture look like? As mentioned elsewhere in this book, one of the indicators that an organization is making progress toward implementing a transnational strategy is its development of a global mindset both for its employees and for the firm as whole. Extrapolating from the research on the global mindset of individuals, one would expect that an organization with a global mindset culture would have one or more of the following characteristics:

- Flexibility—an ability to react quickly, to be nimble, and to quickly adapt in the different markets where it is doing business.
- Acceptance—a recognition across the organization (but especially among senior managers) that approaches may differ across markets, and a rejection of an ethnocentric strategy in favor of a geocentric strategy (Perlmutter 1969).
- Curiosity—an eagerness to learn about different markets, to share that knowledge, and to transfer learnings across borders to employees in different subsidiaries as well as different functions.
- Empathy—a willingness to seek differences and conflicts in a constructive, win-win manner across the organization.

Based on these characteristics, the following are recommended organizational practices for organizations that want to create a global mindset culture:

1. Top management commitment toward a global mindset culture. How regularly do the senior executives in your company reinforce the importance of thinking globally and recognizing the importance of markets other than the home market? How often do executives travel overseas to learn about the importance of these markets—especially from their overseas subsidiaries? How frequently do managers and executives from overseas subsidiaries come to HQs to participate in strategy meetings? Are key executives from overseas represented in important task forces and corporate initiatives?
2. Structures and processes for global alignment and coordination. What formal and informal mechanisms has the company put in place to facilitate efficient and effective coordination across countries where the company does business? How well defined are the company's formal structures, such as matrix relationships, global and regional roles, and roles and responsibilities of HQs and subsidiaries? When global teams are created, how well represented are subsidiaries from relevant countries in these teams?
3. Infrastructures for global communication. Has the company invested in the necessary technologies to enable efficient communication across countries? How much communication, training, and

support are being provided so managers globally can take advantage of these new tools and technologies?

4. Assessment of global mindset potential. How important does the company consider global mindset in selecting internal or external candidates for positions that will require cross-cultural interactions? Is cultural fit one of the criteria used before assigning individuals to global roles? Unfortunately, many companies consider technical skills and business experience as the critical factors for selecting managers for global assignments while ignoring or downplaying interpersonal and cross-cultural factors. Somehow, these companies believe either that interpersonal skills are not as important cross-culturally, or that technical skills and a strong track record can more than compensate for any deficiencies in interpersonal skills.

5. Use of development assignments to build global mindset in individuals and teams. When setting development plans for individuals (especially those who may have high potential), what opportunities are provided to them for learning and acquiring experiences in working across different markets and cultures? In one company, executives there were concerned about building a pool of managers who had had experience in international markets. They had begun to hire people from outside the company with these experiences, but preferred to "grow their own." The executive committee identified a dozen high-potential individuals in different functional areas and gave them six-month assignments to countries where the company had a small presence and where the risk of failure would not be catastrophic. The company wanted to provide these high potentials with development opportunities, while at the same time giving them an opportunity to help the company solve some specific business challenges in these low-risk markets.

Caligiuri and Tarique (2009) showed that leaders who participated in "high-contact" activities (such as being members of a global team, short-term expatriate assignments) tended to be more effective than those who were involved in "low-contact" activities such as coursework or language training programs. Osland et al. (2009) have provided the following sequence of developmental learning from lowest to highest potential for competency development (p. 264):

Self-study
Books
Films
Lectures
Cultural briefings
Business seminars
Basic language training
Cultural assimilator training
Case analysis
Role playing
International exposure trips
Global task forces
Global virtual teams
Global project teams
Strategic business travel
Planned field experiences
Global assessment centers
Sophisticated simulations
Expatriate assignments

While the above learning opportunities are helpful to consider, they seem to apply mainly to executives (e.g., Caligiuri's interviews were primarily from senior-level people). Caligiuri (2006) has suggested that the type of developmental intervention will depend on the specific knowledge, skills, abilities, and other personality characteristics. For example, joining a global project team might work best to improve skills and abilities while international assignments might work best to impact personality characteristics. Second, these developmental experiences (e.g., strategic business travel, planned field experiences) seem to have come from international assignments; in fact, as Caligiuri et al. point out, the average expatriate service of their sample is nine years. We need to look beyond this current segment of expatriates, and consider the types of development assignments that are most effective for different types of global leaders. Companies intending to build a global mindset culture need to at least consider providing a targeted array of development experiences for employees with different global roles.

6. Reduction of the HQs "center of gravity." Has the company considered relocating some key functions out of HQs into one of its key markets overseas? Are at least some of the company's centers of excellence or expertise located overseas? Are regional heads and

their staffs still based in HQs or have they moved out to regions? In 2012, P&G announced that it was moving its global skin, cosmetics, and personal-care business unit from its Cincinnati HQs to Singapore.[2] This was not a cost-cutting move, but a recognition that a significant percentage of P&G's sales in this segment are in Asia. In 2008, IBM created a growth-markets HQs in Shanghai (responsible for Asia, Latin America, Russia, Eastern Europe, the Middle East, and Africa).[3] General Motors (GM) has moved the responsibility for global purchasing from Detroit to Shanghai. In 2001, Bayer moved the base of its general medicines division to Beijing, and General Electric's (GE's) health care unit moved its business from Waukesha, Wisconsin to Beijing. Irdeto, a leading company in media protection for pay media companies, set up dual HQs in the Netherlands and in Beijing, with its CEO and his family moving to China.[4] Both Hyundai and Ford plan to make India their global hub for compact car production for the former and for diesel and petrol engines for the latter (Mahidhar et al. 2009). Microsoft, Intel, GE, BASF, and GM are among other global companies that have created established business units and specific centers of expertise in cities such as Bangalore, Beijing, and Mexico City. Recently, Toyota announced plans to build a separate robotics unit in Silicon Valley; it plans to hire 200 employees and invest $1 billion to set up the Toyota Research Institute, which plans to focus on artificial intelligence and robotics.[5]

7. Cross-cultural awareness and sensitivity as a key element in the company's learning strategy. How available and accessible are resources for employees to improve their cross-cultural awareness (e.g., online courses on doing business in different cultures, reimbursement for language training, etc.)? Consulting firms offer many kinds of cross-cultural training to corporations and individuals, but few are able to demonstrate the efficacy of their programs. One promising type of training is the cultural assimilator, of which there are several variations (Bhawuk 2001). In general, this program presents participants with a set of critical incidents that occur between a foreigner and a host national. Trainees select from various alternatives and then receive feedback. Another type of training is Sanchez-Burks et al.'s (2007) program based on their theory of Protestant Relational Ideology. In their view, this ideology refers to "deep-seated beliefs that affective and relational concerns are inappropriate in work set-

tings and, therefore, are to be given less attention in professional, work settings than in social, non-work settings." (p. 259) The training consists of a self-assessment and then a directed discussion focusing on differences between participants' responses to those found in East Asia and Latin America. Although the results seem promising, the outcome measures were based on self-reports and more research on the efficacy of this approach needs to be conducted. While companies may decide to implement different types of education and training for employees, those who do have a learning strategy to offer employees opportunities for expanding their global mindset will have a decided advantage over others who have not considered integrating cross-cultural awareness and sensitivity into their learning and development programs.

8. Identification of a global talent pool. How inclusive is the company's global talent management process? For example, when considering internal candidates for key positions, does the slate of candidates include highly qualified employees from different locations? Does the company have a global database of employees that captures key data about their experiences, background, and competencies? Companies need to think about their talent multidimensionally. While there should be an overall corporate talent strategy (much like an overall corporate business strategy), companies should also consider talent strategies for at least four segments of its employee population (as reflected in the examples above):

- Building successors and creating a pipeline for the *senior levels* of the company
- Retaining the *solid performers* and the B-players
- Recruiting and developing talent at the *junior* levels
- Motivating the *critical skills employees* in the company

There is no one best strategy or approach for each of these, partly because the answers depend on the particular industry of the company and its competitive position within that industry, the strategic direction of the organization, and its talent philosophy (Henson 2009). Regardless of the particular approach and talent strategy, however, it is important for companies to keep in mind the outcome: to have an organization with a pipeline of the best talent that will help the company innovate and achieve sustainable competitive advantage. Beechler and Woodward (2009), for example, cite research by McKinsey that managers from top-performing companies had a higher average of cross-border moves than companies that were not top-performing.

When I visited one of Colgate Palmolive's US centers for a business meeting with some executives, I was surprised to learn that over 70 % of its revenues come from outside the USA. To its credit, Colgate Palmolive has a talent program where their high potentials are designated as either regional or global talent. According to Charan (2007), " … the high-potentials receive assignments that stretch their abilities and expand their knowledge, exposing them to a variety of markets, cultures consumers, and business circumstances, in tune with Colgate Palmolive's evolving leadership requirements." (p. 151) Even in its US-based offices, there are quite a few managers who are on assignment from their subsidiaries.

Hong and Doz (2013) have described L'Oreal's approach to building global talent; it refers to these individuals as "multiculturals." L'Oreal is in over 130 countries and over half its sales come from outside Europe and North America. It has to maintain a steady stream of new products (approximately 20 % of products are new every year), and invests significantly in R&D. Because of the importance of making sure that their brands are global yet appeal to different consumer groups in different regions, L'Oreal developed a strategy to "internationalize" its management team. Focusing on product development teams (there are about 40), the company decided to recruit multiculturals, individuals who are rooted in more than one culture, either because their family backgrounds are multicultural, and/or because they have lived in different countries. They draw from three pools. The first is internal, individuals with at least five years of experience in sales and marketing in the subsidiaries. The second is external, recruits from other global companies. The third comes from graduates of leading international business schools. According to Hong and Doz, L'Oreal has had success with new product launches because of the cross-cultural sensitivity and awareness of these multiculturals. They demonstrate, among other things, cultural empathy, multilingual skills, and an ability to switch among cultural frames of reference and communication modes.

While being exposed to multiple cultures and having lived overseas certainly are promising indicators or antecedents, it is also important to identify an individual's global mindset. More research needs to be done to validate some of the existing instruments, such as Thunderbird's Global Mindset Inventory. Another instrument, the Overseas Assessment

Inventory (Dodd 2007) seems useful but is limited to those being considered for overseas assignments and there needs to be more research on its validity.

A company's approach to managing talent and human capital—especially managing those who are being assigned to global roles—can be described as one of two types. The first is what I would describe as a "sink-or-swim" approach to the development of its human capital. These companies seem to be sending an implied message: you are on your own. It's up to you to succeed or fail, and to fix any problems that you may encounter. If you do fail, then there are others who can take your place, and the "cream will rise to the top." When I describe this approach in the abstract to executives and business school students, and I ask them whether this is an approach that they personally favor, I am somewhat surprised to see the majority seem to agree. With global assignments, research has shown that only about a third of organizations provide any kind of formal cultural preparation for expatriates, and I suspect much less for managers going into other kinds of global roles.

This was true of one interviewee, Dennis, who was a global leader for a shipping company with major operations in Finland, Germany, and Sweden. Dennis manages a global software development team and he is based in the USA. His team members are diverse, coming from different countries including Russia, Israel, China, the USA, the UK, and Germany. When he was first assigned to the team, Dennis recalls that there was no formal process that the company had, and he had to reach back to what he learned from his MBA classes, as well as his own instincts. He decided to visit each of the sites, and spent time meeting with and having dinners with the key team members in each site. In previous virtual team meetings before his visit, Dennis had defined a team goal, and asked each team member representing a different country to identify differences between the country's current state with respect to the goal and the ideal state. He referred to this as a gap analysis. Although he has been relatively successful with his approach, this was despite of, and not because of, the company's approach (or lack thereof) to providing support for global team leaders.

Horst had an even more challenging assignment. His company, a global agribusiness and food company known for international soybean exporting, food processing, and fertilizers, sent him (along with his family) to Singapore as CFO of the Asia-Pacific region, leading a team of approximately 30–40 employees in Singapore, plus another 20 or so employees in China. There was no corporate shared services model at the time, so Horst was responsible for the full set of regional financial reporting. Since the company's global structure was still evolving, and this was going to be a new position, Horst had some personal concerns: Could I do this? Could I do this work? Could I be successful?

Adding to his concern was that this was going to be his first international assignment, albeit to an expatriate-friendly place like Singapore. Like others, Horst did not receive much pre-departure training (specifically, one day) that he described as pretty much worthless. Like Tom, Horst decided to spend time actually working in each of the countries in the region, including India, Vietnam, Indonesia, Thailand, and Malaysia. He found that each location came with different challenges. For example, he found that in India, there were generally two types of employees: those who were local entrepreneurs and those who worked for large multinational companies. When his company started to acquire local businesses in the country, he found that many of the employees of these small businesses would resign almost immediately since they had no desire to work for a large multinational and had strong loyalty to local entrepreneurs. In China, he was surprised at the lack of "institutional loyalty" and employees in his team seemingly jumped from company to company with minimal increases in salary. Horst's flexibility, reflected by what he described as a "learn as you go" mindset, served him well. He adopted the approach that, just as managers are advised to manage their own career, he had to manage his own assignment.

At the other extreme to managing talent and developing human capital is what I describe as a "development" philosophy. The implied message here is that the global manager is an investment for the company, and therefore the company wants to protect this investment by providing the manager with support and resources. Despite the soundness of this approach, I continued to be intrigued as to why many students and managers still seemed to favor the former "sink-or-swim" approach. However, introducing another dimension, an organization's performance orientation, helped to add some clarity. At the one extreme are organizations that emphasize and reward meritocracy, where individuals are recognized for their performance and accomplishments. These organizations tend to have processes and systems in place to measure performance more or less objectively and to establish a "pay-for-performance" approach to rewarding and promoting employees. At the other extreme are organizations that are paternalistic, and tend to reward loyalty and seniority among employees. Many of these companies do not have processes and systems for evaluating

Paternalistic

Country Club   Political

Development ——————————————————————— Sink-or-Swim

High
Performance   Cutthroat
and High
Involvement

Meritocratic

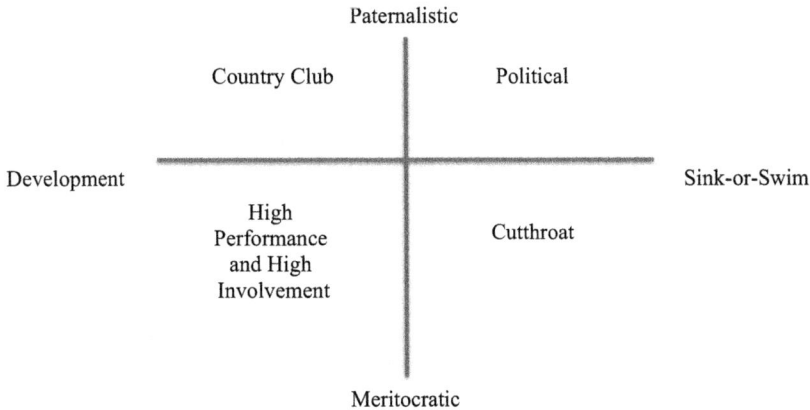

Fig. 8.1 Development and performance approach

employees, and some of them tend to be run by company founders who do not necessarily believe in building a "human resource bureaucracy." Unfortunately, the unintended consequence of this approach results in decisions about people and their performance that are sometimes subjective and biased, and facilitates a culture that breeds favoritism.

Thus, four organizational types can be conceptualized in this 2 × 2 model in Fig. 8.1:

Cutthroat companies attract a certain type of individual, and those who perform will find themselves recognized and rewarded. However, this kind of organization also tends to discourage collaboration, since it creates an intensely competitive atmosphere. The "rank-and-yank" system that GE introduced and that Enron embraced eventually led to many dysfunctional behaviors. Individuals were reluctant to share information or to help others since this would not be in their best interests. One executive I interviewed described how mistakes were handled in his company. When managers were sent overseas or were assigned to a special project, any failures were not tolerated; employees who did not succeed in their assignments were "red circled" in succession planning charts; two circles and these employees were then asked to leave the company.

Country Club companies provide support and many opportunities for development for its employees. Because these companies tend to lack rigorous and objective processes for evaluating people and their potential or performance, employees don't feel much pressure to improve their performance. Rewards tend to be distributed, as one executive described it, in a "peanut butter" way, spreading it evenly across the board. Large and small companies that have become very successful and continue to enjoy large profit margins will tend to have considerable resources for training and development, and facilities that are sometimes lavish. In such companies, employees feel little pressure to perform, and the complacency and lack of urgency is palpable in these organizations.

A lack of performance focus combined with a "sink-or-swim" approach results in a Political company. Employees will seek to ally themselves with those who have the power to control their fates. Employees will tend to avoid risks, and will hesitate to speak out for fear of reprisal. This sometimes devolves into a company of "haves" and have-nots."

In a High Performance–High Involvement organization, on the other hand, employees are provided the appropriate support, training, and guidance to improve their performance, especially those who have demonstrated a track record of results. However, employees are still held accountable although not in a punitive way. When these four types of companies are laid out, the High Performance–High Involvement type of organization is what many say they prefer, despite the gap with their own experiences.

Ultimately, your development as a global leader is up to you; you have to take responsibility for developing the global mindset, skills, and attitudes you need to become successful in your global role. However, in these High Performance–High Involvement companies, senior management invests in providing the "infrastructure" necessary to help you succeed. Professional sports teams, for example, take seriously their responsibility to spotting and building talent. Once a highly regarded athlete is drafted and signed, most sports organizations will make sure that their athletes are coached and trained properly. They don't expect these athletes to make it strictly on their own. In fact, many teams build world-class facilities so their athletes can train with the latest equipment and techniques. Of course, the athlete has to have the talent, motivation, and the drive to succeed, and that is ultimately his or her responsibility.

High Performance–High Involvement companies also focus on coaching and preparation when they send their managers overseas, while recognizing that this is a dual responsibility. As mentioned previously, many multinationals still fall short in their approach to global talent. A recent study by McDonnell et al. (2010) of multinationals based in Ireland found that 35 % of them did not have any global succession planning in place, and that many of them rely on an ad hoc approach to assignments.

9. Recognition and rewards for those with global mindsets. How valued are those individuals who have proven themselves in overseas assignments, not just in improving business results but also in being recognized as someone who has worked effectively in different cultures? When these individuals complete their assignments, to what extent does the company leverage their experience? Does the company's competency model and performance evaluation system include global mindset behaviors as a key element?

In a recent study by Price Waterhouse Coopers,[6] 4108 return migrants from 81 countries of origin who had spent between three months and two years in the USA at some point during the years between 1997 and 2011 under a category of the J-1 visa designated for professional training completed a survey. These respondents all had bachelor's or master's degrees, and had work experience in many industries with companies such as Google and JPMorgan Chase, as well as thousands of small startups and midsized companies.

They found that, while almost all of the respondents reported that they learned about practices overseas they could implement in their home countries, only 67 % reported having shared any of this knowledge upon their return, and only 48 % reported having shared knowledge and then having seen this knowledge implemented. The study concludes that on average, for every two workers with international experience hired by a given firm, only one will successfully share knowledge from overseas at some point during his or her tenure.

Interestingly, countries like China, India, and Brazil are creating incentives to entice their foreign-trained nationals to return. A recent *Wall Street Journal* article[7] described the emergence of these "sea turtles," the term used for a Chinese native who is returning home after several assignments in the West. The article mentions several such Chinese businessmen who, after working for multinationals like Coca-Cola and Nike in the USA, have decided to return to China, often in much larger roles and with much greater compensation than they had in their former companies' HQs. Aside from these considerations, there is the perception that the opportunities with a Chinese company are greater, as are the psychic benefits. For example, Guo Xin, a sea turtle who joined a Chinese recruiting firm, said, "You're making global decisions rather than having these decisions made for you" by Western HQs.

High Performance–High Involvement organizations also recognize and reward those managers who themselves identify and develop individuals in their teams to build their global mindset.

10. Support for individuals on overseas assignments. Does the company provide ongoing support for individuals on overseas assignments—before, during, and after the assignment is over? KPMG surveyed over 600 organizations for its latest Global Assignment Policies and Practices Survey and found that 39 % of companies do not have formal assessments in place to identify and select assignees, while 56 % rely mainly on informal assessments (primarily from HR or from line managers).[8] In Ernst & Young's Global Mobility Effectiveness Survey (2013), they found that on average, 16 % of assignees left the company within the first two years after repatriation, and another 41 % returned to their pre-assignment position.

Does the company require some form of cultural training for managers' families prior to their overseas assignments? For example, BASF works with an outside vendor that helps international assignees adjust to their new surroundings. The vendor also provides "cultural attaches" who will help BASF employees with the day-to-day logistics of settling in a new country, for example, finding apartments, completing mandatory state registrations, and setting up bank accounts. In another company, I helped develop an expatriate mentorship program whereby international assignees were assigned to senior executives as mentors, with the condition that these senior executives had to be outside these individuals' functions. For example, the CIO volunteered to mentor an individual in Marketing and a manager in Finance who were both in overseas locations on expatriate assignments. He kept in contact with them throughout their assignments, and helped facilitate their transition back to their next assignments. Mezias and Scandura's (2005) research suggest that multiple mentors for different stages in an expatriate's international assignment (e.g., pre-departure, on-site repatriation) are important. Extending their concept, global leaders with different types of global assignments might also do well to have different types of mentors to help with their development and effectiveness.

Eduardo was a Brazilian expatriate who worked in an Asian country for two years before returning to his home country. While overseas, his company assigned him a Program Champion, a Brazilian who had served in a number of international assignments. Eduardo and he met monthly through teleconference to discuss his current assignment, the support that he needed, and to keep him up to date on business and related issues back in the subsidiary. Eduardo was also able to pass on the tacit knowledge that he was acquiring while on assignment.

More recently, as reported in the *New York Times*,[9] some corporations have been experimenting with "talent swaps," whereby individuals from the same company but in different countries temporarily switch jobs. "Talent swaps, which typically last less than a year, can involve less paperwork and expense than traditional expatriate assignments, in which companies have the added cost of moving a family and dealing with schools and costly housing ... The swaps are also effective for career development, to promote cross-border mobility earlier and to attract and retain employees who are seen as having high potential." One example is Karen Jung, a manager at PriceWaterhouse Coopers in its Virginia office, who swapped jobs with Marie-Claire Delpin, a manager with the same company in Paris. Dow Chemical is another company that has a talent swap program; 126 employees have participated since the company started the program in 2012.

Other than the benefits cited by the article, this approach represents another mechanism for building a global mindset in an organization. Appealing as this might be for individuals and for companies, there are some risks involved, and the cross-cultural preparation should not be underestimated. It cannot be assumed that just because two individuals are from the same function or doing similar jobs, their knowledge and skills are easily transferrable.

11. Formal and informal processes for sharing best practices globally. When he was CEO of GE, Jack Welch was relentless in promoting knowledge management, and he held people accountable to make sure that they were proactive in communicating and sharing best practices (Slater 1998). How much sharing of information and best practices goes on internally in the company, and are there formal and informal mechanisms for facilitating the dissemination of these best practices? Somewhat belatedly, for example, GM has just begun to implement this. In an interview,[10] President Dan Ammann described what the company has started to do:

A couple months ago we brought about 25 of the top sales leaders from around the world together in Charlotte, N.C. We conducted workshops where each discussed the tactics they are using in their home markets to drive sales, work with dealers and interact with customers. This is the first time anyone can remember that happening.

Perhaps next time they should meet in Beijing, Sao Paolo, or Mexico City. Sutton and Rao (2014) wrote about a sergeant who had been fighting in Iraq for 15 months since 2004 and who was very concerned about the lethal dangers of improvised explosive devices (IEDs). While Master Sergeant Chad Walker was visiting the US embassy in Baghdad, he saw a handbook on one of the staff member's desks that was essentially an IED defeat manual, describing the lessons learned from many combat units and gathered by the Center for Army Lessons Learned (CALL). Sergeant Walker was furious that this kind of knowledge was not widely disseminated. Eventually, CALL apparently became much better at sharing and passing on critical knowledge to the troops.

Ryan was an American expatriate in Asia who was helping his company build a brand new chemical plant. He has had this role for at least 20 years, going from country to country for the company and gaining valuable knowledge and experience along the way. Ryan had established many connections in different countries and with the FDA, who had to review the requirements of the plants he was helping to build. Yet in all this time, the knowledge seemed to be all in his head. He had not trained anyone in the company who could eventually replace him and understandably, there was no incentive for him to do so. He enjoyed traveling and being the unique expert in the company on building and opening new chemical sites. There was no question that he was adding a lot of value to the company, but it was unfortunate that the company had not developed mechanisms for knowledge transfer. Only when he announced his coming retirement did the company begin to identify a replacement and train that person.

Organizations will need to prioritize which of these practices are most important to implement, taking into account its overall strategic and business goals, as well as where the best payoffs are. For example, if an organization is planning a major expansion into China over the next three to five years, then assessing cultural fit among high-potential employees (#5) and establishing an office in one of its cities (#6) should be high on the list of actions. Each of these practices will require resources and focus for any company and therefore prioritization is an important step to take for any organization wanting to create a global mindset culture. However, top management commitment is key and should be the starting point for companies in their journey toward creating a global mindset culture.

NOTES

1. "How Companies Can Profit from a Growth Mindset" in Harvard Business Review,pp.28–29:https://hbr.org/2014/11/how-companies-can-profit-from-a-growth-mindset
2. http://www.wsj.com/articles/SB10001424052702304070304577396053688081544
3. https://angel.co/ibm-growth-markets-unit-headquarters-shanghai-china
4. http://www.managementexchange.com/story/overcoming-mothership-syndrome-story-irdeto
5. Andy Sharman, "Toyota To Set Up Robotics Institute in Silicon Valley, Financial Times, November 6, 2015.
6. Dan Wang, "The Untapped Value of Overseas Experience," Strategy + Business, Winter 2014, Issue 77: http://www.strategy-business.com/article/00283?gko=419e2
7. See Kathy Chu et al.'s article, "Chinese Firms Bring More Natives Home", 2014,http://www.wsj.com/articles/chinese-firms-lure-native-executives-home-1409671081
8. See KPMG's report on Global Assignment Policies and Practices: Survey 2015: https://www.kpmg.com/Global/en/IssuesAndInsights/Articles-Publications/Documents/global-assignment-policies-and-practices-survey-2015-v2.pdf
9. Tanya Mohn's article on May 18, 2015, "Across Borders, Talent Swaps Help Develop Skills and Careers,http://www.nytimes.com/2015/05/19/business/talent-swaps-help-develop-skills-and-careers.html?_r=0
10. See Jeff Bennett's article, "GM's Ammann Drives for Change in the Wall Street Journal, November 11, 2014: http://www.wsj.com/articles/gms-ammann-pushes-for-change-1415751611

REFERENCES

Beechler, S., and I. Woodward. 2009. The Global "War for Talent". *Journal of International Management* 15: 273–285.

Bhawuk, Dharm P.S. 2001. Evolution of Culture Assimilators: Toward Theory-Based Assimilators. *International Journal of Intercultural Relations* 25(2): 141–163.

Caligiuri, Paula M 2006. Developing Global Leaders. *Human Resource Management Review* 16(2): 219–228.

Caligiuri, Paula, and Ibraiz Tarique. 2009. Predicting Effectiveness in Global Leadership Activities. *Journal of World Business* 44(3): 336–346.

Charan, Ram. 2007. *Know-How: The 8 Skills That Separate People Who Perform from Those Who Don't*. New York: Crown Books.

Chattopadhyay, A., R. Batra, and A. Ozsomer. 2012. *The New Emerging Market Multinationals: Four Strategies for Disrupting Markets And Building Brands.* New York: McGraw Hill Professional.

Denison, Daniel R., Stephanie Haaland, and Paulo Goelzer. 2004. Corporate Culture and Organizational Effectiveness: Is Asia Different from the Rest of the World? *Organizational Dynamics* 33(1): 98–109.

Dodd, Carley H. 2007. Intercultural Readiness Assessment for Pre-Departure Candidates. *Intercultural Communication Studies* 2: 1–17.

Drucker, Peter. 1973. *Management: Tasks, Responsibilities, Practices.* New York: Harper & Row.

Dweck, Carol. 2006. *Mind Set: The New Psychology of Success.* New York: Random House.

Erez, Miriam, and Efrat Gati. 2004. A Dynamic, Multi-Level Model of Culture: From the Micro Level of the Individual to the Macro Level of a Global Culture. *Applied Psychology: An International Review* 53(4): 583–598.

Fischer, Ronald, Maria Cristina Ferreira, Eveline Maria Leal Assmar, Paul Redford, and Charles Harb. 2005. Organizational Behaviour across Cultures: Theoretical and Methodological Issues for Developing Multi-Level Frameworks Involving Culture. *International Journal of Cross Cultural Management* 5(1): 27–48.

Ghemawat, Pankaj. 2012. Developing Global Leaders. *McKinsey Quarterly.* http://www.mckinsey.com/insights/leading_in_the_21st_century/developing_global_leaders

Henson, Ramon. 2009. Key practices in identifying and developing potential. *Industrial and Organizational Psychology: Perspectives on Science and Practice* 2(4): 416–419.

Hong, H., and Yves Doz. 2013. L'Oreal Masters Multiculturalism. *Harvard Business Review* 91(6): 114–118.

Mahidhar, Vikram, Craig Giffi, and Ajit Kambil. 2009. Rethinking Emerging Market Strategies: From Offshoring to Strategic Expansion. *Deloitte Review* 4: 30–43.

McDonnell, Anthony, Ryan Lamare, Patrick Gunnigle, and Jonathan Lavelle. 2010. Developing Tomorrow's Leaders - Evidence of Global Talent Management in Multinational Enterprises. *Journal of World Business* 45(2): 150–160.

Mezias, John M., and Terri A. Scandura. 2005. A Needs-Driven Approach to Expatriate Adjustment and Career Development: A Multiple Mentoring Perspective. *Journal of International Business Studies* 36(5): 519–538.

Osland, Joyce, Sully Taylor, and Mark Mendenhall. 2009. Global leadership progress and challenges. In *Cambridge Handbook of Culture, Organizations, and Work*, eds. Rabi Bhagat and Richard Steers, 245–271. New York: Cambridge University Press.

Perlmutter, Howard V. 1969. The Tortuous Evolution of the Multinational Corporation. *Columbia Journal of World Business* 4(1): 9–18.

Sanchez-Burks, Jeffrey, Fiona Lee, Richard Nisbett, and Oscar Ybarra. 2007. Cultural Training Based on a Theory of Relational Ideology. *Basic and Applied Social Psychology* 29(3): 257–268.

Schein, Edgar. 2010. *Organizational Culture and Leadership*, Fourth edn. San Francisco, CA: Jossey-Bass.

Slater, Robert. 1998. *Jack Welch & The G.E. Way: Management Insights and Leadership Secrets of the Legendary CEO: Management Insights and Leadership Secrets of the Legendary CEO*. New York: McGraw Hill Professional.

Sutton, Robert, and Huggy Rao. 2014. *Scaling Up Excellence*. New York: Crown Business.

CHAPTER 9

The Road Ahead: The Future of Global Leadership and Implications for Research and Practice

In the business world, the subject of leadership has long been of interest not just to scholars but also to managers and students worldwide. Type in the word "leadership" on Amazon and there are over 230,000 results.[1] In the past 40 years or so in particular, there has been substantial progress in the study of leadership and leadership effectiveness. Among organizations and other institutions, the importance of having effective leaders is well acknowledged, although as Pfeffer (2015) has indicated, the gap between rhetoric and reality on what makes for effective leadership continues to be significant.

There has also been progress in our understanding of global leadership. The research has evolved from studying Western leaders to leaders in different global environments, as well as a greater focus on contextual factors. In practice, Western multinational organizations are learning not just about business strategies of emerging market multinationals (e.g., Chattopadhyay et al. 2012), but also about how leaders from different countries lead (e.g., Bennett and Bell 2004).

Cultural variations do not matter in all types of cross-national transactions. They matter in some situations more than others: they matter more in situations where fundamental cultural values are either challenged or questioned in the process of expanding global operations of multinational firms. (R. Bhagat 2009, p. 523) (Reprinted with the permission of Cambridge University Press.)

© The Editor(s) (if applicable) and The Author(s) 2016   285
R. Henson, *Successful Global Leadership*,
DOI 10.1057/978-1-137-58990-3_9

Still, there is much more to learn. It is somewhat disconcerting that a leading scholar in the field (Osland 2008) wrote recently that " ... there is no consensus on the construct definition of global leadership." (p. 61). The following are a number of areas of research and practice that might help both scholars and practitioners gain a better understanding of global leadership over the next decade.

(1) Future success factors for various global leadership roles. Much of the early research was focused on Western managers who took on overseas assignments (the traditional expatriate model). As reported in this book, while there have been a number of studies focusing on expatriates and others on overseas assignments and on their adjustment, there are relatively fewer studies focusing on their performance or effectiveness. In addition, organizations are using their managers in various types of global leadership roles, with many of these managers coming not just from the home country headquarters but also from various locations around the world. Do these different global leadership roles require similar attributes, dispositions, and competencies but perhaps to a lesser degree than expatriate roles, or are there different ones required for these different roles? In one of the few studies examining different kinds of global leadership roles, Tay et al. (2008) collected data from business travelers working in large multinational corporations in Singapore, Israel, and Brazil. They focused on which experiences and aspects of cultural quotient (CQ) might impact the adjustment of these "short-term business travelers." They found that the amount of cultural exposure (as defined by the proportion of work time spent outside of home country, and the product of the number of business trips and average duration of business trips made in the year) that these short-term business travelers experience on business trips was positively associated with cognitive CQ only. Janssens and Cappellen (2008) interviewed managers who had fulfilled more than one global assignment (not necessarily as expatriates) and showed continued willingness to work globally. This broad definition of global manager is in alignment with the approach that we have taken here as well. They found some differences in these managers' CQ beyond the traditional definition (and consistent with some of the practices laid out in a previous chapter) perhaps due to the short-term but

frequent cross-cultural interactions. Specifically, their sample of global managers used such tactics as:

- Acquiring knowledge on a few cultural artifacts to compensate for a limited cognition
- Distancing themselves from their own frame of reference
- Becoming more mindful
- Listening and taking the time to coordinate their tasks worldwide
- Becoming conscious about integrating different perspectives

Doing research with and learning from populations such as these will further expand our understanding of these success factors. We have mentioned that there is encouraging research on the importance of psychological capital (Luthans et al. 2015) and its impact on global mindset (Clapp-Smith et al. 2007). Luthans et al. (2008) surveyed 456 workers from the largest copper refining state-owned enterprise (SOE) and the largest private copper refining factory in China on their psychological capital, and analyzed the relationships between their scores and performance ratings by their supervisors. Psychological capital was significantly related to performance, with no significant differences in the relationship between psychological capital and performance in the SOE and in the private firm.

Yunlu and Clapp-Smith (2014) modified Luthans' concept and introduced the construct of cultural psychological capital. They used Luthans' same four dimensions—hope, optimism, self-efficacy, and resilience—but introduced a cross-cultural element. For example, an item from the Hope subscale was modified to read, "When in another country, I think that I can obtain goals that are important to me," and from the Optimism subscale, "I always look on the bright side of things regarding what I experience in other cultures." In their sample of 236 alumni of a school of international management (most of whom have lived abroad), they found positive relationships between cultural psychological capital and motivational cultural intelligence, as well as with metacognitive awareness. The importance of psychological capital cross-culturally is a potential area for further investigation, especially with regard to global leadership outcomes.

In summary, we need to have a better understanding of the unique requirements of the different global leadership roles over and above the requirements of effective leaders in general. Our model suggested an overall process for global leadership, but we acknowledge that there is no magic formula, and certainly not one that will fit the different kinds of global leadership roles discussed here.

There is also much to learn about the kinds of cultural fit that work best with these global leadership roles. Tung and Verbeke (2010) have suggested that companies may err in making assumptions about cultural distance based on geography. They refer to the inverse resonance hypothesis by suggesting that in some cases, host subsidiaries may be actually more receptive to global leaders from culturally distant countries. Note the example given earlier of the South American leader who was assigned to manage a German subsidiary. We need a better understanding of when and why this happens, but this does suggest that considering cultural distance alone when making decisions on whom to assign for international assignments might not be sufficient.

We noted earlier some interesting studies on biculturals, and one trend at least in some countries like China is to hire Chinese nationals who have spent time overseas to manage Chinese-owned global companies. There has also been an increase in the number of female leaders in global leadership roles, and there is some research indicating that female expatriates have better interaction adjustments than male expatriates (Hechanova et al. 2003).

The foundational requirements for global leaders outlined in a previous chapter seem consistent with what research and practice suggest. They also seem consistent with the types of skills expected to be in high demand over the next five to ten years (Oxford Economics 2012). It is likely that there is no one combination of global leadership requirements that is appropriate for all kinds of global leadership roles, and on what the appropriate weighting of these elements should be. These are all areas for further study and understanding.

(2) The impact of the continued growth or emerging markets and their impact on global leadership. We have seen from research and practice that while there are some universally accepted leadership attributes, there is great variability in the importance of various leadership characteristics. How will these change as more non-Western companies grow and expand? Aycan et al. (2000) surveyed managers in ten countries (Canada, the USA, Romania, Russia, Germany, Israel, China, Pakistan, Turkey, and India) on their cultural environments (e.g., power distance, paternalism) and their relationship to human resource management (HRM) practices. They found, not surpris-

ingly, "cultural fits" between these cultural dimensions and HRM practices. These findings are in line with those found by Fischer et al. (2014) where they examined the effects of national culture on various organizational practices. They found, for example, that innovation practices were less frequently perceived in tighter societies than in looser societies.

In another study, Galanou and Farrag (2015) surveyed a sample of the members of the Qatar Chamber to study relationships between Islamic leadership and various other measures of leadership, such as transformational leadership. Using the portrait value questionnaire (or PVQ) developed by Schwartz (1994) to measure Islamic leadership, they found Islamic leadership to be related to transformational, ethical, and authentic leadership. Further studies focusing on how leadership is re-interpreted in different cultures and different contexts, and evidence of successful practice, would help improve our understanding.

As emerging market multinationals continue on their path to growth and expansion to overtake some Western multinationals and become among the world's biggest companies, will their leadership models and practices dominate and even displace some of the traditional Western models? Will their leadership models begin to shift and become more like the Western models, or is there a third alternative, which is some kind of integration between the two?

We also need to learn more about the global leadership of non-Western individuals working in global companies from the developed and emerging countries. Studies like those by Bücker et al. (2014), which examined the cultural intelligence of Chinese host country managers working for foreign multinationals, would help improve our understanding.

(3) The implications of new technologies and innovations for how a new generation of managers will lead globally. As the younger generation moves up to global manager roles in companies, how will their familiarity with technology and social media, especially in communications, impact their leadership of virtual teams? Will these leaders tend to be less sensitive to cultural cues and nuances, or will team members not be as concerned about cultural differences? Will the role of the global virtual team leader change with the use of crowdsourcing and user-generated media models?

With advances in computer technology and robotics, there are fears—and some evidence—that computers and robots are replacing people for many jobs. However, as Colvin (2015a, b) has mentioned, the biggest increases in jobs, at least in the USA, have been in professional and business services, as well as in leisure and hospitality. Along with the increases in virtuality with global teams, these suggest that the global leaders of the future will need to be even more interpersonally and culturally competent:

> It used to be that you had to be good at being machine-like. Now, increasingly, you have to be good at being a person. Great performance requires us to be intensely human beings. To put it another way: Being a great performer is becoming less about what you know and more about what you're like. (p. 110)

Innovations and disruptive forces coming from these technologies also have significant implications for organizations and the types of leaders needed in these types of companies. Gates (1996) described the future of business as "friction-free capitalism," where the traditional factors creating friction (e.g., distance, restrictive regulations, imperfect information, numerous suppliers) will dissipate. Many organizations today, both large and small, seem to be making the shift to become more friction-free. Colvin (2015b) provides a couple of examples of this:

> In a friction-free economy, a company doesn't need nearly as much as it used to ... Apple gets most of its revenue from selling physical products. Yet the company says "substantially all" of its products are made by others ... Apple has even rented other companies' servers to host its iCloud service so it can add or remove capacity easily, paying only for what it needs. (p. 106)

He goes on to state that this kind of friction-free economy has allowed companies with very little physical capital to compete with those with significant capital investments. Note that Airbnb owns no real estate, and Uber owns no cars, although both do have significant intellectual capital.

The capability that these friction-free companies have to expand globally underscores the need for more successful global leadership, although the business models will certainly be a lot different than the traditional model of setting up subsidiaries in various countries. It seems reasonable to suggest that the global leaders of the future will be required even more than before to have a global mindset, and the global leadership competencies that will enable them to inspire others to work on collective goals to achieve organizational objectives, collaborate quickly using the latest technologies, and build a sense of identity with their far-flung staffs.

(4) Future developmental paths and experiences for global leaders. Cross-cultural training generally does not have a positive relationship with the adjustment of expatriates (Hechanova et al. 2003), although some types of training are more effective than others. As cited previously, a survey by the American Management Association concluded that only about a third of companies even offer formal global leadership development programs (American Management Association 2012), although a greater proportion of high-performing companies provide such programs than low-performing companies. Even so, only slightly over half (57 %) of high-performing companies indicated that their leadership development programs were effective, while 37 % of low-performing companies indicating that their programs were effective.

Osland and Bird (2008) have proposed three models of global leadership development. The first, called the Chattanooga model, was developed by a group of scholars and describes how managers can become global leaders through a series of high-level international challenges, and moderated by such factors as spouse/family adjustment. The model also acknowledges that entering managers' characteristics, such as their sociability, tolerance for ambiguity, and self-efficacy are predictors of success. The second model is the Global Leadership Expertise Development model, and is similar to the first in identifying antecedents (such as the manager's individual characteristics and cultural exposure) and transformational processes (or experiences), but differs in its focus on levels of expertise as its dependent variables, such as intercultural competence and global knowledge. The third model, cited earlier, is McCall and Hollenbeck's (2002) in which they identify the themes and lessons of international experience that help develop global executives. In their interviews with global executives, McCall and Hollenbeck (2002) summarized developmental experiences of global executives into four categories: foundation assignments (such as early work experiences and first managerial responsibilities), major line assignments (such as business start-ups and joint ventures), shorter-term experiences (such as special projects and staff jobs), and perspective-changing experiences (such as career shifts and mistakes in errors and judgments).

All three models acknowledge the complexity of becoming a global leader, and the importance of learning agility. Many aspects of these models still need to be researched and applied to different situations. They all assume a traditional model of international assignments, with managers (often from the home country) being sent overseas to international assignments in host countries.

In practice, several organizations are developing their own global leadership programs to prepare their leaders. As noted elsewhere in this book, L'Oreal focuses on selecting multiculturals. Gagnon and Collinson (2014) described two similar but separate leadership development programs in two different organizations. The first, renamed by the authors as Top Global Managers Programme, was designed for senior local managers of newly acquired plants with the purpose of educating them in Western management techniques and developing the most promising candidates into corporate-level leaders. The company then expanded the program to include managers from around 70 countries. The second, renamed by the authors as Global Agency Leaders, consisted of groups of managers working on projects over a five-month period, and supplemented by workshops.

We still have a lot to learn about how global leadership development can be accelerated under different assignment conditions. Barrett (2013) proposed a theory of psychological construction of emotion, in which emotions are viewed as not necessarily somewhere inside an individual's brain that get activated, but emerges dynamically from our interactions with others, and that "emotions are the results of individual meaning making …" (Boiger and Mesquita 2015, p. 380). They suggest that our emotions are grounded in relationships and that they can shape the relationships in which they take place. Positive and negative emotions can influence the development of relationships. Boiger and Mesquita cite research that shows that experiencing gratitude (a positive emotion) toward a partner can predict long-term healthy relationships, while experiencing contempt (a negative emotion) is predictive of divorce among married couples seven years later (Gottman and Levenson 2000).

One implication for global leadership is that those who develop through generating and getting positive emotions in their interactions with colleagues from different cultures are more likely to become effective leaders. Even though individuals may have a predisposition to seek out activities or people somewhat compatible with their cultural values, this theory suggests that much can be gained by building on the interactions through some of the practices described in this book. Nonetheless, there is a need to explore further the implications of this and other concepts to the practice of global leadership. As McCall and Hollenbeck (2002) have stated, "Learning to work across cultures is an essential competency of the global executive, and it is for most people an emotional education as well as an intellectual one" (p. 9).

To supplement these development experiences, researchers and practitioners could also apply some innovative learning strategies applied in other areas. For example, Salas et al. (2008) suggest applying scenario-based training, where learning opportunities are embedded within scenarios and trigger events elicit the targeted behaviors. These could range from role-playing exercises to high-fidelity simulations. This is not to neglect the important role that senior executives play in creating a global mindset culture as well in developing their own global mindset. Mannor (2008) has proposed some hypotheses on the competitive advantages of executives with what he calls executive CQ:

- Greater breadth of information scanning behaviors in culturally diverse settings
- Selecting more direct and proximal sources of information in cultural diverse settings
- Improving the quality of information top executives are able to gather when making decisions in culturally diverse contexts
- Providing larger equity stakes to foreign partners
- Engaging in alliances with strategically valuable foreign partners that are more culturally distant than other executives
- Improving the quality of investment decisions in culturally diverse contexts

(5) The relationships among national cultures, corporate cultures, and institutional forces. Erez and Gati (2004) point to the dynamic relationships among different levels of culture—global culture, national culture, organizational culture, group culture, and the individual. They describe top-down (from global to individual) and bottom-up processes (from individual to global), and propose that these are reciprocal relationships that influence individuals working in organizations. With increasing globalization, we need to understand better

how these processes interact, and whether there are some national cultures that can more readily align with global cultures than others. Will global leaders with a sense of identity toward a global culture be more effective than those with a stronger sense of identity to their national cultures? How does national culture help or hinder this sense of identity? Arnett (2002), for example, suggests that many young people today develop a global identity in addition to retaining their local identity. Their global identity gives them a sense of belonging to a worldwide culture, while they continue to retain their local identity.

Shokef and Erez (2008) have suggested that working in multicultural teams may enhance this sense of global identity. In a study of MBA students from five countries, they used an eight-item measure of global identity developed by Erez and Gati (2004). This included items on an agree–disagree scale such as: "I see myself as part of the global international community." The students worked in 55 virtual multicultural teams on a joint project for four weeks, and they measured their global identity in two points in time. They found significant changes in levels of global identity from Time 1 to Time 2. Can a sense of global identity be fostered merely through working in a multicultural team? Could this be a temporary effect that might dissipate once the members are no longer working with the team? What other experiences and factors build a sense of global identity, and how important is this to successful global leadership? At the same time, we know that there are people around the world who choose to become part of a self-selected culture that often is at odds with the global culture. Arnett (2002) cites religious groups such as Orthodox Jews and fundamentalists, as well as certain non-religious groups. Will these groups continue to exist outside of the corporate world for the most part, or can these groups' beliefs be compatible with working in global organizations? Will mere exposure to the global environment shape a global identity, as Erez and Gati (2004) suggest? If so, what are the implications for global leaders? These are questions that are important to address.

Take Alex for example, who is a Singaporean HR manager working for a French company based in Singapore and who has a regional role. He has a network of colleagues from his company all around the world, as well as other HR professionals from other countries and other industries. Yet he is also deeply rooted in Singapore, with a wife and two children, plus parents and in-laws and other relatives. Are managers like Alex, who have a bicultural identity, more likely to be successful as a global manager than those who do not? How important is this sense of identity as an antecedent to global mindset, relative to other factors?

As Gelfand et al. (2007) have suggested, research is increasingly taking on contextual factors, and we need to view these contextual factors from a multilevel perspective. From the viewpoint of global leaders, understanding macro conditions at a national as well as industry level is important. While the research on the impact of national cultures on organizational behavior is considerable, there is also a line of research that suggests that institutional factors such as the regulatory context, the level of education, the labor market, and strength of labor laws also impact the behavior of employees and organizations, especially HR practices (Brewster 1999; Richbell et al. 2011; Wood et al. 2014). Koopman et al. (1999), in reviewing the GLOBE study findings for Europe, have suggested that such factors as technological development and economic systems can also impact European countries' different perceptions of leadership practices. As Vaiman and Brewster (2015) have argued, we need a better understanding of the relative importance of the cultural and the institutional on management and HR practices, and the practical implications for multinationals, especially those with subsidiaries in different countries.

In addition, as our model proposes, contextual factors at the organizational level (e.g., the organizational climate and support, development experiences) are also important to consider. Gelfand et al. (2007) suggest that we need a better understanding of the dynamics of cultural differences in intercultural encounters. Such encounters are especially relevant for global teams, where individuals from different nationalities and cultures within an organization work together to produce a defined deliverable or to solve a specific problem. With such teams, the role of corporate culture can be significant; in practice, team members may vary in their identification with such corporate cultural norms. Understanding the impact of corporate culture and how to leverage it to improve the effectiveness of global teams is important.

(6) Increasing use of joint ventures, strategic alliances, partnerships, networks, and other forms of cross-border collaboration and cooperation within and across organizations. Within organizations, we have already seen the evolution of various organization designs, from matrix to more complex forms of design networks. This will no doubt continue, as organizations continue to expand their global

reach with their supply chains and expansion of their customer base. Across organizations, the use of joint ventures and strategic alliances (e.g., Allianz and Google), even among rivals (e.g., Apple and Samsung, Ford and GM, Toyota and BMW), shows no sign of abating.[2] We have much to learn about the role of national culture and organizational culture in the success of these kinds of integration. For example, Hajro (2015) found, in her in-depth case study analysis of the merger between an Austrian and a German company, that both tended to play a role but that "organizational cultural differences are more central to M&A outcomes than national cultural differences." (p. 211)

Social identity theory would predict that the success of such collaborations and joint ventures might depend on the degree to which different groups view the similarities or differences among them. As Stahl and Javidan have suggested (2009), employees of one organization may exaggerate the differences between their own and the other party's culture, creating in-group and out-group friction. On the other hand, employees may not necessarily perceive such arrangements negatively. Some cooperative alliances may indeed work to the benefit of both parties (such as the Fiat-Chrysler merger).[3] In other cases, the cultural differences might also benefit the two organizations, especially if there is management support for recognizing and valuing diversity. Still, there is much more that we need to learn about the kinds of alliances and collaborations involving cultural differences that lead to successful outcomes.

In an earlier chapter, we mentioned that some global companies are reducing their center of gravity, thus "disaggregating" their headquarters functions (Ambos and Mahnke 2010; Baaij and Slangen 2013). Other recent examples of these include Chinese handset maker Xiaomi moving its R&D headquarters to India,[4] Samsung's R&D center in Silicon Valley,[5] and GE's John F. Welch Technology Center in India.[6] How will this increasing disaggregation impact communications and organizational design, and how can organizations best take advantage of this trend to accelerate development of their global leaders? Practice may be ahead of theory here, although there is much to learn from both perspectives.

In their meta-analysis of the Hofstede research, Taras et al. (2010) conclude, among other things, that cultural values can in fact predict certain individual outcomes as well as personality traits and demographics. However, the predictive power of cultural values versus personality traits and demographics varies by outcome. More research needs to happen in this area before it can be useful to organizations, especially for selection or development.

The starting point in the journey to becoming a global leader consists of the following: self-awareness and cultural awareness; a deep desire to learn and improve; and involving yourself in experiences and situations where elements of your global mindset can be nurtured. These parallel the cognitive, attitudinal, and behavioral aspects of global mindset and global leadership. As Gelfand et al. (2007) have written, "In a world that offers global opportunities as well as global threats, understanding and managing cultural differences have become necessities."

NOTES

1. As of October 15, 2015.
2. *The Economist*. 2015. "Managing Partners," May 23. http://www.economist.com/news/business/21651895-pressure-companies-form-alliances-rivals-growing-inexorably-managing-partners.
3. "Fiat Gains Full Control of Chrsyler in $4.35 Billion Dollar Deal" from Bloomberg Business Week, January 1, 2014: http://www.bloomberg.com/news/articles/2014-01-01/fiat-agrees-to-buy-rest-of-chrysler-in-4-35-billion-deal
4. "Xiaomi to Set up R&D Centre in Bangalore; Will Focus on India-Specific Products, Says Manu Jain." 2015. *Tech2*. Accessed August 29. http://tech.firstpost.com/news-analysis/xiaomi-to-set-up-r-will-focus-on-india-specific-products-says-manu-jain-251990.html.
5. "Samsung." 2015. Accessed August 29. http://www.samsung.com/us/sjexpansion/.
6. http://www.ge.com/in/oil-and-gas/JFWTC

REFERENCES

Ambos, Björn, and Volker Mahnke. 2010. How Do MNC Headquarters Add Value? *Management International Review* 50(4): 403–412.

American Management Association. 2012. *Developing Successful Global Leaders*. AMA Enterprise Report. https://cdns3.trainingindustry.com/media/13267033/ama_developing_global_leaders.pdf

Arnett, Jeffrey Jensen. 2002. The Psychology of Globalization. *American Psychologist* 57(10): 774–783.

Aycan, Zeynep, Rabindra Kanungo, Manuel Mendonca, Kaicheng Yu, Jürgen Deller, Günter Stahl, and Anwar Kurshid. 2000. Impact of Culture on Human

Resource Management Practices: A 10-Country Comparison. *Applied Psychology: An International Review* 49(1): 192–221.

Baaij, Marc.G., and Arjen H.L. Slangen. 2013. The Role of Headquarters-Subsidiary Geographic Distance in Strategic Decisions by Spatially Disaggregated Headquarters. *Journal of International Business Studies 44*(9): 941–952.

Barrett, Lisa Feldman. 2013. Psychological Construction: The Darwinian Approach to the Science of Emotion. *Emotion Review* 5(4): 379–389.

Bennett, Mick, and Andrew Bell. 2004. *Leadership and Talent in Asia: How the Best Employers Deliver Extraordinary Performance*. New York: Wiley.

Bhagat, Rabi. 2009. Culture, Work, and Organizations: A Future Research Agenda. *In Cambridge Handbook of Culture, Organizations, and Work*, eds. Rabi Bhagat and Richard Steers, 518–525. New York: Cambridge University Press.

Boiger, Michael, and Batja Mesquita. 2015. A Sociodynamic Perspective on the Construction of Emotion. In *The psychological construction of emotion*, eds. Lisa Barrett and James Russell, 377–398. New York: The Guilford Press.

Brewster, Chris. 1999. Strategic Human Resource Management: The Value of Different Paradigms. *Management International Review* 39: 45–64.

Bücker, Joost J.L.E., Olivier Furrer, Erik Poutsma, and Dirk Buyens. 2014. The Impact of Cultural Intelligence on Communication Effectiveness, Job Satisfaction and Anxiety for Chinese Host Country Managers Working for Foreign Multinationals. *The International Journal of Human Resource Management* 25(14): 2068–2087.

Chattopadhyay, Amitava, Rajeev Batra, and Aysegol Ozsomer. 2012. *The New Emerging Market Multinationals: Four Strategies for Disrupting Markets And Building Brands*. New York: McGraw Hill Professional.

Clapp-Smith, Rachel, Fred Luthans, and Bruce J. Avolio. 2007. The Role of Psychological Capital in Global Mindset Development. In *The global mindset: Advances in international management*, vol 19, eds. M. Javidan, R. Steers, and M. Hitt, 105–130. Oxford: Elsevier Press.

Colvin, Geoff. 2015a. Humans Are Underrated. *Fortune* 172(2): 100–113.

———. 2015b. The 21st Century Corporation: Every Aspect of Your Business is About to Change. *Fortune* 172(6): 102–112.

Erez, Miriam, and Efrat Gati. 2004. A Dynamic, Multi-Level Model of Culture: From the Micro Level of the Individual to the Macro Level of a Global Culture. *Applied Psychology: An International Review* 53(4): 583–598.

Fischer, Ronald, et al. 2014. Organizational Practices Across Cultures: An Exploration in Six Cultural Contexts. *International Journal of Cross Cultural Management* 14(1): 101–125.

Gagnon, Suzanne, and David Collinson. 2014. Rethinking Global Leadership Development Programmes: The Interrelated Significance of Power, Context and Identity. *Organization Studies* 35(5): 645–670.

Galanou, Aikaterini, and Dalia Abdelrahman Farrag. 2015. Towards the Distinctive Islamic Mode of Leadership in Business. *Journal of Management Development* 34(8): 882–900.

Gates, Bill. 1996. *The Road Ahead.* New York: Penguin Books.

Gelfand, Michele J., Miriam Erez, and Zeynep Aycan. 2007. Cross-Cultural Organizational Behavior. *Annual Review of Psychology* 58(1): 479–514.

Gottman, John Mordechai, and Robert Wayne Levenson. 2000. The Timing of Divorce: Predicting When a Couple Will Divorce Over a 14-Year Period. *Journal of Marriage and Family* 62(3): 737–745.

Hajro, Aida. 2015. Cultural Influences and the Mediating Role of Socio-Cultural Integration Processes on the Performance of Cross-Border Mergers and Acquisitions. *The International Journal of Human Resource Management* 26(2): 192–215.

Hechanova, Regina, Terry A. Beehr, and Neil D. Christiansen. 2003. Antecedents and Consequences of Employees' Adjustment to Overseas Assignment: A Meta-Analytic Review. *Applied Psychology* 52(2): 213–236.

Janssens, Maddy, and Tineke Cappellen. 2008. Contextualizing Cultural Intellignece: The Case of Global Managers. In *Handbook of Cultural Intelligence: Theory, Measurement, and Applications*, eds. Soon Ang and Linn Van Dyne, 356–371. Armonk, NY: M.E. Sharpe.

Koopman, Paul, Deanne Den Hartog, Edvard Konrad, et al. 1999. National Culture and Leadership Profiles in Europe: Some Results from the GLOBE Study. *European Journal of Work and Organizational Psychology* 8(4): 503–520.

Luthans, Fred, James B. Avey, Rachel Clapp-Smith, and Weixing Li. 2008. More Evidence on the Value of Chinese Workers' Psychological Capital: A Potentially Unlimited Competitive Resource? *The International Journal of Human Resource Management* 19(5): 818–827.

Luthans, Fred, Carolyn M. Youssef-Morgan, and Bruce J. Avolio. 2015. *Psychological Capital and Beyond.* New York: Oxford University Press.

Mannor, Michael. 2008. Top Executives and Global Leadership: At the Intersection of Cultural Intelligence and Strategic Leadership Theory. In *Handbook of Cultural Intelligence: Theory, Measurement, and Applications*, eds. Soon Ang and Linn Van Dyne, 91–106. M.E. Sharpe: Armonk, NY.

McCall, Morgan, and George Hollenbeck. 2002. *Developing Global Executives: The Lessons of International Experience.* Boston, MA: Harvard Business School Press.

Osland, Joyce S. 2008. An Overview of the Global Leadership Literature. In *Global Leadership: Research, Practice, and Development*, eds. Mark Mendendhall, Joyce Osland, Allan Bird, Gary Oddou, and Martha Maznevski, 34–63. New York: Routledge.

Osland, Joyce S., and Allan Bird. 2008. Process Models of Global Leadership Development. In *Global Leadership: Research, Practice, and Development*, eds.

Mark Mendendhall, Joyce Osland, Allan Bird, Gary Oddou, and Martha Maznevski, 81–93. New York: Routledge.

Oxford Economics. 2012. Global Talent 2021: How the New Geography of Talent Will Transform Human Resource Strategies. http://www.oxfordeconomics.com/Media/Default/Thought   percent20Leadership/global-talent-2021.pdf

Pfeffer, Jeffrey. 2015. *Leadership BS: Fixing Work Places and Careers One Truth at a Time*. New York: Harper Business.

Richbell, Suzanne, Michael Brookes, Chris Brewster, and Geoffrey Wood. 2011. Non-Standard Working Time: An International and Comparative Analysis. *The International Journal of Human Resource Management* 22(4): 945–962.

Salas, Eduardo, Katherine Wilson, and Rebecca Lyons. 2008. Designing and Delivering Training for Multicultural Interactions in Organizations. In *The Influence of Culture on Human Resource Management Processes and Practices*, eds. Dianna Stone and Eugene Stone-Romero, 115–134. New York: Lawrence Erlbaum Associates.

Schwartz, Shalom H. 1994. Beyond Individualism/Collectivism: New Cultural Dimensions of Values. In *Individualism and Collectivism: Theory, Method, and Applications*, vol 8, eds. Uchol Kim, Harry Triandis, C. Kagitchbasi, S. Choi, and G. Yoon, 85–119. Thousand Oaks, CA: Sage Publications.

Shokef, Efrat, and Miriam Erez. 2008. Cultural Intelligence and Global Identity in Multicultural Teams. In *Handbook of Cultural Intelligence: Theory, Measurement, and Applications*, eds. Soon Ang and Linn Van Dyne, 177–191. Armonk, NY: M.E. Sharpe.

Stahl, Günter, and Mansour Javidan. 2009. Cross-Cultural Perspectives on International Mergers and Acquisitions. In *Cambridge Handbook of Culture, Organizations, and Work*, eds. Rabi Bhagat and Richard Steers, 118–147. New York: Cambridge University Press.

Taras, Vas, Bradley L. Kirkman, and Piers Steel. 2010. Examining the Impact of Culture's Consequences: A Three-Decade, Multilevel, Meta-Analytic Review of Hofstede's Cultural Value Dimensions. *Journal of Applied Psychology* 95(3): 405–439.

Tay, Cheryl, Mina Westman, and Audrey Chia. 2008. Antecedents and Consequences of Cultural Intelligence Among Short-Term Business Travelers. Developing Cultural Intelligence: The Roles of International Nonwork Experiences. In *Handbook of Cultural Intelligence: Theory, Measurement, and Applications*, eds. Soong Ang and and Linn Van Dyne, 126–144. Armonk, NY: M.E. Sharpe.

Tung, Rosalie, and Alain Verbeke. 2010. Beyond Hofstede and GLOBE: Improving the Quality of Cross-Cultural Research. *Journal of International Business Studies* 41: 1259–1274.

Vaiman, Vlad, and Chris Brewster. 2015. How Far Do Cultural Differences Explain the Differences between Nations? Implications for HRM. *The International Journal of Human Resource Management* 26(2): 151–164.

Wood, Geoffrey, Chris Brewster, and Michael Brookes. 2014. *Human Resource Management and the Institutional Perspective*. New York: Routledge.

Yunlu, Dilek Gulistan, and Rachel Clapp-Smith. 2014. Metacognition, Cultural Psychological Capital and Motivational Cultural Intelligence. *Cross Cultural Management: An International Journal* 21(4): 386–399.

INDEX

A

acceptance, 23, 32, 124, 126, 135, 138–41, 158, 161, 203, 208, 217, 229, 231, 267
adaptability, 57, 130, 137, 264, 266
adjustment, 79, 114, 124–8, 130, 167, 198, 210, 230, 284, 289
affective-based trust, 234, 235
aging, 17
agreeableness, 127
aligning goals, 234, 237–8
antecedents, 124–31, 140, 234, 235, 273, 289
assertiveness, 51, 67, 75, 87, 88, 217, 219
authentic leadership, 168–71, 287
authoritarianism, 67, 68

B

bargaining styles, 228
best practices, 30, 279, 280
biculturals, 131, 286
big five, 127, 128, 143
boundary-spanning, 245

C

center of gravity, 270, 294
centers of excellence, 35
centralization, 26, 43, 109, 265
Chattanooga model, 289
checklist, 190, 225, 248–50
coconut cultures, 88, 208
cognitive-based trust, 234, 235
cognitive bias, 186
cognitive complexity, 134, 135, 139, 140
cognitive empathy, 146–8, 212, 213
collaboration, 56
collectivism, 55, 59, 75, 76, 87, 96, 153, 168, 219, 230, 233
comfort zone, 92, 93, 140, 145, 171, 183, 199–202
communication barriers, 234, 237
company culture, 166, 265
competencies, 3, 103, 117, 118, 124, 127, 133, 159–62, 163, 171, 183, 271, 284
connectors, 185, 186
conscientiousness, 127, 128, 131

© The Editor(s) (if applicable) and The Author(s) 2016
R. Henson, *Successful Global Leadership*,
DOI 10.1057/978-1-137-58990-3

Printed by Printforce, the Netherlands